D1229996

Life and Society in the Hittite World

Life and Society in the Hittite World

TREVOR BRYCE

OXFORD
UNIVERSITY PRESS

OXFORD
UNIVERSITY PRESS

Great Clarendon Street, Oxford OX2 6DP

Oxford University Press is a department of the University of Oxford.
It furthers the University's objective of excellence in research, scholarship, and education by publishing worldwide in

Oxford New York

Auckland Bangkok Buenos Aires Cape Town Chennai
Dar es Salaam Delhi Hong Kong Istanbul Karachi Kolkata
Kuala Lumpur Madrid Melbourne Mexico City Mumbai Nairobi
São Paulo Shanghai Singapore Taipei Tokyo Toronto

with an associated company in Berlin

Published in the United States
by Oxford University Press Inc., New York

First published 2002

British Library Cataloguing in Publication Data
Data available

Library of Congress Cataloging-in-Publication Data

Bryce, Trevor, 1940–
Life and society in the Hittite world / Trevor Bryce.
p. cm.
Includes bibliographical references (p.).
ISBN 0-19-924170-8
ISBN 0-19-926047-8 licensed bookclub edition
1. Hittites—Social life and customs. 2. Hittites—Civilization. I. Title.
DS66 .B755 2002
909'.49199—dc21 2002025032

1 3 5 7 9 10 8 6 4 2

Typeset by SNP Best-set Typesetter Ltd., Hong Kong
Printed in Great Britain
on acid-free paper by
Biddles Ltd, Guildford & King's Lynn

Acknowledgements

I would like to express my sincere thanks to Professor Silvin Košak for the time he has given to reading this book in its draft stages and for the many valuable comments and suggestions he has made. My thanks also to Mr Geoff Tully for his illustrations and to Mr Feza Toker of Ekip Film for kindly providing several of the photographs. A general word of thanks is due to Dr Stephanie Dalley, whose initial suggestions to me about a book on the Hittites prompted the writing of *The Kingdom of the Hittites* as well as the present volume.

Once again I would like to acknowledge the invaluable support and advice which I have received from Professor Oliver Gurney over many years. His passing is a great loss to the world of Hittite scholarship, as it is to me personally.

T.R.B.

August 2001

Contents

List of Illustrations

Maps

Figures

Abbreviations

AA	*Archäologischer Anzeiger*
AfO	*Archiv für Orientforschung*
ÄHK	Edel, E., *Die Ägyptische-hethitische Korrespondenz aus Boghazköi*, 2 vols. (Opladen, 1994)
AO	*Archív Orientální*
AOAT	*Alter Orient und Altes Testament*
AOF	*Altorientalische Forschungen*
AS	*Anatolian Studies*
BA	*Biblical Archaeologist*
BiOr	*Bibliotheca Orientalis*
CTH	E. Laroche, *Catalogue des textes hittites* (Paris, 1971)
EA	*The El-Amarna Letters*, most recently ed. W. Moran (Baltimore, London, 1992)
Fs Alp	H. Otten et al., *Hittite and Other Anatolian and Near Eastern Studies in honour of Sedat Alp* (Ankara, 1992)
Fs Güterbock I	K. Bittel, Ph. H. J. Houwink ten Cate, E. Reiner, *Anatolian Studies presented to H. G. Güterbock* (Istanbul, 1974)
Fs Güterbock II	H. A. Hoffner and G. M. Beckman, *Kaniššuwar: A Tribute to Hans G. Güterbock on his Seventy-fifth Birthday* (Chicago, 1986)
Fs Houwink ten Cate	T. Van den Hout and J. De Roos, *Studio Historiae Ardens (Ancient Near Eastern Studies Presented to Philo H. J. Houwink ten Cate on the Occasion of his 65th Birthday)* (Istanbul, 1995)
Fs Jacobsen	*Sumerological Studies in Honor of Thorkild Jacobsen*, Assyriological Studies 20 (Chicago, 1974)
Fs Laroche	*Florilegium Anatolicum, Mélanges offerts à Emmanuel Laroche* (Paris, 1979)
Fs Otten	E. Neu and C. Rüster, *Documentum Asiae Minoris Antiquae (Festschrift Heinrich Otten)* (Wiesbaden, 1988)
Fs Polomé	*Perspectives on Indo-European Language, Culture, and Religion: Studies in Honor of Edgar C. Polomé*, vol i, *JIES* Monograph 7 (Bochum, 1991)

Fs Sachs	E. Leichty et al., *A Scientific Humanist: Studies in Memory of Abraham Sachs*, Occasional Publications of the Samuel Noah Kramer Fund 9 (Philadelphia, 1988)
IBoT	*Istanbul Arkeoloji Müzelerinde Bulunan Boğazköy Tabletleri (nden Seçme Metinler)* (Istanbul, 1944, 1947, 1954; Ankara, 1988)
JAC	*Journal of Ancient Civilizations*
JAOS	*Journal of the American Oriental Society*
JCS	*Journal of Cuneiform Studies*
JEA	*Journal of Egyptian Archaeology*
JHS	*Journal of Hellenic Studies*
JIES	*Journal of Indo-European Studies*
JNES	*Journal of Near Eastern Studies*
KBo	*Keilschrifttexte aus Boghazköi* (Leipzig, Berlin)
KRI	K. A. Kitchen, *Ramesside Inscriptions, Historical and Biographical I–VII* (Oxford, 1969–)
KUB	*Keilschrifturkunden aus Boghazköi* (Berlin)
MDOG	*Mitteilungen der deutschen Orient-Gesellschaft*
MIO	*Mitteilungen des Instituts für Orientforschung*
MVAG	*Mitteilungen der Vorderasiatisch-Aegyptischen Gesellschaft*
OA	*Oriens Antiquus*
OLZ	*Orientalische Literaturzeitung*
Or	*Orientalia*
PRU IV	J. Nougayrol, *Le Palais Royal d'Ugarit IV*, Mission de Ras Shamra Tome IX (Paris, 1956)
RAI	*Rencontre Assyriologique Internationale*
RHA	*Revue hittite et asianique*
RlA	*Reallexikon der Assyriologie und vorderasiatischen Archäologie*
RS	Tablets from Ras Shamra
SMEA	*Studi Micenei ed Egeo-Anatolici*
StBoT	*Studien zu den Boğazköy-Texten* (Wiesbaden)
TUAT	*Texte aus dem Umwelt des Alten Testament*
UF	*Ugarit-Forschungen*
WO	Die Welt des Orients
WVDOG	*Wissenschaftliche Veröffentlichungen der Deutschen Orient-Gesellschaft*
VBoT	*Verstreute Boghazköi-Texte*
ZA	*Zeitschrift für Assyriologie und Vorderasiatische Archäologie*

List of Hittite Kings

Old Kingdom

King	Dates	Relationship
Labarna	–1650	
Hattusili I	1650–1620	(grandson?)
Mursili I	1620–1590	(grandson, adopted son)
Hantili I	1590–1560	(brother-in-law)
Zidanta I		(son-in-law)
Ammuna	1560–1525	(son)
Huzziya I		(brother of Ammuna's daughter-in-law)
Telipinu	1525–1500	(brother-in-law)
Alluwamna		(son-in-law)
Tahurwaili		(interloper)
Hantili II		(son of Alluwamna?)
Zidanta II	1500–1400	(son?)
Huzziya II		(son?)
Muwatalli I		(interloper)

New Kingdom

King	Dates	Relationship
Tudhaliya I/II		(grandson of Huzziya II?)
Arnuwanda I	1400–1360[a]	(son-in-law, adopted son)
Hattusili II?		(son?)
Tudhaliya III	1360–1344	(son?)
Suppiluliuma I	1344–1322	(son)
Arnuwanda II	1322–1321	(son)
Mursili II	1321–1295	(brother)
Muwatalli II	1295–1272	(son)
Urhi-Tesub	1272–1267	(son)
Hattusili III	1267–1237	(uncle)
Tudhaliya IV	1237–1228	(son)
Kurunta	1228–1227	(cousin)
Tudhaliya IV[b]	1227–1209	(cousin)
Arnuwanda III	1209–1207	(son)
Suppiluliuma II	1207–	(brother)

Note: All dates are approximate. When it is impossible to suggest even approximate dates for the individual reigns of two or more kings in sequence, the period covered by the sequence is roughly calculated on the basis of 20 years per reign. While obviously some reigns were longer than this, and some shorter, the averaging out of these reigns probably produces a result with a reasonably small margin of error.

[a] Includes period of coregency
[b] 2nd period as king

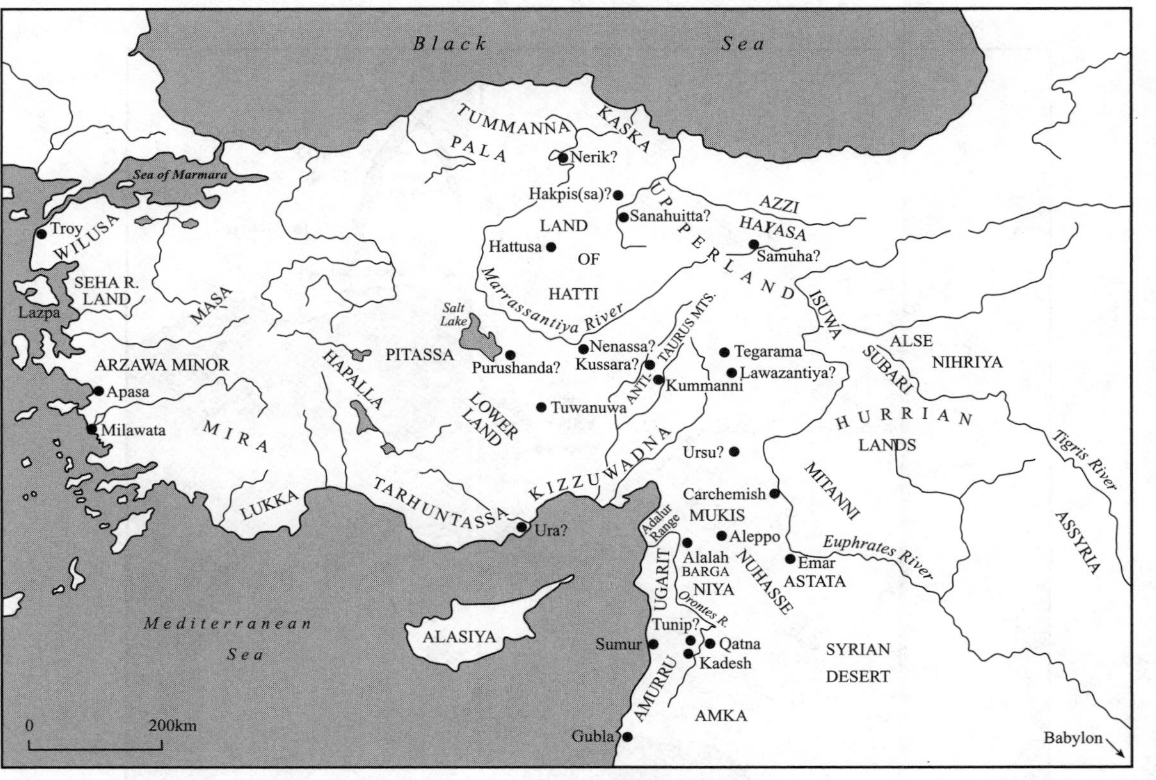

Map 1. The World of the Hittites

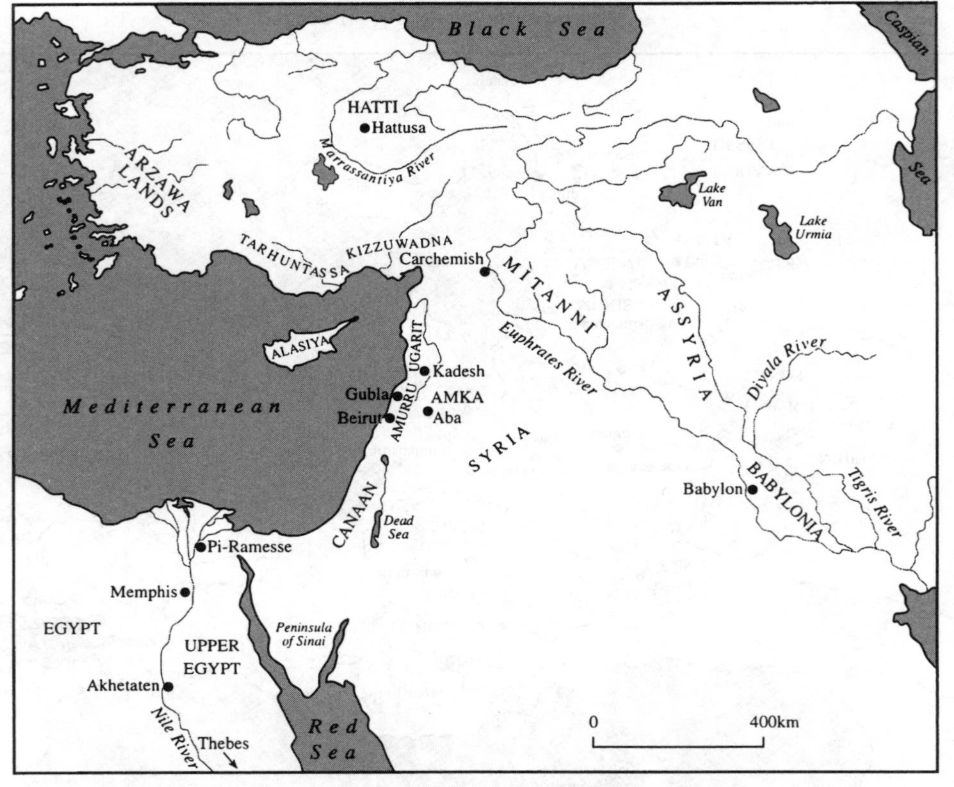

Map 2. The Near East in the Late Bronze Age

Introduction

Some 28 kilometres east of the city of Izmir on Turkey's western coast, there is a mountain pass called Karabel. Overlooking the pass is a relief cut in the face of the rock. It depicts a male human figure armed with bow and spear, and sword with crescent-shaped pommel. On his head is a tall peaked cap. A weathered inscription provides information about him—for those able to read it. Herodotos visited the monument in the fifth century BC. He describes it in his *Histories* and provides a translation of the inscription which, he declares, is written in the sacred script of Egypt: 'With my own shoulders I won this land.'[1] The conqueror does not tell us his name, but his costume is part Egyptian, part Ethiopian, and he is to be identified with Sesostris, prince of Egypt—at least that is what Herodotos would have us believe!

Twenty-three centuries later, in the year 1834, a French adventurer-explorer called Charles Texier is searching in central Turkey for the remains of a Celtic city called Tavium, referred to in Roman sources. The locals tell him of some ancient ruins 150 kilometres east of Ankara. Texier visits the ruins. They are vast—far exceeding in size anything described in Classical sources. One of the entrance gates to the city bears a relief of a warrior—armed, beardless, with long hair, wearing a tasselled helmet and a kilt. Texier is mystified. It is like no other figure known from the ancient world. The locals tell him that there are more figures nearby. They lead him to an outcrop of rock, about thirty minutes' walk from the ruins. This brings further surprises. The rock walls are decorated with relief sculptures—processions of human figures clothed in strange garments, of hitherto unknown types. The reliefs are accompanied by mysterious inscriptions, totally unintelligible. They can be neither read nor identified. But they are dubbed 'hieroglyphic' because of a superficial resemblance to the hieroglyphic script of Egypt. The whole thing remains a bewildering mystery.

We move forward four decades, to the year 1876. In London a

British scholar called Archibald Henry Sayce delivers a lecture to the Society of Biblical Archaeology. It is about a group of people referred to in the Bible as the Hittites. They are apparently a small Canaanite tribe living in Palestine. At least that is what the Bible has led everyone to believe. In his lecture, Sayce puts forward a bold new theory—that the Hittites, far from being an insignificant Canaanite tribe, were in fact the masters of a great and widespread empire extending throughout the Near East. The centre of this kingdom probably lay in Syria—so Sayce believes. But its capital has yet to be discovered.

Two more decades bring us to the first years of the twentieth century. In Turkey the German archaeologist Hugo Winckler has begun excavating the site which had so mystified Charles Texier seventy years earlier. He sits in a hut on the site examining the large quantities of clay tablets which the excavations are bringing to light. They are inscribed in the cuneiform script. Winckler is able to read a number of these since they are in the language called Akkadian, the international language of diplomacy in the second millennium BC. Winckler suspects that the site he is excavating may be part of Sayce's so-called Hittite empire. As he picks up one tablet, he reads it with increasing excitement. It is the Akkadian version of a treaty which the pharaoh Ramesses II drew up with Hattusili, king of the Hittites, in the twenty-first year of his reign. This, combined with other evidence, makes it clear that the site under excavation is the Hittite capital, later to be identified as Hattusa. Unfortunately the great majority of tablets unearthed from the site cannot be read. They are in a strange, unintelligible language. Presumably it is the language of the Hittites themselves.

Moving forward another decade, we find ourselves in a politically turbulent Europe. A Czech scholar called Bedřich Hrozný has taken up the challenge of deciphering the Hittite language. The task is proving a frustrating one and is likely to come to an abrupt end as war breaks out. Hrozný is drafted into the army. But he is given exemption from military duties in order to continue with his scholarly pursuits. As he peruses the Hittite tablets, he returns to a conclusion proposed a few years earlier by the Norwegian scholar J. A. Knudtzon, but generally rejected, that Hittite is an Indo-European language, quite different from the Bronze Age languages already known, like Babylonian and Assyrian. Beginning with a few basic examples, most notably a line from a religious text which refers simply to the eating of bread and the drinking of water, Hrozný demonstrates beyond doubt that Knudtzon's theory is correct. With this first crucial step, the door to the language is unlocked. A once obscure, almost forgotten civilization of the ancient Near East is opened up to the world of modern scholarship.

'They're a biblical tribe, aren't they?' reflects a popular perception of the Hittites that has changed little in the last 150 years, despite all that has happened in the world of Near Eastern scholarship in that time. Indeed many readers who know of the Hittites only from biblical references may wonder how a whole book could be devoted to the handful of Old Testament tribespeople so called, like Uriah, the cuckolded husband of Bathsheba, Ephron, who sold his field to Abraham as a burial plot, and the sons of Heth, who was one of the sons of Canaan.[2] Up until the last decades of the nineteenth century practically everything known about the Hittites was contained in the Bible. Today anyone venturing beyond this source into the world of modern Hittite scholarship will readily understand the astonished reaction which the pioneering 'Hittitologist' A. H. Sayce must have provoked 120 years ago in his lecture to the Society of Biblical Archaeology in London. He claimed that far from being a small Canaanite tribe who dwelt in the Palestinian hills, the Hittites were the people of a great empire stretching across the face of the ancient Near East, from the Aegean Sea's eastern shoreline to the banks of the Euphrates, centuries before the age of the Patriarchs. The Karabel monument, first described by Herodotos, lies at the western end of this empire. It depicts not an Egyptian prince but a local western Anatolian king called Tarkasnawa, a thirteenth-century vassal ruler of the Hittite Great King.[3] In fact our biblical Hittites with their Semitic names have little if anything to do with the earlier people so called, who occupied central Anatolia in the period we now refer to as the Late Bronze Age. Of mixed ethnic origins—Indo-European, native Hattian, Hurrian, Luwian, and numerous smaller groups—they called themselves by the traditional name of the region in which they lived; they were the 'people of the Land of Hatti'. Largely for the sake of convenience, and because of their long-assumed biblical connections, we have adopted for them the name 'Hittite'.

There *may* in fact be a genuine connection. Early in the twelfth century the Hittite capital Hattusa went up in flames, and with its destruction the central Anatolian kingdom was at an end. Elements of the civilization did, however, persist in southern Anatolia, and particularly in Syria, where in the fourteenth century viceregal kingdoms were established, at Carchemish and Aleppo, under the immediate governance of sons of the Hittite Great King. In these regions collateral branches of the royal dynasty survived the upheavals which marked the end of the Bronze Age and continued to hold sway for some centuries to come. Along with this dynasty, elements of the Bronze Age civilization persisted in the Syrian region through the early centuries of the first millennium, as illustrated by the Hittite-type monuments and sculptures and 'Hittite' hieroglyphic inscriptions found at Carchemish and other sites. Yet the traditions of Hittite civilization were influenced by and blended with those of local Syrian origin, and it was this admixture which gave rise to what are commonly known as the Neo-Hittite or Syro-Hittite kingdoms. It is possible that these kingdoms appear briefly in the Bible.

On two occasions the Old Testament refers to a group of Hittites who appear to be quite distinct from the hill tribesmen of Palestine. In 2 Kings 7: 6, Hittite kings are hired by Israel along with the kings of Egypt to do battle against an army of Syrians. In 2 Chronicles 1: 17, Hittite and Syrian kings appear together as recipients of exports from Egypt. These passages give the clear impression that the Hittite kings so mentioned enjoyed considerable status in the Syrian region and may even have been commensurate in importance and power with the pharaohs. In these two instances, then, biblical tradition *may* reflect the continuing Hittite political and military and cultural presence in Syria, albeit in an attenuated and hybrid form, during the early centuries of the first millennium BC.[4]

I have devoted some space to the history of these latter-day Hittites in my general historical survey of the Hittite world.[5] However, a full discussion of their society and culture is better dealt with in the context of a broadly based treatment of the first millennium successors to the Bronze Age civilizations, with all their blends, interactions, and cross-cultural links. The focus of this present book will be almost entirely on the life and society of the Late Bronze Age Hittites whose kingdom spanned a period of some 500 years, from the early seventeenth to the early twelfth century BC.

In compiling a history of the Hittite world, one becomes very conscious of how much of it is a history of warfare in and beyond this world. To a large extent that is due to the nature of our sources, a reflection of what aspects, what achievements of his reign a Hittite king chooses to relate to us. As Professor Hoffner notes, it is clear that many historical works were primarily works of royal propaganda.[6] In seeking to demonstrate his prowess as a Great King worthy of his illustrious predecessors, the ruler of the Hittite world will almost always emphasize his military successes in the records he leaves for posterity. Hence the picture frequently presented of a kingdom geared to chronic warfare. That may indeed have been the case more often than not in the Hittite world. But the picture is only part complete. In fact the great majority of texts from the Hittite archives have little or nothing to do with the military side of Hittite life. They provide information on a wide range of other aspects which help create a more balanced view of life and society in the Hittite world. In dealing with a number of these in the pages which follow I hope that this book will provide a useful complement to my account of Hittite history.

Many books have been written about ancient peoples and places. But even the most comprehensive treatments sometimes lack an important perspective: while providing a wide range of information about a particular society, they fail to convey any clear sense of what it must have been like to live in it, to participate directly in the life of its villages and cities, to meet its people on the streets and in their homes. It is rather like reading a book of facts and figures about Istanbul which though accurate and thorough in its details communicates little of the essential experience of a visit to Aghia Sophia, or a walk through the bustling alleys of the Covered Market or a ferryboat trip along the Bosporus, or a ride in a dolmuş. Of course no matter how graphic the description of such experiences, it can never be a satisfactory substitute for the experience itself—which as far as the ancient world is concerned will be forever denied us, at least until time travel becomes possible. Nevertheless, in using the factual data on which our knowledge of an ancient society is based we should attempt to build up a picture of this society not merely as detached modern commentators but by seeing it through the eyes of someone actually living in it, taking part in its daily activities, its festive occasions, its celebrations, its crises and conflicts, experiencing its whole mix of sights, sounds, and smells.

We find that no fewer than eight languages are represented in the tablet archives of the capital. Probably as many if not more languages were spoken in the streets of the capital every day, some of them quite different from the languages of the archives. What did this mean in practical terms? By imagining ourselves in the city's midst, we are likely to ask questions which we might otherwise never have thought of. How did people of different ethnic origins and speaking different languages communicate with each other on everyday matters? What language did one use in buying a loaf of bread or a pair of shoes, arranging lodgings for the evening, negotiating a business deal or the price of a gold pendant? Was there an informal city *lingua franca*, a kind of pidgin or 'street-speak'? Records of festival programmes survive in abundance in the archives. What was it like to participate in one of these festivals? To what extent can we recreate the festival experience from the tediously repetitive formulaic instructions in the texts—the colour and noise and pageantry of the festival processions and the feasting and entertainment and sports contests associated with them? Military annals routinely list the peoples taken from subject territories in the aftermath of military conquest and resettled in the Hittite homeland. We have only bald statistics. What of the human experiences behind the statistics, as hundreds, sometimes thousands, of men, women, and children are uprooted from their homes and forced to walk hundreds of kilometres often in the harshest conditions to servitude in an alien land? These are the sorts of questions we need to ask if we are to make any genuine attempt to reconstruct the life of the people of the Hittite world. In many cases we can provide no more than tentative or incomplete answers, and in our reconstructions we may sometimes stray beyond the bounds of evidential support. That may *on occasions* be acceptable—provided we remain within the bounds of possibility.

A further point needs to be made. To those to whom this book serves as an introduction to the Hittite world, many of the customs, beliefs, practices, and institutions referred to in the following pages may have a familiar ring about them. The Hittites were an eclectic people. They borrowed freely from predecessor as well as contemporary civilizations in the Near East, weaving strands from a number of different cultures into the fabric of their own. And quite possibly they played an important role in the transmission of Near Eastern cultural traditions and concepts to the European world. Similarities and parallels can readily be found between Hittite and Greek traditions and customs, as illustrated by literary and mythological motifs, ritual practices, and methods of communicating with the gods. Some of these may well have come to Greece via the Hittite world. Of course the Hittites were but one of a number of possible agents of east–west cultural transmission. As we have noted, their civilization was a highly derivative one, and much of what they had in common with the Greek world had been adopted by them from other sources. Indeed the very fact that many of their cultural traditions were widely in evidence in other civilizations of the Near East makes it extremely difficult to identify which of these civilizations were directly responsible for the transmission of particular traditions to the west—or in what period the transmissions took place. The considerable influence of the Near Eastern world on the evolving civilization of Greece can now hardly be denied. But the specifics of cultural transmission still remain debatable.

Chapter 14 deals with some of the possible links between the Near Eastern world and the world that lay in and across the Aegean, and the role which the Hittites may have played in establishing these links. Otherwise there will be no specific discussion, except in a few cases, of what aspects of Hittite civilization were of genuine native origin, what were attributable to foreign sources, and what were passed on to others. A number of books and articles have already been devoted to such matters, both in the past and again in quite recent years. Indeed there is every likelihood that research spanning different time periods and different civilizations will become increasingly common as the disciplinary barriers between the various Near Eastern civilizations and particularly between the Near East and Greece are progressively broken down.

Inevitably in writing a book of this kind, one has to be highly selective in the material chosen for discussion. Inevitably there will be criticisms because of what has been left out. The limitations imposed by the publisher can be pleaded as part excuse. But even if the publisher were indulgent enough to allow a book three times the current length, it would not significantly reduce the element of selectivity, given the substantial body of material which ongoing research in the field of Hittite studies is constantly generating. Other experts in the field may well have included different material or used different emphases. Nevertheless, the book will have succeeded in its main aim if its readers on completing it feel that it has brought them closer to a knowledge and understanding of the life of the people, and the people themselves, who dominated a large part of the Near Eastern world throughout the Late Bronze Age.

Synopsis of Hittite History

The kingdom of the Hittites rose in the central Anatolian plateau, in the region called the Land of Hatti, during the early decades of the seventeenth century BC. In the course of the next 500 years, the period we call the Late Bronze Age, the Hittites built an empire which extended across much of the Anatolian landmass and from there through northern Syria to the western fringes of Mesopotamia. Throughout its history it was ruled by a royal dynasty from the city of Hattusa (modern Boğazköy/Boğazkale), the religious and administrative capital of the empire. The official language of the kingdom was an Indo-European language called Nesite, which we commonly refer to today as the 'Hittite' language. Its use harks back to the dominance of an Indo-European group in the region during the so-called Assyrian Colony period. From its base in the city of Nesa, the leaders of this group gained control over large parts of the eastern half of Anatolia a century or so before the emergence of the Hittite kingdom. Indo-European speakers may have first entered Anatolia during the third millennium, or even earlier. After their arrival one branch of them intermingled with a central Anatolian people called the Hattians (hence the name Hatti), and to begin with, the Hittite population and civilization were primarily an admixture of Indo-European and Hattian elements. Throughout their history, however, the Hittites absorbed many other ethnic and cultural elements within the fabric of their civilization, through the system of transportation in the wake of military conquest as well as through a range of foreign cultural influences and commercial contacts.

Scholars commonly divide Hittite history into two, or three, main phases. These are largely arbitrary divisions, and views differ widely on where one period should end and another begin. Nevertheless in accordance with the modern convention I have divided the Late Bronze Age civilization into two phases, an Old Kingdom (down to *c.*1400 BC) and a New Kingdom (from *c.*1400 to the early twelfth century). In the latter period, sometimes referred to as the Empire, the kingdom of Hatti reached its pinnacle of power and influence throughout the Near Eastern world. Its ruler was one of the Great Kings of this world, corresponding on equal terms with his counterparts who sat upon the thrones of Egypt, Babylon, Mitanni, and Assyria.

Beyond the core territory of its homeland in central Anatolia, the Hittite empire consisted largely of a network of vassal states, whose rulers enjoyed considerable local autonomy but were bound by a number of obligations to their Hittite overlord, formalized in the personal treaties he drew up with them. In the latter half of the fourteenth century, direct Hittite rule was extended to parts of northern Syria with the establishment of viceregal kingdoms at Aleppo and Carchemish.

Early in the twelfth century, the royal capital Hattusa was destroyed by fire, and with its destruction the Anatolian kingdom of the Hittites came to an abrupt end. This occurred within the context of the widespread upheavals associated with the collapse of many Bronze Age kingdoms throughout the Near East and mainland Greece. However, some kingdoms and civilizations survived the upheavals, and elements of the Hittite civilization were to continue for some centuries to come in peripheral areas of the former kingdom. As we have noted, these were reflected particularly in the so-called neo-Hittite or Syro-Hittite kingdoms of Syria, which lasted for almost 500 years and were culturally and politically prominent in the period from *c.*900 BC until the last of them fell to the Assyrian king Sargon II between 717 and 708 BC. In the neo-Hittite kingdoms members of the Hittite royal dynasty held power in unbroken succession through the early centuries of the Iron Age. It was they who ensured that the dynasty had the rare distinction of spanning almost 1000 years of history, equivalent to the entire life-span of the empire of Byzantium.

CHAPTER I

King, Court, and Royal Officials

The king is close to death. His chief warriors and dignitaries have been summoned to his bedside in Kussara, ancestral home of the Hittite royal dynasty. A scribe is standing by, to record what the dying man has to say to those gathered around him. This will be no carefully composed document, the product of numerous drafts and revisions. There is no time for that. But the fate of the kingdom may well depend on its monarch's final words. The scribe has been instructed to ensure that every one of these words is committed to permanent record, exactly as he speaks them. A crisis is in the making, for arrangements for the royal succession have been plunged into disarray after the sudden fall from favour of the king's nephew, his recently proclaimed heir. Earlier the king's own sons and daughter had rebelled against their father, perhaps because of favouritism shown to his nephew. Now even the favoured one has proved unfit for the throne, for he is 'an abomination to the sight', 'without compassion', 'cold and pitiless', 'heedless of the word of the king', and likely to plunge the kingdom into bloodshed and chaos. Now there is only the king's grandson to turn to. He is still a child, but there is no-one else. In what may be his last hour, the king proclaims his grandson as successor to his throne and calls upon the great men of the land to uphold his decision, to guide, nurture, and protect the child until he is old enough to grasp the reins of power. There is advice for the child too, and the king orders that his words be read out to him every month. For all these reasons the scribe must be sure to take down every word.

It is a disjointed, meandering composition. Rational, lucid directions from the king to his subjects alternate with rambling reminiscences about a family which has consistently defied and betrayed him—his own family. His sister, mother of his disgraced nephew, figures as arch villain. She above all is to blame for what her son has become. It is against her that the king's anger is principally directed. In a bizarre mix of images, she is both 'a serpent', and a creature who 'bellows like an ox'.

The document ends on a curious note. The king has done speaking, or so it seems, and the scribe rules a paragraph line at the bottom of the text. But then unexpectedly His Majesty stirs and speaks again. The scribe hastily picks up his stylus. He has to listen hard to catch his master's words. They are barely coherent—indeed they almost defy translation. They are not meant to be recorded; but the scribe is obeying his instructions to the letter. The king is appealing to a woman called Hastayar, perhaps a daughter, or a favourite concubine. 'Do not forsake me,' he pleads in a barely audible whisper. And then, finally, 'Hold me to your bosom. Keep me from the earth.'

The king is Hattusili I, the Great King, the Tabarna, King of the Land of Hatti, surpasser of the achievements of the mighty Sargon, the lion who pounces without mercy upon his prey—but now a pathetic, lonely old man, forsaken by his family, seeking final comfort in a woman's embrace, terrified by the imminence of his own death.

The Men behind the Masks

The so-called Testament which records Hattusili's speech[1] provides us with one of our very rare glimpses into the actual personality and character and emotions of a Hittite king. Mostly these features lie well concealed behind an official façade presented in formal, carefully worded texts—annals, letters, decrees, treaties, and the like—on which we depend for much of our knowledge of Hittite royalty and the Hittite kingdom in general. Sometimes these texts contain what may appear to be expressions of personal feelings on the part of a king—anger, sorrow, regret at the behaviour of a rebellious vassal or disloyal official—and occasionally they highlight an apparent act of compassion or chivalry, extended to a courageous old woman who seeks forgiveness for her rebellious son, or a beautiful and resolute young one left vulnerable to her enemies by her husband's death. But that is all part of the diplomatic rhetoric which characterizes Hittite kings' dealings with their subjects and foreign counterparts, and which often disguises the real and very pragmatic motives underlying a particular policy or course of action.

Sometimes, however, the mask of officialdom slips momentarily, giving us an occasional brief glimpse of the actual person behind the mask: the politically astute Suppiluliuma, greatest of all Hittite warlords, suddenly nonplussed by an extraordinary appeal to him from Tutankhamun's young widow;[2] Mursili II, a deeply pious man, thrown into abject depression by the death of his beloved wife; Hattusili III, a scheming and ruthlessly ambitious man, yet betraying in his letters a desperate need for the approval of his royal peers. There is of course a danger, in the absence of more substantial evidence, of seizing upon a tiny clue, a passing reference, and using it to construct an entire persona. But we have little else to turn to, especially as we have almost no idea of what a king's own subjects thought of him. This in particular gives us cause to regret the lack of an independent contemporary chronicler who might have presented us with a more comprehensive picture of the lives and conduct and personal idiosyncracies of the kings of the Hittite world and their families—at least from an outsider's viewpoint. For all the bias of a Thucydides or a Tacitus (in spite of their claims to the contrary), or even the scandal-mongering of a Suetonius, such writers do at least provide us with popular perceptions of the leaders of their day, valuable complements to the images presented through the official sources.

Interestingly, though not surprisingly when one thinks about it, we know rather more about some of the female members of the royal family than we do about their sovereign lords. That is largely because of comments by other people. Thus Hattusili I's remarks about his sister, including his gloriously mismatched metaphors, provide a vivid thumbnail sketch of what this woman was like, at least in her brother's eyes. The tyrannous behaviour of which Suppiluliuma I's Babylonian wife stood accused, along with her extravagance, her currying of favourites, and her introduction of undesirable foreign customs, are graphically described by her stepson Mursili II. And towering over all other females is the magnificent Puduhepa, wife of Hattusili III, probably no less a tyrannical figure in the royal household than Suppiluliuma's imported spouse, but a major source of strength to her husband and on many occasions his partner in the administrative, judicial, and diplomatic activities of the kingdom. She was royal matchmaker *extraordinaire*, took personal responsibility for bringing up the hordes of little Hittite princes and princesses in the palace, and corresponded on equal terms with the pharaoh Ramesses II. It is indeed through this correspondence that we learn much about the esteem in which she was held internationally, even by Ramesses himself.

Official records tell us much about the public achievements of the individual kings. But throughout the entire Hittite period, right down to the last of the neo-Hittite kings in Syria, one thing is conspicuously absent. We never hear of a king who was actually a bad ruler. Even the kings who came to the throne by usurpation, by murdering their predecessors and sometimes their families as well, are never accused of corruption or mismanagement by any of their successors once they were actually enthroned. It was not the misrule but the bloody coups of his predecessors that King Telipinu held responsible for the fragile state of the kingdom at the time of his accession (*c.*1525).[3] He has not a word of criticism about any of their regimes once they were installed in office. In fact to judge from the few scraps of information that we have, none of them appear to have abused their office, but rather to have attempted to exercise the responsibilities of kingship as ably as they could. A case in point is King Hantili I, assassin and successor of Mursili I, an energetic ruler who seems to have been intent on maintaining his predecessors' influence in Syria and whose ultimate failures were probably due much more to circumstances beyond his control than to any lack of ability or application on his own part. Many years later Hattusili III usurped the throne from his nephew Urhi-Teshub and attempted to justify his action in a long and singularly unconvincing document we call the *Apology*.[4] His action plunged the kingdom into civil war. Yet nowhere in his defence of this action can we find a single negative comment about Urhi-Teshub's exercise of kingship. Hattusili's only justification for unseating him is a personal one. Urhi-Teshub had stripped him of the offices which his father Muwatalli, Hattusili's brother, had bestowed upon him—and if the truth be known, he probably had good reason to do so.

In general, if we were to judge our kings purely from their monuments, their annalistic records, their letters, their proclamations, we might conclude that they led unremittingly austere and upright lives. But that is because they present us only with their public face, the face they wish others to see. So too we might conclude about the monarchs of Byzantium had we only their icononography and public pronouncements to judge them by. The world of the Hittite royal court was probably no less byzantine in its character and behaviour than the court at Constantinople during its thousand-year Reich.

And it would indeed be surprising if the royal Hittite dynasty in the course of its own thousand-year history failed to come up with at least one or two corrupt paranoid despots when imperial Rome managed to produce a whole crop of them (if we are to believe our sources) within the space of a few decades, to say nothing of the succession of grotesque monsters who occupied the throne of Byzantium. Any long-lasting monarchy which is absolute and unaccountable almost inevitably spawns a few creatures of this sort in the course of its history. Why should the Hittite royal dynasty have been an exception to this? Unfortunately by their very nature most of the tablets in the archives at Hattusa ensure that we remain forever screened from the private lives and idiosyncracies and defects of the kings whose public exploits they extol.

If anything, the kings were as little known to most of their own subjects as they are to us. When in residence in the capital they lived in Oz-like seclusion from the general populace behind the walls of the acropolis, which effectively cut off the palace district, sprawling over the summit's sloping surface, from the rest of the city. And the barrier between palace district and everything else in the city became even more pronounced in the extensive building operations of the last century or so of the kingdom when the acropolis enclosure wall was substantially fortified. Of course when the king came forth at the time of festival processions, the inhabitants of the capital may have caught a distant glimpse of him in the midst of his entourage of attendants and bodyguards as he passed along the processional way. So too his subjects in the provincial towns during the course of his pilgrimages to religious centres outside the capital. But he remained a remote figure. Even on his regular and often lengthy military campaigns there was probably little scope for any camaraderie to develop between king and troops. The royal pavilion was no doubt well segregated from the camps of the common soldiers, few if any of whom were likely to have had the good fortune of experiencing a little touch of Hattusili in the night, or at any other time for that matter.

Much of it had to do with keeping the king free from contamination. The obsessive concern with ensuring that he was totally removed from all forms of contact with any persons or objects likely to cause defilement must have established an impassable barrier between him and the great majority of his subjects, in both military and non-military contexts. Even the king's shoes and chariot could be made only from the leather of animals slaughtered in the palace precincts and prepared under the strictest conditions of hygiene in the palace kitchen.

The King's Officials

While in a physical sense the king seems to have been kept well insulated from the majority of his subjects, in an administrative sense he maintained close personal involvement in the affairs and daily activities of his kingdom. A great many of the officials and functionaries throughout the land were directly accountable to him, and reported regularly to him. Such persons ranged from his highest-ranking administrators and military officers to the holders of what to our way of thinking were relatively lowly posts. Their relationship with the king was regulated by contracts or sets of instructions which spelled out their official duties and obligations. Twenty or so of these documents have survived.[5] They contain instructions for district governors and military commanders, for the *hazannu*, the chief administrator of Hattusa, for the king's bodyguard, for temple officials, palace functionaries, and gatekeepers. All serve as valuable sources of information on the day-to-day operations and activities of those who were quite literally On His Majesty's Service.

One of the most important persons in the administration was the BĒL MADGALTI (Hittite *auriyas ishas*) (literally 'lord of the watchtower'), a term used of the king's district governors. The duties and obligations of these officials were wide-ranging. In Hatti's outlying regions they were responsible for the security of the frontiers and had charge of the garrisons stationed in the area. They were strictly required in the instructions issued to them to ensure that fortresses and towns under their control were securely locked in the evenings. They had to keep an adequate supply of timber on hand in case of siege. They were warned to keep particularly on the alert against one of the Hittites' greatest fears—the outbreak of fire. They had to ensure that all who left the fortified community in the morning, probably mainly peasant farmers, and returned in the evening after working in the fields were carefully scrutinized, to ensure there was no enemy presence among them. They were responsible for the maintenance of buildings, roads, and irrigation canals. They managed the king's lands and collected his taxes. They were responsible for the upkeep and restoration of temples. They had judicial functions which entailed travelling around their district to preside at local assizes. And they were obliged to submit reports on all these activities to the king himself.

Our information on what their appointment entailed comes largely from the so-called *BĒL MADGALTI* text, a kind of job description which sets out in considerable detail the governor's duties and responsibilities.[6] We can supplement it with further material that has come to light at Maşat-Höyük, a site which lies some 116 kilometres north-east of Hattusa and is almost certainly to be identified with the Hittite city called Tapigga.[7] In the course of excavating the palace area of the site, Professor Özgüç's team discovered a cache of seal impressions and clay tablets, which can be dated to the reign of King Tudhaliya III in the early fourteenth century.[8] The tablets range in their contents from land-grants and inventories of goods and personnel to matters relating to oracular consultation. But the great majority are letters (a total of ninety-six have been discovered) dispatched by the king to his local officials in the region and copies or drafts of letters sent by the officials to the king; there are also some interesting and sometimes acerbic exchanges of correspondence between the officials themselves.[9] The most frequent recipient of the royal missives was a man called Kassu, whose impressive logographic title UGULA NIMGIR.ÉRIN.MEŠ literally means 'overseer of the military heralds'. He apparently had prime responsibility for the defence of the region.[10] Next to him in importance in the correspondence was the local *BĒL MADGALTI* Himuili.

The cache, which has the distinction of being the first Hittite archive to be discovered outside the capital, provides us with a valuable record of day-to-day administration in the outlying areas of the Hatti land. Quite noticeably, the king himself makes most of the decisions on even the most routine matters, apparently leaving little scope to his local officials to show any initiative at all. But this may not be typical of his dealings with all his provincial officials. His particularly active interest in this region may have been very much due to its precarious situation on the verge of the Kaska zone. The correspondence is largely taken up with the problems of maintaining an effective defence, by military and other means, against the ever-increasing menace of the Kaskan forces. Indeed the letters may foreshadow what was soon to come. The archive probably covers a maximum period of ten years. It is very likely that the city was destroyed at the end of this period by enemy action, when the massive invasions of the homeland began which forced Tudhaliya and his court to flee the capital while his land fell victim to the forces advancing against it from all directions.[11]

Strategic considerations relating to the defence of the realm may explain why even the $^{\text{LÚ.MEŠ}}$AGRIG, the keepers of the royal storehouses (literally 'seal-' or 'tablet-houses') located in various parts of the kingdom (a hundred or more are attested), were directly appointed by the king and dealt with him on a one-to-one basis. The storehouses were of considerable importance to the kingdom, both militarily and economically. They served as clearing houses for income due to Hattusa, as produce redistribution centres in the local area, and it seems too that they constituted a network of armouries for the Hittite militia.[12] It was clearly essential that their keepers be utterly trustworthy. These were no doubt the reasons why such relatively lowly officials were required to report directly to the king, and were directly accountable to him.[13]

Relationships between the King and his Gods

The king was in his turn accountable to the Storm God, the divine Chief Executive Officer who had delegated to him his power on earth and whose servant or slave the king frequently calls himself. The king thus occupied the *second* highest rung in the line management structure. He held his appointment by divine right. But he ruled merely as the steward of the Storm God, for 'the land belongs only to the Storm God; Heaven and Earth together with the army belongs only to the Storm God. And he made the Labarna, the king, his deputy and gave him the whole land of Hattusa.'[14] Divine endorsement conferred the status of sacrosanctity upon the king: 'May the Storm God destroy whoever approaches the king's person (with hostile intent)', the above text continues. His appointment gave him a special *ex officio* relationship with the Storm God, as his deputy on earth. But the divine patronage which he enjoyed was quite comprehensive in its scope, for a common royal epithet informs us that he was 'favoured by (all) the gods'.[15] He could also lay claim to a particular personal tutelary deity, who protected and nurtured him through his life, and ran before him and struck down his enemies in battle. Seal impressions and rock-cut reliefs sometimes depict king and protective deity benevolently linked, with the latter extending his arm around the king or holding his hand. Mursili

II was the special favourite of the Sun Goddess of Arinna, Muwatalli II of the Storm God of Lightning, Hattusili III of Ishtar, Tudhaliya IV of Sharruma, offspring of the Hurrian divine couple Teshub and Hepat.

Though theoretically a new king was the gods' appointee, whenever a current king refers to his successor there is never any indication that the gods had any part in his selection. Thus Suppiluliuma I declares to his vassal ruler Huqqana: 'Now you, Huqqana, recognize only My Majesty as overlord! My son of whom I, My Majesty, say, "Let everyone recognize this one," and whom I thereby distinguish among (his brothers)—you, Huqqana, recognize him!'[16] We must assume that the king's choice of successor, within the parameters laid down by Telipinu,[17] had the benefit of divine guidance, or that he at least ensured, through divination or other means, that his choice was acceptable to his divine masters. Some scholars believe that the king may originally have been elected by the nobility. But even if this were so, the principle of hereditary succession had been firmly established by the time of Hattusili I, the king with whom our earliest written records are associated. By implication, this principle also had divine endorsement, since the gods' appointee was invariably a member of his predecessor's immediate family.

The king's remoteness from his common subjects and his direct links with his kingdom's divine overlords no doubt greatly enhanced the sense of mystique which surrounded him. To many of his subjects, his image must have been that of a being who hovered somewhere between heaven and earth. It was an image which was deliberately cultivated, and reinforced by royal titles like 'My Sun', which is already attested in the Old Kingdom, and was regularly used during the New Kingdom in addition to or in place of the traditional royal name Labarna. It was very likely the standard formal appellation used in addressing the king, equivalent to an expression like 'Your Majesty'. Probably derived from northern Syria rather than Egypt,[18] and closely associated with the image of a winged sun-disc,[19] the title serves to reinforce the divine nature of the king's position.

His elevation from the world of the profane to a higher plane of existence must have been formally marked and celebrated at his coronation ceremony, his 'Festival of Enthronement'. Unfortunately we know little of the ceremony beyond the fact that the new king donned special royal vestments for the occasion, and was anointed with fragrant oil and formally given his throne-name.[20] Our surviving scraps of written information tell us no more, and as far as we know none of the extant reliefs depict scenes from a coronation. In those reliefs in which the king does appear, he is generally depicted wearing a skull cap and long ankle-length robe, symbolizing his office as high priest of the Hittite world. He also carries a curved staff (Hittite ^{GIŠ}*kalmuš*), often referred to by the Latin word *lituus* (from the similarly shaped staff carried by Roman augurs). The Hittite staff has been interpreted as a stylized shepherd's crook[21] or a symbol of judicial power.[22] In either case it is one of the insignia closely associated with the Sun God—as 'shepherd of

Fig. 1. King Tudhaliya IV as priest, relief from Yazılıkaya

humankind'[23] or as supreme lord of justice. The king is so accoutred and equipped not as a god himself but as the gods' agent-in-chief on earth. He is none the less a god in the making, for on his death he is said to 'become a god', a clear indication of his *post mortem* promotion to the ranks of those he formerly served.

Members of the Royal Court

Though the king may have been strictly isolated from direct contact with most of his subjects, there was a select group of people who were in regular close contact with him. These were the people of the royal court, living and working in a community totally shut off from the outside, in the fortified and heavily guarded acropolis now known as Büyükkale (literally, 'big castle'). It was a part of the city of Hattusa, yet it was a world apart from it. At the topmost level was the king himself, and the most immediate members of his family—what was called 'the Great Family'. There was the Tawananna, the reigning queen and chief consort of the king, high priestess of the Hittite realm and sometimes a politically powerful figure in her own right, who retained her status until the end of her life even if she outlived her husband.[24] There was the king's most favoured (though not necessarily his eldest) son—the crown prince, the *tuhkanti*, heir designate to the throne, the son on whose shoulders the burdens of empire would sooner or later come to rest. Already his extensive military training had equipped him to command a division of the army under his father's general command, or even to take the field as the army's commander-in-chief. Already his schooling in the complexities of a king's religious duties had enabled him to fulfil his father's role as his deputy at a number of the kingdom's important state festivals.

There were other roles, scarcely less important, to be filled by other sons—diplomatic missions to foreign states, a range of military commands, major posts in the kingdom's administrative bureaucracy, both civil and religious. Above all there were the vitally important appointments to the viceregal kingdoms of Carchemish and Aleppo, first established by Suppiluliuma I in the fourteenth century and always held, to the kingdom's last days, by sons of the Great Kings. Other key posts were assigned first and foremost to other members of the royal family. Of these the post of GAL *MEŠEDI*, 'Chief of the Bodyguards', was probably the most prestigious and the most important. The man appointed to it had to be one on whose ability and loyalty the king could rely implicitly. For he above all others had responsibility for the king's personal safety and security. He was generally if not invariably a close member of the king's family, on a number of occasions one of the king's brothers. Suppiluliuma appointed his brother Zida to the post, Muwatalli his brother Hattusili, and Hattusili on himself becoming king his son Tudhaliya.

The *MEŠEDI* formed an elite guard, armed with spears, whose prime responsibility was the protection of the king.[25] We might think of them as roughly comparable to the praetorian guard of imperial Rome, the personal bodyguard of the Caesar. However, they differed from the praetorians in at least two important respects. In the first place, their numbers seem to have been very much smaller. We hear of no more than twelve assembled at one time—those who formed a guard in the courtyard adjoining the royal palace. Of course their total number must have been somewhat larger since constant guard duties would have necessitated their working in shifts. There may also have been separate detachments of *MEŠEDI* stationed in royal villas and regional palaces visited by the king in the course of his religious pilgrimages, though it seems more likely that the detachments so assigned travelled with the king from his capital in order to provide him with a constant escort throughout his itinerary. The other respect in which the *MEŠEDI* differed from the Roman praetorians was that they shared their duties with another security force known as 'the golden spearmen'. They too provided guard duty in the palace courtyard, they too were twelve in number. One member of each group was detailed for sentry duty on one of the main gates in the south-west and south-east corners which separated the palace complex from the outside world. The purpose in appointing two sets of guards, suggests Professor Beal, was so that each would ensure the loyalty of the other.

But there is no doubt that the *MEŠEDI* constituted the king's elite and most trusted security force. It was they who provided an inner ring of protection around the king during festival processions and at festival venues, sometimes themselves participating in the festival activities. And no doubt they too had the prime responsibility for the safety of their sovereign lord during his military campaigns, very likely providing an impenetrable security screen around him whenever battle was joined. One can appreciate the enormous power and influence which their chief, the GAL *MEŠEDI*, must have enjoyed, both in the political sphere, and as a high-ranking military commander in the field of battle. Our records do not reveal whether the post was ever exploited to the point where it produced a Hittite Sejanus or Tigellinus. But Hattusili III's ambitions beyond his allotted station in life, his desire to wear one day his brother's crown, may well have been spawned and nurtured by his tenure of that post while his brother was still on the throne.

Prominent amongst other officials of the kingdom was the man designated as the GAL (LÚ.MEŠ) GEŠTIN, 'the Chief of the Wine (Stewards)', an unpretentious-sounding but in fact highly prestigious title. Its holder was assigned important military commands either under the general command of the king or as commander-in-chief in his own right. The use of such a term, which goes back to the early days of the Old Kingdom, no doubt reflects a time in early Hittite history when the king's most trusted confidants and advisers were those who attended him in a range of capacities, some quite humble, on a daily basis. With time, the increasing importance of the persons upon whom the king came particularly to depend also enhanced the status of the positions which they held. Some of these positions, while retaining their original names, were gradually divested of their original characteristics as their holders acquired more influence in the court and increasingly higher levels of responsibility.

Even in the kingdom's early days all members of the palace establishment, down to the most menial functionaries, must have seen themselves as members of an elite, exclusive community, set apart from all other subjects of the king. And no doubt the kings themselves fostered this notion. It made good sense to do so, for it was in a king's interests to bond as closely as possible to those in closest contact with him, that is, to those to whom he was most vulnerable—an important consideration in the days of chronic plots and coups and struggles for the royal succession prior to the accession of King Telipinu. In his famous Proclamation, Telipinu included a comprehensive range of palace staff, from highest to lowest, in the assembly called the *panku*. To this assembly he assigned extensive executive and disciplinary powers, even over members of the royal family. It was to include 'the Palace Servants, the Bodyguard, the Men of the Golden Spear, the Cup-Bearers, the Table-Men, the Cooks, the Heralds, the Stableboys, the Captains of the Thousand'.

By the New Kingdom, the *panku* had become all but defunct[26] as more formal bureaucratic structures developed. None the less the sense of superiority that came from belonging to an elite, exclusive community must have continued to be one of the defining features of membership of the royal court. To be Chief of the Table-Men in the king's palace was a title its occupant could bear with pride. Even the most menial functionaries could claim a status which elevated them far above those engaged in similar employment outside the palace walls. Probably not without justification. In many cases their positions may well have been hereditary, passed on from father to son. But all must have been obliged to undergo rigorous training before being considered fit to enter His Majesty's service. We have seen the meticulous attention paid to ensuring that everything with which the king came in contact was totally free of contamination—the food he ate, the clothes he wore, the items he used, the water in which he washed. To be in the king's service was a matter of great privilege and great pride. But there was a downside to this as we shall see. To be found negligent in the king's service, even over an apparently trivial detail, could attract the severest penalties.

In a broad sense, then, we might think of the royal court as including all those who were members of the king's own family and/or who were in the direct service of the king in one capacity or another. The latter included the king's chief military commanders, the Chief of the Scribes, tablet archivists, bureaucratic officials, medical consultants of both local and foreign origin, the royal bodyguards, and the wide array of household staff—cooks, domestic servants, doorkeepers, pages, heralds, prayer-reciters, barbers, cleaners, craftsmen, and grooms.

Where did they all live? The area on which the palace complex on Büyükkale was built was some 250 by 150 metres in extent. Its irregular surface required the construction of a number of artificial terraces to level the site, and on the east and west sides to extend it, in order to maximize the space available for the erection of the palace buildings. The final building phase of the acropolis, carried out under Hattusili III and Tudhaliya IV, was its most extensive and most impressive. Then indeed there arose a complex of monumental proportions, worthy of a Great King. In overall concept, it has been likened to an Ottoman seraglio, with its series of free-standing buildings linked to form an architecturally coherent whole by successive courtyards and colonnades, each giving access to the next through portals flanked by porters' lodges or guard rooms. But impressive though all this undoubtedly was, it is somewhat ironic that the capital's most splendid material phase, both on the acropolis and in the upper city, should correspond with the beginning of an irreversible decline in the kingdom's political and military fortunes. One may see a certain symbolism in the strengthening of the acropolis fortifications at this time, including its total enclosure within walls. Undoubtedly this was a great engineering achievement, one which must have greatly enhanced the imposing character of the site, like the walls of contemporary Mycenae and Tiryns across the Aegean. Yet it is difficult to escape the feeling that here as in Mycenaean Greece substantial new fortifications were a reflection of growing insecurity. Perhaps those with foresight were already looking to the day when all else would be lost and the citadel would have to stand alone against enemy onslaught, its fortifications serving as a last line of defence.

In the early days of the kingdom, the great majority of officials and attendants who directly served the king may have resided in the acropolis precincts. But as the kingdom expanded and its bureaucracy became increasingly complex, this grew less and less feasible. Particularly in the last century of the kingdom, the architectural emphasis in the acropolis on space and monumentality, as reflected in the open courtyards linked with large free-standing buildings, would have been quite incompatible with the provision of adequate residential areas for a large number of live-in service personnel. It seems likely, then, that permanent residents of the acropolis were by and large limited to members of the royal family and to those staff whose services were required virtually at any time, particularly those responsible for food preparation and general household maintenance. It is possible that some of the king's closest advisers, like the Chief of Scribes and the royal physicians, also lived permanently in the acropolis precincts. But other officials may have lived elsewhere in the city, travelling to the acropolis either each day or whenever there was a call upon their services. Many of the high-ranking military officers and other dignitaries who were also in a sense members of the royal court may well have lived like baronial lords on estates outside the city, estates which they or their forebears had received as gifts from the king for services rendered. In terms of their allegiance to the king, they were obliged to render him service and meet with him in council as and when required.

On Büyükkale, the chief royal residential quarters lay at the far end and highest part of the site.[27] Here were accommodated the principal residents of the acropolis—those who were members of, or had an attachment of one sort or another to, the royal family. Their numbers were probably not inconsiderable, especially by the last century of the kingdom. In one of her letters to Ramesses II Queen Puduhepa speaks of a royal household full of little princes and princesses, many of whom were probably the offspring of royal *Nebenfrauen*, secondary wives, or concubines. For these too palace accommodation was required, as also for the king's sons and their families, possibly too in some cases for members of collateral branches of the royal family. There was no doubt a reasonably constant turnover of royal personnel, as sons were assigned to viceregal posts or to other administrative positions which took them and presumably their families from the capital, and as daughters were married off to foreign rulers. Many family members were probably housed in other royal residences in Hattusa (several are attested) or elsewhere in the kingdom. The ranks of those with royal connections, and royal pretensions, swelled rapidly with each succeeding generation, much to the consternation of one of the last kings Tudhaliya IV, who in constant fear of being unseated in a coup bemoans the fact that the kingdom is 'full of the royal line: in Hatti the descendants of Suppiluliuma, the descendants of Mursili, the descendants of Muwatalli, the descendants of Hattusili are numerous!'[28]

Since strictly speaking Tudhaliya had no right to the throne, which his father had illegally wrested from his cousin Urhi-Teshub, his concerns may have been well justified. A king's claim to divine protection actually counted for very little in the face of a determined challenge to seize his throne from him. Even in the most stable periods there is little doubt that intrigues and family faction disputes constantly simmered within the royal court. Generally these are kept well hidden from our scrutiny, and we can only guess at them from, say, the sudden disappearance of a prominent royal person from our records, like Henti, wife of Suppiluliuma I, prior to his marriage to the Babylonian princess. But there are occasions when a king rattles his family skeletons quite openly. We have already learnt something of the behaviour of Hattusili I's dysfunctional family from his 'death-bed' Testament. And we also learn of an Old Kingdom Tawananna, whose conduct so outraged the king that he banished her from the palace and henceforth forbade even the mention of her name, or that of her children, on pain of death.[29] Further examples are provided by later kings' prayers and oracle enquiries. Thus we come to hear from Mursili II of his stepmother's scandalous conduct in the palace both before and after her husband's death, and her alleged responsibility for the death of her stepson's wife. From an oracle text we learn of faction strife between the women of the royal court, probably in the reign of Tudhaliya IV. Squabbles appear to have erupted between the king's mother Puduhepa and her supporters on one side, and his wife and her mother and supporters on the other.[30] The trouble was no doubt due to Puduhepa's apparently obsessive desire to control all that went on in the royal household, and much that went on in the kingdom at large. Her arrogation, or at least her assumption, of the roles of royal matchmaker and rearer of little princes and princesses probably had as much to do with consolidating her personal control over members of the royal court as it did with the kingdom's greater good.

Concubinage

Numerous though the royal progeny were, at least in the thirteenth century to judge from Puduhepa's claims and Tudhaliya's concerns, it was no easy task to ensure that the supply of such could always meet demand. A Great King needed substantial numbers of offspring for a variety of purposes—including the provisioning of princesses for establishing family unions with vassal kingdoms or foreign royal houses. Princes might also be used for this purpose, as well as for administrative, religious, military, and diplomatic posts within the kingdom. Indeed particular situations could often arise where a royal prince was required, whether to fulfil an important administrative role, to sort out a serious judicial dispute in the vassal states, or to lead a high-level diplomatic mission to a foreign kingdom. When one was dealing with status-conscious foreign kings and vassal rulers a royal pedigree could be essential to the success of the undertaking.

But problems could arise if there were insufficient princes of the blood available for such purposes. Hence the extension of the title DUMU.LUGAL, 'son of the king', to other persons, including certain scribes, who though of high status had not actually been born in the purple.[31] The essentially honorific title conferred upon such persons full authority to deputize for the king—especially, it seems, in the Syrian vassal states where they were apparently employed for particular tasks rather than appointed to a specific post. Professor

Beckman notes the commissions they performed in Ugarit, redrawing the borders of the state, arbitrating between the queen and a tax official, and even ordering the vassal king ʿIbiranu to appear in person before the Great King. They could also be used to validate legal documents, as at Emar, with their name appended first in the list of witnesses to the documents.[32]

But this was at best a compromise. The elevation of an enterprising subject of lesser status to the ranks of surrogate princedom was still no substitute for a genuine product of His Majesty's own loins. Hence there must have been a considerable obligation on the king to go forth and multiply. Which of course raises the question of precisely whom he could go forth and multiply with.

We must remember that he often spent a good deal of each year on military campaigns far from home. This obviously limited his opportunities for procreational activity, at least on the official level, and necessitated a maximization of these opportunities in the few months of the year that he was at home. Yet if he were confined to only one official wife his siring output was inevitably going to be very limited, regardless of how physically desirable or fecund she may have been. This is where the institution of concubinage comes into its own. No doubt the king was expected to devote a good deal of his 'home' periods to distributing his royal seed as frequently as possible amongst his officially recognized bedmates of child-bearing age. This in order to ensure a continuing supply of royal offspring, for marriage alliances with foreign or vassal rulers, or (in the case of males) for representing the king on diplomatic missions, holding important military commands, or occupying important posts in the palace bureaucracy. A harem of secondary wives and concubines was probably not so much a perk of the job of being king as a requirement of it.[33]

Princes and princesses were graded according to the status of their mother. The most important responsibilities were reserved for the highest-ranking offspring. Sons whose mothers belonged to one of the top two ranks were eligible to inherit the throne, according to the principles of succession laid down by King Telipinu: 'Let a prince, a son of the first rank, become king. If there is no prince of the first rank, let him who is a son of the second rank become king. But if there is no prince, no heir, let them take a son-in-law (that is, a husband) for her who is a daughter of the first rank, and let him become king.'[34] That is to say, the sons of the king's chief wife, in most cases the Tawananna, had first claim on the throne. If she had no sons the succession passed to a son of the second rank—presumably the offspring of the so-called *esertu* wife, a woman inferior in status to the chief wife though still of free birth.[35] If she too was without sons, the succession passed to a son-in-law of the king, the husband of the daughter of the king's chief wife. Clearly the offspring of the king by concubines of lower status, designated as *naptartu* and SAL SUHUR.LAL (literally 'attendant woman' in the Hittite context), were ineligible to succeed to the throne, but as genuine 'sons of the king' they may well have filled other important posts in the kingdom's administrative hierarchy.

Yet they were clearly distinguished from those sons who came out of the king's top drawers. Rank, status, pecking order were very important in the Bronze Age world. Even a royal *pahhurzi*, a son of the second rank[36] and therefore perfectly eligible for the throne, did not inspire the same respect as a first-rank son. Indeed this was the ostensible reason why Masturi, ruler of the western vassal state Seha River Land, refused support to King Urhi-Teshub, the son of an *esertu* wife, when the latter had his throne contested by his uncle Hattusili: 'Should I protect a (mere) second-rank son?' sniffed Masturi. His air of superiority may have been partly due to the fact that he himself had been honoured with the hand of a Hittite princess of the *first* rank in marriage, Massanauzzi (Massana-ÌR-i), daughter of Mursili II. Princesses of this status were probably normally reserved for marriage alliances with other Great Kings, and Masturi may indeed have been privileged in his marriage alliance. Unfortunately, despite all their efforts the couple were to remain childless.

The Responsibilities of Kingship

There can be no doubt that in the management of the affairs of the Land of Hatti the Hittite king's role was very much a hands-on one. He was chief priest of his people, the gods' deputy on earth, and each year he was the principal celebrant in a demanding round of religious festivals, which often took him on pilgrimages to the main religious centres of his kingdom. He was commander-in-chief of the Hittite armies, and regularly led his troops on campaigns far from the homeland. He deputized for the Sun God as the supreme earthly judge of his people, and personally sat in judgement on disputes between vassal rulers, on cases which could only be tried by the king's court, and on appeals against judgements made by a lower court. Encapsulated in these duties is the classic threefold functions of kingship in the Near East, as well as in Homeric society, which combines the king's religious, military, and judicial roles. The responsibilities of empire also required the king to maintain regular contact both with his vassal rulers throughout his subject territories and with his royal counterparts in Egypt, Mesopotamia, and occasionally Mycenaean Greece. And there were vassal treaties and parity treaties with foreign kings to be revised and drawn up afresh every time a new vassal ruler or royal Brother came to power through the death or displacement of his predecessor.

Some kings were notable for their building achievements, like the otherwise almost obscure Old Kingdom Hantili II, who was responsible for the first extensive fortification of the capital, or Tudhaliya IV, to whose credit lie the massive expansion and redevelopment of Hattusa in the final decades before its fall. Suppiluliuma I and Mursili II reported fortifying cities and lands. But building achievements were never incorporated into the ideology of kingship in the Hittite world as they were in Egypt and Mesopotamia. Nor did Hittite kings ever seem to have followed the Mesopotamian practice of placing foundation tablets beneath public buildings, identifying themselves as the builders and giving details of the time and occasion on which the buildings were erected.

Speaking merely in relation to the king's religious obligations, Professor Güterbock wondered how he found time to do anything else! The answer must lie in one word—delegation. We do know that many of his functions could be delegated, particularly to other members of his family including the surrogate 'sons of the king'. Quite possibly a great deal more was delegated than we are currently aware of. We know that viceroys and other officials regularly deputized for the king in the judicial affairs of the vassal states, especially in Syria, and it might well be that the great majority of cases that came before the king's court in Hattusa were conducted in his name rather than by him in person. There were occasions too when a son could deputize for his father in religious festivals, though this was a rather more sensitive area, and a king had to be very careful to avoid offending a deity by failing to honour his rites in person. On the other hand military commands could be regularly delegated, both to the king's sons and to other officers—generally though by no means always with positive outcomes. Above all, we can scarcely overestimate the importance of delegated authority to the king's scribes, in the routine administration of the kingdom, in the preparation of drafts and final versions of treaties, decrees, and diplomatic correspondence, and on a broad range of matters which constantly came before the king and required his decision. The Chief Scribe in particular must have assumed much of the workload involved in managing affairs of state which were officially the responsibility of the king. It was only through the services of all these persons, acting as the king's delegates, that the king himself could hope to fulfil all the demands that his office imposed upon him.

It is perhaps fitting that we should end this chapter by noting a quality of kingship which though not strongly emphasized in our texts does surface from time to time. It is the quality of mercy or compassion. We have seen that Hattusili I declared his nephew unfit to succeed him for lack of this quality. It is the quality which Mursili II claimed in yielding to the appeals of a rebellious vassal's aged mother. It is the quality which a king sought to instil in those charged with judicial responsibilities, instructing them to protect the weak and vulnerable members of society. So too the Old Kingdom prince Pimpira, acting probably as regent for the boy-king Mursili I, called upon his officials to 'give bread to the one who is hungry, oil to the one who is chapped, clothing to the one who is naked. If heat distresses him, place him where it is cool. If cold distresses him, place him where it is warm.'[37] Simple though this statement is, it may well reflect an important element in the ideology of kingship, albeit one which finds little explicit recognition in the record of royal qualities and achievements.[38]

CHAPTER 2
The People and the Law

> A man has been injured. His injury is neither permanent nor life-threatening, but it is sufficient to incapacitate him so that he is unable for a time to engage in his normal work. The person who has caused the injury, whether deliberately or accidentally, is legally responsible for providing his victim with appropriate medical care, covering his doctor's bills, supplying someone to work in his place during his convalescence, and paying him compensation after his recovery.

We learn a great deal about how a society functions, or is supposed to function, by studying the laws it has devised for guiding and regulating the behaviour of its members. By their very nature, a society's laws tell us much about the ethical norms and codes of conduct which operate within the society, and they often provide important insights into the overall philosophy and principles which helped shape them; for many laws are in effect specific applications of general principles. In the centuries before the rise of the Hittite kingdom, the Mesopotamian lawgivers generally made explicit the principles and purposes of their programmes of legal reform. Thus in the prologue to his Laws Lipit-Ishtar, a king of the Isin-Larsa dynasty (*reg. c.*1934–1924 BC), indicates the chief intent of his reform programme by highlighting his achievements in the field of social justice and welfare: 'I established justice in Sumer and Akkad in accordance with the word of (the god) Enlil. I procured the freedom of the sons and daughters of Sumer and Akkad upon whom slaveship had been imposed.'[1] So too in the epilogue to his famous 'law code' the Babylonian king Hammurabi (*reg. c.*1792–1750) states that his laws have been designed to ensure 'that the strong may not oppress the weak, that justice be given to the orphan and the widow'.

No such general statement of policy or overall intent introduces or is appended to the Hittite collection of laws (which we will henceforth refer to as The Laws).[2] But from its individual clauses we can identify a number of the principles which underlie it. The most fundamental is the right of all subjects of the state to legal redress for offences committed against their persons or their property.[3] This principle, illustrated by our introductory paragraph,[4] is embodied in many parts of The Laws. And with it is associated one of The Laws' most characteristic features—fair compensation to the victim of an offence, to be made by the person who has offended against him. In contrast to Hammurabic law, the emphasis in Hittite law is not so much on retributive justice or vengeance for its own sake, which is rarely of any material benefit to the victim, as on compensatory justice. An offender will have satisfied the demands of justice and paid his penalty in full once he has discharged his legal obligations to his victim.

The Hittite term *handantatar* seems to have been the closest the Hittites came to designating law as an abstract concept. Comparable in some respects to the Egyptian concept of *maat*, *handantatar* is a difficult term to translate. Approximating to the meaning 'justice', or 'just behaviour', it encompassed both divine justice and the power to impose that justice.[5] Within the sphere of human activity, justice has to do with the restoration of order and balance and equity, which have been disrupted by an offender's action. This will not be achieved merely by punishing the offender without benefit to his victim; the penalty must equate to full restitution for the victim, to ensure that he will be as he was before the offence took place. When this is achieved, balance will be restored, justice will have been done.

Sources of Information

Our knowledge of Hittite law and its application is based on a range of sources. These include minutes of court proceedings which record the testimony of the participants involved in litigation (for example, defendants accused of theft or of having misappropriated certain items placed in their charge),[6] instructions issued by the king to provincial administrators who have been assigned judicial responsibilities in their regions, records of cases arising from disputes in and between vassal states, especially in Syria where they were generally dealt with by one of the king's representatives in the region (often the viceroy), and an occasional reference to court cases in the homeland, like the lawsuits involving the prince Hattusili (later King Hattusili III) and his rival and distant relative Arma-Tarhunda. We might also include in our list of sources the collection of anecdotes from the so-called Palace Chronicle, dating back to the reigns of Hattusili I and Mursili I, which record various offences committed by palace officials, and the penalties for these offences.[7]

However, the collection we have called The Laws is by far our most important source of information on the operation of law and justice in the Hittite world. It consists of some 200 clauses, the earliest surviving version of which dates to the Old Kingdom, around 1650 BC. From references it makes to revisions to previous laws we know that there must have been an even earlier version, probably going back to the reign of the original Labarna, the earliest known Hittite monarch, in the kingdom's first days. In the centuries that followed, the collection's integrity was carefully maintained as it was repeatedly copied by successive generations of scribes. Many such copies have survived,[8] four dating to the Old Kingdom,[9] the remainder to the New, from *c.*1400 to the kingdom's final days. The later versions sometimes modernize the language, and sometimes refine or flesh out details of the earlier versions, but only one New Kingdom version, the so-called 'Late Parallel Version',[10] contains any substantive revisions.

The Nature and Content of The Laws[11]

Even though The Laws was carefully preserved and repeatedly copied with little change over the centuries, the collection seems not to have been treated with any special veneration or regarded as having any special authority. We have noted that there is no *apologia*, no philosophical rationale attached to it (at least none that has survived), and unlike its Mesopotamian predecessors or its biblical parallels there is not the slightest suggestion that it was seen as either divinely inspired or divinely endorsed. It is a plain, straightforward secular document. It was never presented in monumental form or put on public display for all to see, like the stele inscribed with Hammurabi's Laws.

Nor does it really warrant being called a code, except purely as a matter of convenience. (Of course the same can be said of any of the ancient Near Eastern compendia of laws.) Its coverage of areas which must have required due legal process is far from comprehensive, the areas it does deal with are only partially covered, there appears to be no logical pattern in the way the clauses are ordered,[12] there are numerous inconsistencies and anomalies in the levels of specificity in the various prescriptions and rulings, and when seen from the point of view of modern Western law, the collection presents a largely unsystematic jumble of civil and criminal law. It has all the signs of being a hodge-podge of a number of separate contributions, perhaps accumulated over a period of many years. And from the hundreds, perhaps thousands, of court judgements on which it might have drawn there appears to have been a considerable element of randomness in what actually went into it.[13]

In the area of criminal activity, The Laws deals with a range of offences extending through accidental or unpremeditated homicide, assault, abduction, theft, damage to property, and sorcery, to various categories of forbidden sexual liaisons. In the area of civil law, it contains a series of provisions relating to marriage, and it often stipulates prices to be paid for particular goods and services, the latter including hire rates for human labour, livestock, and equipment. There are some surprising omissions, in terms of what we might expect to find in a compendium of laws. Items not covered or barely touched upon include, in the criminal area, premeditated homicide and rape (only one clause refers to rape), and in the civil area contract and commercial law, and laws relating to family succession and inheritance. In a fully developed legal system which the Hittites obviously had, we must assume that such matters were either subject to customary law[14] or dealt with in other legal contexts—or in the case of certain crimes against individuals left to the discretion of the victim or his (or her) family.

In a case of murder, for example, it was apparently the prerogative of the victim's relatives to decide the murderer's fate. 'Whoever commits murder, whatever the heir of the murdered man says (will be done),' declares the Old Kingdom Proclamation of King Telipinu. 'If he says: "Let him die," he shall die; if he says "Let him make compensation", he shall make compensation.'[15] In later times, the choices available to the victim's family seem to have been limited to either compensatory payment by the murderer or his enslavement to the family.[16] The death penalty was apparently no longer an option, except in districts where it had the sanction of customary law. In a case of adultery, however, if a cuckolded husband took the law into his own hands and executed his faithless wife and her lover the law condoned if not actually legitimized his action (clause 197).

All this depends of course on the assumption that the murderer was actually caught. In the event that he avoided capture or his identity remained unknown, The Laws invoked a principle, first attested in Mesopotamian law, that a person or community on whose land or in whose neighbourhood a crime was committed must bear the responsibility and make due restitution for the crime:[17]

> If a man is found dead on another's property, the property owner shall give his property, house, and sixty shekels of silver. If the dead person is a woman, the property owner shall give (no property, but) 120 shekels of silver. But if the place where the dead body was found is not private property, but uncultivated open country, they shall measure three DANNAS in all directions,[18] and the dead person's heir shall take those very (people who inhabit the village). If there is no village within that radius, the heir (of the deceased) shall forfeit his claim.[19]

This clause leaves no doubt that the inhabitants of a particular district or community were themselves held responsible, in part at least, for the maintenance of law and order within their territory, and faced serious consequences for failing to do so. The harshness of these consequences must have acted as a powerful incentive for local property owners and communities to make sure that the actual perpetrators of serious crimes like murder were promptly apprehended and brought to justice. Community responsibility for the prevention of crime and apprehension of criminals features also in the judgements handed down by the Hittite viceroys in Syria when dealing with cases of murder in the vassal states. Substantial penalties were imposed on states or communities held responsible for the murder of merchants travelling through their territory. Ugarit seems to figure frequently in cases of this kind. For example, the town of Apsuna in Ugarit was required to pay one talent of silver to the merchant Talimmu for the murder of his business associates (see Chapter 5). The basic principle involved goes back at least to Hammurabic law, and quite possibly originated in the customary law of the nomadic forebears of Hammurabi's subjects.

The Application of The Laws

In view of its contents and overall character The Laws might best be described as a manual of legal precedents. In the area of criminal law, an offence was committed, a judgement handed down, and a record of that judgement kept, for guidance when future cases of a similar nature arose. The degree of specificity in many of the clauses lends weight to this assumption.[20] However, in the manner of case law, the clauses are formulated as a series of hypothetical propositions: 'If someone commits such-and-such an offence, the penalty the court will impose upon him will be. . . .' Precedents for this type of formulation occur in a number of Mesopotamian legal texts, notably Hammurabi's Laws, and later parallels can be found in Old Testament Law. But the 'manual' went well beyond the area of criminal law, providing guidelines on wages and prices and social contracts as well as listing criminal offences and penalties. Its overall value as a source of reference on legal matters probably led to its wide distribution throughout the homeland. No doubt all local judicial authorities had their own copies to hand when dealing with cases which came under their jurisdiction.

But what influence did The Laws actually have on their deliberations? Records, which were certainly kept, of judgements handed down in specific cases might have given us some indication of how closely these judgements matched up with what The Laws actually specified. But unfortunately none of these records have survived. Even so, The Laws must with few exceptions have been intended to guide rather than to prescribe, allowing considerable discretion to the local judicial bodies. Indeed in a large number of cases it could hardly have been otherwise. Our introductory paragraph describes a general situation involving bodily injury. Nothing specific is said about the circumstances in which the injury was inflicted or its degree of severity. The types of compensatory action which the offender is obliged to take are specified. But in each individual case the actual payment to be made must have been scaled to take account of the severity of the injury, the extent to which there was any apportionment of blame between the offender and his victim, the length of time of recovery, the completeness of recovery, and the status of the victim (whether slave or free). In the interests of ensuring that justice was fully and fairly done, the local authorities must have been allowed considerable leeway in doing it. That is clearly the import of clauses like 94 and 95, which state a specific penalty to be imposed for the offence of burglary, but then add the rider: 'If (the offender) steals much, they shall impose much upon him. If he steals little, they shall impose little upon him.'

In the regional and rural districts of the homeland the administration of justice was one of the responsibilities of the town or village authorities known as the Council of Elders, probably consisting of the heads of prominent local families, wealthy local landowners, and the like.[21] In the judicial area as no doubt in other areas the councils were obliged to collaborate closely with the regional governor, the *BĒL MADGALTI*, an appointee of the king whose many duties included the dispensing of justice in the region to which he had been appointed. Minor cases may have fallen entirely within the competence of the local council. But something like assizes were probably held for more serious cases during the governor's tours of inspection of his region. On such occasions he must have presided as the king's representative over local courts with the local mayor (LÚMAŠKIM.URUKI) (Akk. *rābisu*) and members of the village council acting as his advisers. The manual of legal precedents (if we may so call The Laws) no doubt provided him with a handy source of reference in dealing promptly and expeditiously with the incessant squabbles and disputes which must have been as much a feature of Hittite village and rural life as of any closely settled agricultural society in any age.

It is this which provides us with one of The Laws' defining features. Its concern was much less with the elite elements of Hittite society than with the little people of the state—the villager injured in a tavern brawl or in a dispute with his neighbour over boundaries, the small farmer seeking to buy some pigs or a small orchard, the hired labourer, the herdsman, the cattle rustler, the slave, the local romeos and lotharios, the participants in family weddings, the partners in mixed and common law marriages. There was potential for conflict and litigation in every aspect of life in the village and farming communities, and no doubt the 'city-gates', the venue of the local courts, were thronged with clamorous appellants, seeking justice for real or supposed wrongs, laying claim to stray livestock which their discoverer has refused to hand over, seeking the return of the 'bride-price' for a reluctant bride who had absconded on her wedding day, demanding compensation for a crop trampled by a neighbour's unsupervised cattle, or for a favourite working dog brained by an irate neighbour for savaging his ducks.

In the terms of his appointment, the governor was strictly instructed to administer justice fairly and impartially, not favouring the strong over the weak, being sure to protect the interests of vulnerable members of society, like widows and orphans, against exploitation by a powerful neighbour: 'Into whatever city you return, summon forth all the people of the city. Whoever has a suit, decide it for him and satisfy him. If the slave of a man, or the maid-servant of a man, or a bereaved woman has a suit, decide it for them and satisfy them. Do not make the better case the worse or the worse case the better. Do what is just.'[22]

Governors were also enjoined to show due regard for local customs in dispensing justice. Judgements handed down and penalties imposed should not, as far as possible, be contrary to local customary law, which might in a number of instances take precedence over judgements specified in The Laws. The governor might often have had to rely on the village council's knowledge of local traditions to ensure that his judgements were consistent with these. It might well be that local tradition prescribed a harsher penalty than that allowed for in The Laws. For example homicide, as we have already noted, is not categorized as a capital offence in The Laws. But there were apparently districts of the kingdom where this offence did in fact attract the death penalty. In such districts the king's governor had instructions to abide by the local custom: 'If in the past it has been the custom in a town to impose the death penalty, that custom will continue. But if in a town it has been the custom to impose exile, that custom will continue.'[23]

This accords with the impression one frequently has in reading The Laws of the increasing emphasis placed on local communities becoming as self-regulatory as possible, with less and less involvement by the central authority of the state. Where these communities have their own customary law, let their members be tried in accordance with it. In later versions of The Laws, not only are a number of the prescribed penalties substantially reduced but the king waives his share of any part of the proceeds. Such a concession might well have been influenced by practical considerations. The difficulty of ensuring that the king always received his due share of innumerable fines of relatively insignificant amounts must scarcely have warranted the effort in collecting them or the ill-will that such a task no doubt generated. On the other hand, by extending the compensatory principle to almost all cases where an offence had been committed, the state ensured that there were always those with a vested interest in seeing to it that a judgement was carried out. This is in marked contrast to a system in which (a) the victim derives no benefit from the punishment of the person who has harmed him (except the satisfaction of seeing him punished), and (b) the state has the entire responsibility, and the cost, of ensuring that the culprit pays his debt to society in full.

In theory the amount of compensation payable to a victim should exactly equate with the extent of his indisposition or loss. But in practice the compensatory sum or equivalent in kind was determined by a range of factors, including not only the nature of the offence, the extent of the injury or loss, or whether an injury suffered by a victim was permanent or temporary, but also whether the injury or loss was inflicted deliberately or accidentally, the capacity of the offender to pay, and the status of both the offender and the victim. This last is particularly significant, and in fact illustrates another fundamental principle of The Laws. While every member of the state had a right to the protection of the laws, justice was not even-handed in its application. A clear distinction was drawn between slave and free. Thus compensation imposed for offences against the former was generally only half that imposed for offences against the latter. It is not entirely clear who actually received the compensation for injury to a slave—the slave himself or the master. However, it may well have been the master, since the slave was after all his master's property and in this respect any injury he sustained may have been regarded as no different from damage to his master's livestock or crops or orchards. On the other hand, offences committed by slaves attracted only half the penalty of those committed by free persons (for example, clauses 101, 121). If the slaves themselves were responsible for paying the compensation, and that is how the clauses appear to read, then we obviously have to do with slaves who were persons of independent means—as indeed a number of slaves in Hittite society appear to have been (see below). Yet the ultimate responsibility for compensating a victim of a slave's actions must have been borne by the master himself, just as he was responsible for damage done to a neighbour's property by his livestock. The smaller penalty may be intended to reflect either an assumed lesser capacity on the part of the slave to pay compensation, or alternatively a lower level of responsibility on the part of his owner to make good the damage he had done, than if the master himself were directly at fault.

When the court had ruled that compensation be paid to a complainant, there were presumably procedures for enforcing compliance by the offender. In some cases it is not unlikely that complainants or their representatives were allowed considerable latitude in enforcing it themselves, by whatever means. However, there may well have been many cases where the complainant was unable or unwilling to take such measures. Very likely then the council had the overall responsibility for ensuring that the court's judgement was carried out, just as it had the authority to take other punitive measures against recalcitrant members of its community. We might note here that a number of clauses, after stating the offender's liability, end with the phrase *parnassea suwayezzi*, whose interpretation has been the subject of much debate. Various suggested translations include 'he shall pledge his estate as security' (thus Goetze), and most recently 'he shall look to his house for it' (thus Hoffner); that is to say, a person awarded compensation was entitled to recover damages from the estate of the perpetrator of the offence against him. Whatever the precise meaning of the phrase, it probably indicates that an offender's entire estate could be claimed upon if a court found against him, and that if necessary he would be obliged to forfeit part or all of the estate if he could not meet his legal obligations by other means. Such a stipulation would almost certainly imply that there were officials responsible for ensuring that the decisions of the court were fully carried out.

The local council represented in a sense the lowest identifiable level in the judicial hierarchy of the Hittite land. The regional governor represented a higher level of judicial authority, with responsibilities which may have included acting as a court of appeal against judgements made purely at council level. We also hear of officials with the title ^{LÚ}DUGUD 'dignitary, magistrate'. They were judicial authorities appointed by the king and rendered judgement in his name. As such their judgement was final and absolute, as made clear by the penalty for rejecting it: 'If anyone rejects a judgement of the king, his house will become a heap of ruins. If anyone rejects a judgement of a magistrate, they shall cut off his head' (clause 173a). This is one of the very few instances in The Laws where the death penalty is prescribed. It is not a particular offence which attracts this penalty, for none is actually specified in this clause. Rather it is the failure to abide by the judgement handed down, irrespective of the offence. Direct defiance of the king himself attracted the most severe retribution—apparently the destruction of the offender's entire family, if that is the correct interpretation of the first part of the clause.[24] Defiance of the magistrate acting *in loco regis*—rendering judgement in the king's name—was serious enough to warrant the extreme penalty for the offender (to flout his authority was tantamount to an act of defiance against the king himself) though in this case his family was spared.

Did these magistrates try cases of a particular kind? An Old Hittite text informs us that they were charged with investigating complaints of the poor against rich citizens (along with indicating that the magistrates were susceptible to corruption by the latter).[25] Consistent with this, one of their major responsibilities may well have been to act as a final court of appeal with full authority delegated by the king to deal with appeals against judgements made in a lower court. Very likely this was aimed particularly at eliminating or at least reducing the possibility that justice dispensed at district or community level might be biased in favour of the more powerful and influential members of the community. And this may provide us with a third fundamental principle of Hittite law: Justice must be dispensed fairly to all, regardless of wealth or status; and all members of the community have the right of appeal to the king against what they believe to be an unjust judgement. The harsh penalty imposed for ignoring the final judgement of the king or his representatives may well have been intended particularly as a deterrent against powerful local landowners or corrupt local officials who might otherwise be tempted simply to ignore a judgement given against them and to continue to exploit their position over the weaker and more vulnerable members of their community.

The rare occasions on which sentence of death is stipulated in The Laws indicates a general reduction, by the time of the New Kingdom, in the range of offences which attracted the death penalty, when compared with the broader application of this penalty in the earliest period of Hittite society, and particularly when compared with its widespread application in Hammurabic law. This in turn serves to highlight the extreme gravity, in the Hittite perception, of those offences for which it was still applicable. Notable amongst these were acts which caused pollution or defilement, physical or moral, like certain prohibited sexual liaisons. It was also applicable in a number of instances to those who polluted the environment of kings or gods, either by coming before them in an unclean state, or by serving up polluted food or drink to them, or by entering a temple without authorization. Keeping for oneself and one's family sacrifices intended for a god was also punishable by death. So too acts of negligence committed while in the service of king or god, such as careless action leading to the destruction of a temple by fire.

Sometimes the official's family as well as the official himself forfeited their lives in atonement for the latter's negligence. Clearly, offences committed deliberately or inadvertently against the gods ranked amongst the most serious of all crimes, no doubt because of the possible consequences to an entire community of an offended god's wrath. They were for this reason included in the much reduced group of crimes for which the death penalty was still applicable.

The King as Judge

The highest judicial authority in the land was exercised by the king. As deputy of the Sun God, he was the judge supreme in the kingdom. He had very much a 'hands-on' role in the kingdom's judicial activities. Disputes between vassal rulers were brought directly before him for arbitration, as also a range of other disputes arising within or between vassal states. He heard appeals against judgements made in lower courts, and cases originating in lower courts were referred to his court when they were adjudged to go beyond the competence of the lower court. In addition, the king's court, known as 'the king's gate' or 'the palace gate' (clauses 198, 199), was the venue for judging a wide range of offences which had by law to be referred directly to it.

One wonders how the king could possibly have found the time to discharge all his judicial responsibilities, given his other commitments and his regular long absences from the capital on military campaigns and religious pilgrimages. He would certainly have dealt personally with disputes between vassal rulers, who were after all bound by personal oaths of allegiance to him, and whose disputes if not dealt with at the highest level might well have had serious repercussions for the stability of their region as a whole. No doubt too there were many instances where the king's direct intervention in disputes amongst his vassal subjects served as an important means of keeping tabs on them and maintaining his authority over them. But some cases seem so trivial as to hardly warrant his personal attention, like that of a priest of Emar on the Euphrates, who had appealed a decision made against him by the local garrison commander over property and taxes. In a letter dispatched to the authorities at Emar, the king ordered that the appeal be upheld.[26] In fact we know from a second letter which has recently turned up in the Bible Lands Museum in Jerusalem that the case was dealt with by the viceroy as well as by the Great King. Dr Singer, who has published the second letter, comments thus: 'The two Hittite letters provide an important insight into the Hittite judicial system in the Syrian provinces. It is remarkable that a clergyman from a distant city had the possibility to appeal directly to the emperor, and be granted not only a hearing, but also a just verdict against the abuses of the very administration that served the Hittite state.'[27]

Within the homeland there were a number of apparently minor offences that according to The Laws had to be referred to the king's court, like the failure to keep a bull penned up (clause 176a), or the theft of three talents (= *c.*100 kilograms) of timber (clause 102). Of course what may appear minor to us could well have had a significance of which we are unaware. In general we can reasonably assume that only the most serious crimes—that is, those judged most serious by Hittite standards—were dealt with by the king's court. Prohibited sexual liaisons, as we have noted, fell into this category. So too did acts of sorcery (clause 111). For slaves at least sorcery was an offence punishable by death. Capital offences were regularly referred to the king's court, probably for the very reason that they attracted the death penalty, since apparently no lower court had the authority to sentence offenders to death.[28]

In any event, much of the business brought before the king's court cannot have been conducted by the king in person. And very likely many of the cases referred to his court were heard and judged by deputies acting in his name and with his authority. We have seen that officials with the title ᴸᵁ́DUGUD ('dignitary, magistrate') could deputize for the king in the judicial arena and render judgement on his behalf. At the very highest level, members of the king's own family shared a number of His Majesty's judicial responsibilities. Thus Queen Puduhepa passed judgement in a case involving a damaged boat in Ugarit, in the name of the king and actually using the title 'My Sun'. Already very early in her marriage to Hattusili Puduhepa appears to have been active in judicial matters, to judge from her appearance with her husband in the preamble to the text which contains the so-called 'case against Arma-Tarhunda'.[29]

In the Syrian subject territories the viceroys based at Carchemish and Aleppo assumed much of the responsibility, as the Great King's deputies, for dealing with the incessant stream of litigants who brought their complaints and squabbles to their overlord for arbitration. Many of the disputes arose through merchant activities in the region. Thus the merchant Mashanda laid before Ini-Teshub, the viceroy at Carchemish, a complaint against the king of Ugarit for taking from his caravan 400 donkeys, worth 4,000 shekels of silver. His anger and frustration at this appropriation were all the greater since a decision had already been given in his favour by the former Hittite king Urhi-Teshub, who had imposed a substantial fine ($1\frac{1}{3}$ talents of silver) upon the Ugaritic king.[30] Merchant travel through the region was a hazardous occupation, to judge from the various cases of murder, robbery, hijacking which came before the courts with all the accompanying demands for justice and claims for compensation. Particularly when disputes arose between citizens of two different states, or between a merchant of one state and the authorities of another, the king or his viceroy needed to be involved, or at the very least a high-ranking official appointed by the king or viceroy and acting with the full authority of the king. Even so the chances of bringing to justice the perpetrators of crimes against travelling merchants must often have been extremely remote, and the citizens or authorities of the districts where the crimes were committed were held responsible for their safe conduct and forced to pay substantial compensation when they failed to exercise this responsibility.[31]

Penalties

We can often deduce as much about a society's moral and social values from the penalties its laws impose as we can from the laws themselves. Some penalties which a particular society prescribes may surprise us with their apparent mildness, others may shock us by their perceived harshness. But this helps emphasize how widely different the attitudes of different peoples can be on the matter of acceptable and unacceptable, punishable and non-punishable forms of social behaviour. What one society sees as a serious offence, another sees as no offence at all or at worst a peccadillo. One society punishes homosexual activity, another those who discriminate against it. One society relegates adultery to the area of civil litigation, another punishes it with death. One society bestows rights and privileges on parents who produce many offspring, another penalizes those who have more than one. Each set of rewards, each set of penalties has something important to tell us about the nature of the society which bestows or imposes them.

In the Hittite Laws the high percentage of clauses which deal with theft of or damage to property and the penalties which such offences attract clearly reflects the importance which Hittite society attached to the protection of individual property rights, particularly in an agricultural context. The farmer who loses his crops or livestock or equipment through someone else's negligence or malice risks losing his livelihood, which is ultimately to the detriment of Hatti's land-based economy. Penalties have to be sufficiently high to prevent this, or to ensure adequate compensation for the victim.

We have already referred to the increasing emphasis in Hittite society on equating punishment for an offence with compensation for the victim of the offence. This was part of a general movement in The Laws away from more severe forms of punishment, such as execution and mutilation, to milder, more practically useful ones. Monetary penalties, in the form of a certain number of shekels of silver, commonly replaced other forms of penalty, and when monetary penalties originally applied the amounts prescribed were often substantially reduced with no payment to be made, as formerly, to the palace. The reduction in the severity of punishments is typical of many societies in which customary law is replaced by statute law. The former is almost invariably harsher than the latter, probably because it is generally a feature of societies which are in their early stages of development, often struggling to survive, and less willing or less able than more developed societies to tolerate anti-social activities by any of its members. In a pioneering community crimes like theft of livestock are likely to have much more severe consequences than similar crimes in a more stable, settled one. Draconian penalties in the former case may be necessary to safeguard the community's welfare, perhaps its very survival. But as the community develops the techniques and the institutions to exercise greater control over its environment and its members, penalties for offences against it are often reduced, to reflect more accurately their actual consequences for both the individual victim and the community as a whole. Hammurabi's Laws retain many elements of the customary law and rough justice typical of a once nomadic people. The Hittite Laws have moved considerably beyond that stage.

Although in the revised scale of penalties, compensatory payments were generally reduced, by up to 50 per cent, they were still in the order of five- to ten-fold restitution payable to the victim. And in the 'Late Parallel Version' some fines were in certain circumstances substantially increased.[32] They often provide a good indication of the value which Hittite society placed on particular possessions such as livestock which had been damaged, destroyed, or stolen. Trained working animals like sheep- and cattle-dogs were highly prized. Strike and kill an ordinary farmyard dog, and you will pay its owner one shekel of silver. But if you strike and kill a herdsman's dog, you will pay twenty times that amount.

Penalties for the theft or injury of livestock were often expressed in kind. Thus in clause 63, for the theft of a plough-ox the thief 'formerly gave fifteen cattle, but now he shall give ten cattle: three two-year-olds, three yearlings, and four weanlings, and he shall look to his house for it'. We can but speculate on the reasoning behind this very precise breakdown of compensation into three categories of animals. It does, however, have the appearance of a negotiated settlement arising out of a specific case. Since in clause 178 the sale-price of plough-ox is said to be twelve shekels, that of a yearling five, and that of a weanling four, the compensation appears at a rough calculation to be around five times the stolen animal's actual market value. Probably no more than fair return to an owner whose losses caused by the theft or injury of a mature working animal at a critical time of the year may have greatly exceeded what the animal would actually have fetched in the saleyard. Once judgement was handed down, the offender was responsible for 'looking to his own house', that is, paying from his own property the compensation at the level specified by the court—perhaps, we have suggested, five times the stolen animal's market value. Negotiation may have come in at this point. Let us suppose that the offender did not have five plough-oxen or a sufficient number of shekels in hand to discharge his debt to society—to the plaintiff in particular. After some haggling, the plaintiff agrees to accept from him an assortment of animals at different stages of development, which *in toto* have an estimated market value of five times that of his plough-ox. The agreement is recorded, and then preserved in The Laws for future reference.

Sexual Offences

One of the most curious features of The Laws is the relatively large number of clauses which have to do with sexual offences—bestiality, incest, and to a lesser extent rape and adultery.[33] The last fourteen of the 200 clauses deal with sexual liaisons of one kind or another, both forbidden and permitted. That is a high proportion when we consider the range of other activities and offences that we might expect to find in The Laws but which are barely touched upon or are omitted altogether. The bans a number of clauses impose on various forms of sexual activity might argue for a certain fastidiousness in Hittite society on sexual matters. On the other hand the devotion of so much space in The Laws to prohibiting such activity suggests that there was probably a fair amount of it going on.

But what are we really to make of the prominence given by The Laws to sexual deviancy? Are we to conclude that the Hittites were particularly prone to this kind of indulgence in its various forms? The imposition of the death penalty—otherwise extremely rare in The Laws—for intercourse with pigs, dogs, and sheep might reflect Hittite society's repugnance at bestiality. But that seems to be negated by a clause (200a) which explicitly exempts from punishment those who indulge in sexual relations with a horse or a mule. Speculation on why one may have sex with such animals but none others has led to a number of explanations in the scholarly literature which are ultimately inconclusive, even if they have the merit of being ingenious and entertaining. The fact is we simply do not know. All that is clear is that Hittite law, as distinct from biblical law which has a blanket prohibition on all forms of bestiality, did not prohibit bestiality *per se*, any more than the ban which certain societies place on eating the flesh of particular animals amounts to a ban on flesh-eating *per se*.

How then do we explain the severity of the punishment meted out to the man found guilty of illegal bestiality? A man who commits murder may be let off with no more than a fine. A man who has intercourse with a sheep, even in the privacy of his own farmyard, forfeits his life. The difference in the severity of the respective penalties can perhaps be explained thus: the former may have but one victim, the latter may put at risk an entire community; an act of illegal sex not only defiles the person who so indulges but is likely to infect all those with whom he comes in contact.

Sexual intercourse with any partner, animal or human, left those who so indulged in an unclean state. Hittite gods were particularly fussy about this sort of thing—as indeed were other Near Eastern and Egyptian gods. Even sex with a legal spouse rendered a person unfit to communicate with the gods until he had thoroughly bathed himself. King Mursili II was instructed to refrain from sex with his wife the night before undertaking the ritual to cure his aphasia.

Officials on temple duty had to be in an absolutely pure or sterile state before entering into the presence of the god. They were permitted to have sex beforehand, but must then spend the night in the temple, presumably after they had thoroughly cleansed themselves from their sexual activity as well as from any other form of pollution. An official who spent the whole night with his wife and thus came before the god in an unclean state forfeited his life.

If normal, legitimate sexual activity left a person unclean, how much greater his defilement if he had engaged in deviant illegal sexual behaviour. The most alarming feature was that his defilement could spread to others. As we have noted, a whole community could be infected by it, and suffer the full force of divine wrath for harbouring such a creature. The defilement must be eradicated at its source. The simplest and most effective way of doing this was by executing the offender. As with other capital offences, the final judgement was made by the king's court. There was a rider to this. The offender could not enter into the actual presence of the king, for that would put the king himself at risk of defilement, the consequences of which might be terrible indeed. Even a coupling with a horse or mule disqualified a person from entering the king's presence or serving as a priest. Though this form of sexual liaison was legally sanctioned, it was still better to play it safe and not risk defiling the king or incurring divine displeasure.

As a milder alternative to the death penalty some regions of the kingdom prescribed banishment for illegal sexual activity. This might be just as effective in removing a source of defilement from a community. Perhaps even more so, for even after death a sexual deviant continued by his presence to pollute his location, and much care had to be taken to dispose of the body in a place where it could no longer do harm. But a banished person carried his defilement away with him, just as a substitute victim or scapegoat might carry off with it a source of pollution (see Chapter 8). Even after the removal of the defiled person all members of the community from which he came should, to be on the safe side, thoroughly bathe themselves, to ensure that all trace of contamination was removed.[34] Towards the end of the kingdom, and probably under Hurrian influence, it seems that defiled persons could remove their defilement from themselves and their community by performing an appropriate ritual which had the effect of transferring the defilement to a substitute victim. The substitute was henceforth driven from the community in place of the banishment of the actual offender.[35] We shall have more to say about this below (Chapter 11).

The general term used in The Laws for an illegal sexual coupling is *hurkel*. It covers incestuous conduct and other prohibited couplings between humans as well as bestiality. Some of the sexual taboos common to many societies are listed, including relations between mother and son, father and daughter, father and son. The strict bans on incestuous behaviour applied to the Great King's vassal subjects as well. Suppiluliuma I had occasion to rebuke one of his vassal rulers for his country's practice of brother–sister couplings and sex between cousins and other close relatives. The rebuke carried with it a none too subtle warning of the consequences likely to follow if such behaviour continued:

For Hatti it is an important custom that a brother does not have sex with his sister or female cousin. It is not permitted. Whoever commits such an act is put to death. But your land is barbaric, for there a man regularly has sex with his sister or cousin. And if on occasion a sister of your wife, or the wife of a brother, or a female cousin comes to you, give her something to eat or drink. Both of you eat, drink, and make merry! But you must not desire to have sex with her. It is not permitted, and people are put to death as a result of that act. You shall not initiate it of your own accord, and if someone else leads you astray to such an act, you shall not listen to him or her. You shall not do it. It shall be placed under oath for you.[36]

This is the only clearly attested instance of a Hittite king interfering in the local practices of his vassal states. It serves to emphasize the abhorrence with which incestuous conduct was regarded in the Hittite world. However, the blanket prohibition against incest applied only to persons who were blood relatives. Couplings between persons related by marriage, such as brother- and sister-in-law, stepmother and stepson, were tolerated by the law—*provided* that the woman's spouse was not still living. This very likely relates to the provision of levirate marriage in The Laws (see Chapter 7).

We can only speculate on the reasons underlying other *licets* and *non licets* in the clauses dealing with sexual relations. The legal sanctioning of necrophilia, for example (clause 190), seems particularly surprising, given the Hittite concern in other contexts to avoid any form of direct physical contact with corpses because of possible contamination. There are no references at all to homosexuality in The Laws, or any other Hittite document for that matter, which may well indicate that on the *quod non uetatur permittitur* principle ('what is not forbidden is permitted') it was so much an accepted activity in Hittite society that there was no need even to refer to it.[37] There is also the curious provision which permits a free man to have sex with free sisters of the same mother, and with the mother herself, but only if they are not all in the one location (clause 191). Again this provision probably arose out of a specific case and ruling which the compilers of The Laws saw fit to include in the collection for future possible reference.

Slavery

The connotations and conditions of slavery have varied enormously from one society to another. A loyal slave in an Odyssean household had no bad life in comparison to one who worked on an American cotton plantation run by a Simon Legree. The most commonly shared feature of slave-owning societies is that slaves are property owned by a master and are for life bound to that master unless he chooses to dispose of them as chattels or set them free. In the worst slave-owning societies, slaves are no different from other forms of livestock. They have no property of their own, and can be used and abused and even killed on the whim of their master.

How well did slaves fare in the Hittite world? There is little doubt that a significant proportion of the homeland population consisted of slaves, particularly if we include in this category the thousands of 'booty-people' imported as spoils of military conquest.[38] Some of these went on to serve in the king's militia, some were assigned to temple service, others were used to populate or repopulate sparsely inhabited areas of the kingdom, particularly in the frontier zones. But probably the great majority were allocated as an agricultural workforce to the estates of the king's land-owning officers and to the various towns and rural communities throughout the homeland. Particularly in view of the heavy demands imposed on the kingdom's manpower by constant military campaigns, slave labour must have become an indispensable element in the economy of the kingdom.

As in other Near Eastern and some early Greek societies, free persons could be enslaved for failure to pay a debt. But a debt-slave appears to have had a good chance of regaining his freedom, either through paying off the debt, or as the beneficiary of a general release of debt-slaves by royal proclamation. A person might also be enslaved, for the crime of homicide, to his victim's family, or he might be required to give one of his sons into slavery for such a crime (clause 44a), probably for a period to be determined by the court in each individual case. Slaves could also be purchased like other goods in the course of normal trading activity, for example in the markets of the Levant. Yet the great majority of slaves were acquired through military conquest and probably remained bound to their masters for life, unless their masters chose to sell them as they would other forms of livestock. Several of The Laws, if we have correctly interpreted them, refer to the purchase price of skilled and unskilled slaves.[39] The going rate for an unskilled slave, male or female, was twenty shekels of silver (clause 177), the price of a draft horse. A slave trained as an augur could be expected to fetch twenty-five shekels (clause 177), and various skilled craftsmen, including potters, smiths, carpenters, leather-workers, and weavers, perhaps as much as thirty (clause 176b).[40]

An owner appears to have had virtually unlimited power in his treatment of his slaves, which included the right to punish them as he saw fit. Mutilation and execution were included among the punishments an owner might mete out to a slave who had angered him. Indeed the punishment might extend to the slave's entire family:

> A slave who provokes the anger of his master will either be killed or have his nose, eyes or ears mutilated; or his master will call him to account along with his wife, his children, his brother, his sister, his in-laws, his family, whether it be a male or female slave. . . . If ever he is to die, he will not die alone; his family will be included with him.[41]

This passage comes from a set of instructions to temple officials, in which slaves are far from being the only ones for whom draconian penalties are prescribed for misconduct or negligence. The death penalty is stipulated for a range of offences, whether committed by slave or free. In actual fact the slaughter or disabling of a slave by his master was probably extremely rare in Hittite society—as much for practical as for humanitarian reasons.[42] For many owners, slaves represented a valuable asset whose damage or destruction could almost literally be a case of cutting off one's nose (or in this case the nose of a slave) to spite one's face. (One might note, incidentally, that the practice of mutilation referred to in a number of clauses continued in Byzantine times. The removal of nose, eyes, and ears, sometimes with various other parts of the anatomy thrown in, featured amongst the favourite punishments which the emperors of Byzantium meted out to their enemies.) And even if a master was thoroughly enraged by a slave, he might well have stopped short of killing him if he was then obliged to execute the rest of his family as well.

The Laws probably gives an accurate view of how slaves actually did fare under the rule of Hittite law. The large number of clauses that refer to slaves might suggest that they as well as free persons had certain legal rights and that their treatment was subject to a number of judicial controls. There was, for example, a law designed to protect the rights of both partners in a marriage between slaves in the event that the marriage broke down: 'If a male slave takes a female slave (in marriage) and they make a home and children, when they divide their household, they shall divide their goods equally. The female slave shall take most of the children, with the male slave taking one child' (clause 33).

But most of the clauses which deal with slaves probably have little to do with the rights or welfare of the slaves themselves. Nowhere is there any reference to what a master may or may not do to his slave—which may well indicate that this was a matter with which the law was not concerned, reinforcing the notion that a master's power over his slaves was absolute. What apparently *was* subject to some legal control was the legal redress a third party could expect if someone else's slave committed an offence against him. In such a case the law clearly discriminated between slaves and free persons.

Thus when a free man committed an act of burglary, the law required that he return all the stolen goods and pay to his victim a fine of twelve shekels of silver, an amount reduced substantially from an original forty shekels (clause 94). Compare the punishment meted out to a slave for the same offence: 'If a slave burgles a house, he shall make full compensation. He shall pay six shekels of silver for the theft. He (*the victim of the burglary?*) shall mutilate the slave's nose and ears, and the slave shall be returned to his owner. If he steals much, they will impose much upon him. If he steals little, they shall impose little upon him. If his owner says "I will make compensation for him", then he shall make it. But if he refuses, he shall lose that slave' (clause 95).

An initial reading of this clause might suggest that as well as losing his nose and his ears the offending slave was liable to pay his victim monetary compensation, though only half the amount required of a free person. This would clearly imply that the slave had resources of his own from which to pay the compensation, and indeed as we shall see, a number of slaves may well have accumulated such resources. But the likelihood is that it was the slave's owner who was liable to pay the fine[43] (or at least do so if the slave was unable to), the reduced amount in recognition of the fact that he was not directly responsible for the crime. In any case the mutilation of his slave was a further form of punishment for both himself, as the owner of a now substantially depreciated piece of property, as well as his slave.

In the revised versions of The Laws mutilation had been abolished as a punishment for free persons, but still remained in force for slaves for what were considered serious crimes, like house-breaking and arson. Its harshness may be, in part at least, a reflection of the difficulties of maintaining law and order in a society which contained a large motley assortment of persons uprooted from their own homelands and forcibly resettled in their conqueror's. Unless deterred by fear of severe reprisals, and without effective supervision, such persons may well have posed a serious threat to the stability and security of the society in which they had been settled. Facial mutilation stigmatized the slave offender for all time, and for all to see. But the punishment affected the owner as well. His slave was henceforth damaged goods, with quite possibly a reduced work capacity depending on the nature of the work he did, and in any case totally unsaleable. Just retribution, perhaps, against the owner who was ultimately responsible for the behaviour of all his livestock, whether human or animal, and must suffer the legal consequences of any damage or losses they caused to someone else's property. To a society which placed so strong an emphasis on the protection of private property, house-breaking might well rank as a particularly serious crime, though as we have noted, the clauses which deal with it include the rider that the punishment should be scaled to fit the offence. Minor pilfering might still attract a fine, but leave the slave with his features all intact.

The very fact that a slave could have resources of his own set him apart from his counterparts in many slave-owning societies. Indeed as we shall see, he could in some situations accumulate sufficient resources to buy himself a free son-in-law, with the prospect that offered of free grandchildren. In this respect too Hittite society showed a remarkably liberal attitude, placing no legal barriers in the way of marriages between free persons and slaves, and in fact ensuring that in such cases the rights of both partners were properly acknowledged.

Of course the fact that such marriages were legally permitted does not in itself imply that they commonly took place. We do need to bear in mind that many clauses of The Laws reflect not the typical practice but the atypical. A specific ruling on the status of the offspring of a mixed marriage may have come about and been recorded because it was in fact an uncommon occurrence. We can hardly doubt too that mixed marriages could not have gone ahead without the consent of the slave's owner. It is inconceivable that a man who had the power of life and death over his slaves lacked the authority to prevent them from forming marriage alliances to which he was opposed. By approving a mixed marriage he was after all depriving himself in the future of an ongoing supply of young slaves, since by granting his consent to a mixed marriage he was forfeiting control over the offspring of the marriage. Of course a benevolent owner might well be prepared to do this, just as slave-owners in Roman society often manumitted slaves who had given them long and faithful service, without being legally obliged to do so. As we have already commented, a system of rewards and incentives which amongst other things offered a slave the prospect of free descendants might well have been as much to the benefit of the owner in terms of the productivity of his slaves as to the slaves themselves.

We can hardly doubt that many slaves in Hittite society led harsh and miserable existences and longed to be free again and sometimes attempted to escape from their captivity, as attested in a number of clauses of The Laws which deal with runaway slaves. Yet equally there must have been many slaves who benefited from the security which ownership by a benevolent master afforded them, and enjoyed material advancement under the system. As in Homeric society, slaves did not occupy the bottom rung of the social ladder. Like the *thetes* of Homeric tradition, that position must have been occupied by the free but unattached person, without a secure home, or any sense of belonging, a drifter who picked up work wherever and whenever he could. But for all that, he was still a free man.

CHAPTER 3
The Scribe

So into Lycia
he sent him, charged to bear a deadly cipher,
magical marks Proitos engraved and hid
in folded tablets.

(*Iliad* 6. 168–9, transl. R. Fitzgerald)

This well-known passage from Bellerophon's story in the *Iliad* has often been remarked upon as the only reference which Homer makes to writing. In his version of the story Proitos, king of Argos in Greece, sends Bellerophon (whom he wrongly believes to have seduced his wife) to Lycia in south-western Anatolia with a letter inscribed on wooden tablets for delivery to the Lycian king, Proitos' father-in-law. Bellerophon himself is unaware of what the letter says. In fact it contains his death warrant (which fortunately for him was never put into effect).

Taken at face value, the episode indicates at least a knowledge of writing in Homer's time, the late eighth or early seventh century, and an assumption that literacy was a feature of the age in which the *Iliad* is set, the last century of the Bronze Age by our reckoning. In fact Homer's words reflect a typical scenario in Bronze Age international communications: two kingdoms are linked by a marriage alliance; the ruler of one, who is the husband of the other's daughter, makes a request of his father-in-law; he does so in a letter written in a language accessible to both parties, though quite possibly the native language of only one of them, or neither of them.

Of course a Bronze Age king who is credited with authorship of a letter is no more its actual writer than a king who claims to have built a palace is in a literal sense its actual builder. The task of putting stylus to tablet belongs to a scribe.[1] Similarly, the addressee of the letter is not the person who actually reads it. That is the task of his scribe, who reads it to him. So how far did literacy extend in the Late Bronze Age Near East? Who were the literate members of Late Bronze Age society?

The Extent of Literacy in the Hittite World

Literacy skills were probably acquired by many members of the higher echelons of Hittite society, particularly if they were destined for careers in the imperial civil service. Such skills were very likely learned through a training programme in scribal schools (see below). We also hear of priests and doctors with scribal skills, and they too may have received part of their training in such schools. Persons like these, whose professions required them to have at least a basic level of literacy, should perhaps be distinguished from a class of professional, full-time career scribes—though if such a distinction did exist, it was probably a fairly blurred one. Doctors and priests sometimes also used the designation 'scribe', and career scribes sometimes occupied high positions in the administration. No doubt the main difference between the career scribe and other literate professionals was that the former could be expected to devote all his working time to scribal activity of one kind or another, and his training was for this end rather than as a prerequisite for something else. He may well have achieved a higher level of competence than did 'part-time scribes' in the complexities of the cuneiform script, the speed with which he could read and write it, and in the range of languages which used it.

Yet while literacy in Hittite society almost certainly went beyond a purely scribal class, it was still confined to a select minority. We need to bear in mind that near-universal literacy in a society is a comparatively recent phenomenon. In many earlier societies reading and writing were specialized skills restricted to a small proportion of the population, like the skills required for practising medicine or magic or various other professions, arts, and crafts. A modern society which operates on the assumption of universal literacy would not be able to function without it. An ancient society which may have been highly advanced materially and culturally but was not geared to this assumption obviously could, and did.

We should also bear in mind the nature of the cuneiform script, the script most widely used for written records throughout the Bronze Age Near East. It is a syllabic script, made up of wedge-shaped signs. That is to say, each group of signs represents a whole syllable, or in some cases a complete word or concept—what are called logograms. By contrast alphabetic scripts require a separate symbol for each individual sound. The advantage of the cuneiform script is that it is very economical in terms of space required on the writing surface, and that for one fully trained in its use its signs can be produced on a tablet with great rapidity—by a series of woodpecker-like jabbing motions with a wedge-shaped stylus pressed into soft clay at different angles. Speed was an essential requirement in taking dictation from the king, recording legal judgements, ritual enactments, and the like.

But a cuneiform script has a major disadvantage. In contrast to an alphabet which has only a small number of simply devised symbols to be learnt (the largest alphabetic script is that of Russian, with thirty-two symbols), a syllabic script by its very nature requires many hundreds of signs to ensure that every possible combination of sounds from which syllables are formed is individually represented. Thus the cuneiform script used by the Hittites has well over 300 signs (a modest number, in fact, when compared with some other cuneiform scripts), many of which are made up of numerous little wedge-shaped formations. In the early learning stages many signs are easily confused since the distinctions between them are often very small. Thus unlike an alphabetic script which can be mastered relatively quickly and easily, a cuneiform script takes some years to learn and memorize, to the point where it can be read and written easily, quickly, and accurately. This in itself precluded all but a specially trained minority from ever acquiring competence, or at least a high level of competence, in the written language. It seems unlikely that a prince being schooled in the religious, administrative, and military tasks which his royal birth required of him could ever have afforded the time, or indeed have been prepared to submit to the tedium, that training in the art of reading and writing required. Why should he indeed when others were employed to do it for him?

The Training of Scribes

Information from Mesopotamian texts indicates the existence of scribal schools in Mesopotamian societies dating back to the Early Bronze Age. Generally attached to temples, the schools were designated in Sumerian by the term *eduba*, which literally means 'tablet house'.[2] Very likely similar institutions were established by the

Hittites when writing was introduced into the Hittite world.[3] In such institutions those destined for the scribal profession began their training from their early years. The training must have been rigorous, and by its very nature highly repetitive and tedious. Students began by learning simple syllable signs and word signs, copying them over and over again until they stuck in the memory, and then moving on to the more complex signs. If treated like their Mesopotamian counterparts, they could be subject to harsh discipline, with beatings administered for laziness, recalcitrance, or incompetence.

Once the basics of the script had been mastered, the student then progressed to copying, repeatedly, religious texts and great literary classics like the epic of Gilgamesh. Fragments of Hittite, Akkadian, and Hurrian versions of the epic have been found in Hattusa's archives. The exercise may have been intended primarily as a means of mastering the complex script in which the classics were recorded, but it also served to provide the budding scribe with an education in many of the cultural traditions of his society. No doubt too the scribal schools were one of the means by which these traditions were transmitted to the wider community. Sometimes the scribes adapted them for local tastes. Thus in the Hittite version of the Gilgamesh epic, the passages dealing with Gilgamesh's city of Uruk were much reduced, no doubt with the interests of an Anatolian audience in mind. And it may well be that in translating the now lost Hurrian original of the Kumarbi song cycle into Hittite, the scribes substantially edited the composition, to ensure its theological and cultural appropriateness within the context of the religious reform programme of the thirteenth century. In general terms, the scribal schools must have served as powerful agents in the dissemination of cultural traditions throughout the Near Eastern civilizations from the Sumerian period onwards.[4]

The cuneiform script may have been introduced into the Land of Hatti by Babylonian scribes hired or abducted during the course of early Hittite military campaigns, beginning with Hattusili I's Syrian expeditions and culminating in the destruction of Babylon by his successor Mursili I (*c.*1595). Very likely these scribes were instrumental in establishing a local scribal profession by setting up training institutions along the lines of the Old Babylonian model—though as yet we have no direct evidence of such institutions. Training in the art of literacy also involved instruction in the Akkadian and, to a much lesser extent, Sumerian language. Initially the texts in these languages provided the young Hittite scholar with the only 'textbooks' for learning the cuneiform script. Bilingual syllabaries and lexical lists (in Sumerian, Akkadian, and Hittite) found at Hattusa also belong within this context. Through such means the scribe acquired a knowledge of the Akkadian language at the same time as he developed competence in the script which expressed it, as well as in the religious and literary traditions which the script recorded. From a political viewpoint his bilingual skills were of enormous value in the Hittite world as the kings of this world increasingly extended their political and diplomatic links throughout the Near East—for Akkadian became the international *lingua franca* of the age. However, while Akkadian may have been the language primarily used to introduce literacy into the Hittite world, the cuneiform script was quickly adapted to the task of recording texts in Nesite, that is, in the Hittite language, since very likely the first major documents of the Hittite kingdom were composed in this language.

The Employment of Scribes

We have commented that scribal training must have been a long and often tedious process, particularly for those destined to become career scribes. But persistence and application eventually paid off. The profession for which it prepared its pupils was an important and honoured one. For those who reached the top of the profession it offered the prospect of a distinguished career, sometimes at the very highest levels of Hittite society. (We shall have more to say about this below.) On a number of occasions sons followed their fathers into the profession, and indeed there may have been some degree of exclusivity attached to it. Perhaps something approaching a professional caste. There were also on occasion certain privileges attached to being a scribe, such as exemption from taxes and levies.

Even so, demand may well have exceeded supply. In the thirteenth century some fifty-two scribes (including thirty-three scribes of the wooden tablets) were attached to the service of the Great Temple in Hattusa, making up just over a quarter of the temple's total cult personnel.[5] The kingdom's numerous other temples must also have employed a high proportion of scribes amongst their personnel. And there was undoubtedly an ever-increasing demand for well trained scribes to serve in the king's administration as the empire grew in size and complexity. Given the copious records which the Hittites kept of a wide range of activities, and given that literacy in the Hittite world was largely confined to a professional scribal class, it is difficult to imagine any major activity which did not require the involvement of scribes, sometimes in a substantial capacity. On a routine level scribes were employed on the ongoing task of making copies, sometimes multiple copies, of important documents like international and vassal treaties, and correspondence with foreign kings, vassal rulers, and regional governors. Scribes were required for recording royal decrees, land-grants, legal pronouncements, and judgements handed down in lawsuits.

The often long and complex prayers which a king or queen offered up to a deity, sometimes daily, were in many cases read out on their behalf by a scribe, thus avoiding the need for His or Her Majesty to learn them by heart, or the risk of causing divine offence by inadvertently leaving something out. The royal worshipper need not even be present when the prayer was uttered. The daily prayer of King Mursili II to the god Telipinu begins with the words: 'The scribe reads this tablet addressing the deity daily; he praises the deity (saying): Telipinu, you are a mighty and noble deity. Mursili, the king, your servant, and the queen, your handmaid, have sent me (with the request): "Go! entreat Telipinu, our Lord, the guardian of our persons!" '[6] There is no doubt that a number of prayers were quite literally compositions of the king himself. In such cases, a scribe was at hand to take down the king's words as he uttered them. Thus the colophon to Muwatalli's prayer to the Storm God of Kummanni[7] states that the prayer was 'written down from the mouth of His Majesty' by a Junior Incantation Priest called Lurma. It is interesting to compare the two surviving copies of this prayer. One of them, 'copy B', shows signs of having been written down very rapidly—signs unfinished, dislocated words, misunderstanding of what was dictated etc.—whereas in 'copy A' many of the original mistakes have been rectified. It looks, then, as if 'B' really was written down verbatim, by a relatively junior scribe who had yet to master fully the art of taking dictation. Subsequently his hastily composed document was revised at leisure, producing 'copy A'.[8]

Scribes must also have been heavily involved in the preparations for the numerous festivals which occupied a considerable part of the Hittite year (see Chapter 11). The extensive organization which these entailed, including the collection of all the ritual paraphernalia, the gathering of suitable animals for sacrifice, the organizing of the musicians and other entertainers, the collection of all the foodstuffs required for the festival banquets, necessitated the services of those who could consult the relevant manuals in order to advise on what was required, to ensure that nothing was omitted in the festival preparations and in its actual performance, and to check off each item as it was attended to. It was essential that each stage in the festival was carried out meticulously; even the slightest error could invalidate the whole procedure and provoke divine wrath.

Scribes must also have accompanied the king on his military campaigns. During the course of a campaign, the king needed an effective messenger system, to enable him to keep in touch with events in the homeland, and to communicate from a distance with his allies or his enemies if and when the need arose. Communications were sometimes received and delivered orally. But while on the march the king also sent off written dispatches—instructions to his subordinates, threats and ultimatums to his enemies. His campaign staff must have included a number of scribes, on hand to write his dispatches and to read to him any messages delivered to him in writing.

An instance of the former is the written ultimatum which King Hattusili III sent to the renegade Piyamaradu, in an attempt to reach a settlement with his rebel subject while he (Hattusili) was advancing with his army against him.[9] He needed a scribe to write the document at his dictation, and perhaps also to deliver it in person and read it to Piyamaradu—particularly if the latter had no scribe of his own to perform this service; Piyamaradu's messages in reply to Hattusili's dispatches were apparently delivered orally. The services of scribes on the campaign staff must also have been required for keeping records of the enormous logistical operations involved in the transportation of thousands of men, women, children, and livestock back to the homeland in the wake of conquest. The numbers of prisoners-of-war recorded in the Annals of King Mursili II (for example) suggest that precise tallies were made and recorded (just as in Egyptian reliefs scribes are depicted recording the number of enemy slain on the battlefield), probably both at the beginning of the journey and at its end when the prisoners were allocated to various areas and to various jobs within the homeland. Scribes were the obvious officials to undertake such a task.

There is also the more general matter of the employment of scribes in the regions and communities subject to Hittite overlordship. The recently discovered cuneiform archives at (modern)

Maşat, Kuşaklı, and Ortaköy in central Anatolia provide information about the day-to-day administration of the homeland's regional centres and the small scribal staff in each of these centres. We have discussed the tablet records found at Maşat in Chapter 1. Ortaköy, probably to be identified with Hittite Sapinuwa, was another important regional centre of the kingdom.[10] More than 3,000 tablets were unearthed from the site. Their contents include letters exchanged between the king and his officials, inventories, divination texts, and other texts of a religious character. Many of the local scribes had presumably been trained in the scribal schools in the capital, and then perhaps early in their career sent out for a period to serve on the staff of a regional governor.

However, some of the scribes at Maşat seem to have been imported from Syria or Mesopotamia, to judge from their Akkadian names[11]—perhaps an indication that at least in the period of the Maşat archive the demand for scribes in the kingdom exceeded the supply from the local scribal schools. Further afield, scribes of Hittite origin may have been sent by the Hattusa administration as appointees to the courts of vassal rulers, particularly in the west. As yet no tablet archives have come to light in western Anatolia. But the written communications attested by the Hattusa archives with the vassal states in this region, communications particularly in the form of letters and treaties, clearly indicate the presence of scribes in the vassal courts. These men could read to the local ruler documents dispatched from Hattusa, and put in writing the vassal's response, when one was required, and any other matters where written communication was appropriate.

While communications with other parts of the empire or with foreign kings were written in Akkadian, the international language of diplomacy, those with the western vassal states were almost certainly written in Hittite. That at least was the language used in the copies of such communications kept for reference purposes in the capital's archives, and it seems most likely that the originals were in Hittite as well. Since Luwian was the primary language of the western subject states and was closely related to Hittite (both were Indo-European languages), the latter would have been much more easily mastered by native Luwian speakers than the Semitic Akkadian language. Indeed, in a letter sent to the pharaoh Amenhotep III by a king of Arzawa, the postscript contains a request from the scribe that all future correspondence be conducted in Hittite (that is, not in Akkadian): 'You, scribe, write well to me; put down, moreover, your name. The tablets that are brought here always write in Hittite!'[12] If scribes from the Luwian-speaking Arzawan countries had difficulty with Akkadian, or at least were more comfortable with Hittite, then the latter was obviously the appropriate language for communications between the Hittite king and his western vassals.

But the explanation for the use of Hittite may simply be that in the absence of, or in preference to, local Luwian-speaking scribes, the king dispatched some of his own scribes to take up residence in the vassal courts. There would obviously have been no need for a king to write to his western vassals in any language other than Hittite if the western scribes came from Hattusa in the first place. (Of course they would also have needed to be competent in the local Luwian language, to enable them to act as interpreters, if necessary, between their sovereign lord and his vassal subjects.) Besides, a Hittite scribe resident in the local vassal court could have other uses. Given the regular concern expressed by Hittite kings in their treaties that they be forewarned as early as possible of any untoward political developments in their vassal states, particularly in the west, a scribe in the region whose first loyalty was to Hattusa might well serve as a valuable source of information on local conditions. Also noteworthy is the fact that in the one substantial piece of correspondence we have between a Hittite and an Ahhiyawan king, the 'Tawagalawa letter' referred to above, the language used is Hittite. We shall return later to the possible implications of this.[13]

The Tablet Archives

The scribal profession covered a wide range of skills, tasks, and responsibilities. Novices fresh from the training school were no doubt given the most menial and most mechanical tasks, including the routine copying and recopying of hundreds of tablets, for storing in the capital's archives,[14] or in the case of multiple copies for distribution in a number of locations. In the capital alone tablets were discovered in many locations. These included several buildings on the acropolis (A, D, E, and K), a number of houses, and rooms used for tablet storage in the city's temples.[15] The records found on temple sites deal with matters relating to each temple's cultic and administrative activities, including the management of its land-holdings outside the city. The great Temple of the Storm God in the Lower

City was the chief repository for state treaties, because (as we know from information supplied by the texts) their provisions were sacrosanct and under special divine supervision. The building commonly known as 'The House on the Slope' was apparently reserved for works of a scholarly literary nature. A scribal school may have been located here.

Tablets came to light in a number of other locations as well, sometimes totally out of their original context. Indeed it is often very difficult to make any general determination about the original arrangement and location of these documents. This is due to various factors, not least of which was the failure to record precise findspots when the tablets began coming to light during the German excavations early in the twentieth century. But this aside, there must have been major disruptions to the capital's archives on several occasions during its history—when Hattusa was sacked in the early fourteenth century, in the course of the capital's relocation to Tarhuntassa in the late fourteenth or early thirteenth century, in the course of conflicts in Hattusa between the opposing forces of Hattusili and Urhi-Teshub, and perhaps most of all during the major redevelopment of Hattusa in its final years. In this last period, many tablets may have been stored in temporary locations—where they still remained at the capital's end—and many others may simply have been dumped when they were of no further use. The most dramatic instance of a tablet found out of context is the famous bronze tablet discovered in 1986 under a pavement near Hattusa's Sphinx Gate.[16] It was almost certainly buried there deliberately, to ensure that it would never be seen again.

We do know that considerable care was taken with the initial storage of tablets which contained valuable records to be retained for future reference and consultation. It was obviously important to ensure their easy retrieval, when required, from the thousands of written records distributed throughout the capital's tablet repositories. As far as we can determine, the tablets were arranged on wooden shelves supported by rows of stone pillars. This in fact helped ensure their survival. When fire penetrated the archive rooms during the capital's final destruction, the shelves collapsed and the unbaked tablets crashed upon the floor. Though often shattered into many fragments, they were baked in the intense heat generated by the burning timber, and thus preserved for all time. Each shelf's contents were indicated by lists in the form of small clay tablets, which also indicated if there were any gaps in a particular series: 'Two tablets relating to the offering of substitutes to the Sun Goddess of the Earth by the king, the queen, and the princes. First tablet missing.' 'Third tablet of the spring festival at Hurma. How the lord celebrates festivals at Hurma. First and last tablets missing.'[17] Sometimes the contents of a particular tablet were indicated by a brief statement at the end, in what is known as the colophon. Thus Hattusili I's Testament concludes with the words: '(This is) the tablet of Tabarna, the Great King: when the Great King, the Tabarna, fell ill at Kussara and appointed the young Mursili for the succession.' We can imagine that a number of scribes were employed largely if not exclusively on the task of maintaining the tablet collections, and storing and retrieving particular documents as required, no doubt bringing to the job the same degree of dedication and pride—and possessiveness—as many of their modern counterparts.

Upward Mobility in the Scribal Profession

A hierarchy within the profession offered prospects of career advancement commensurate, presumably, with the upwardly mobile scribe's ability, experience, and seniority. Although we have no clear picture of different stages in the career progression, there are, however, indications of the career path of a number of scribes, like Angulli, son of Palla, pupil of Anuwanza, who appears as an ordinary scribe in a couple of documents and later becomes chief of the scribal school.[18] Information of this kind is available to us from the scribe's frequent habit of recording his name at the end of the document which has been dictated to him. Thus: 'The hand of Hapati-URMAH, son of Tuwattaziti, in the presence of Anuwanza, the chief, has written (it).'[19] The scribe's name is probably appended in such cases for future reference, just as a modern business letter is often referenced by inserting the name of the secretary who actually typed it. In this case we also have the name of the dictator of the document, Anuwanza, chief of the scribal school.

It was in fact possible for a scribe to reach the most exalted levels of the Hittite administration—as reflected in the office of the GAL.DUB.SAR.MEŠ, 'Chief of the Scribes'. The importance of this man, the head of the Hittite chancellery, is indicated by his ranking next to the royal couple and the crown prince in the lists of beneficiaries of gifts from vassal rulers. He is also sometimes given the honorary title

DUMU.LUGAL, 'son of the king', a title which, we have noted, was conferred upon a number of distinguished officials who were not actually related by blood to the royal family. Moreover, one of the chief scribes, Mittannamuwa, was appointed by King Muwatalli II as the administrator of Hattusa when the royal seat was transferred to Tarhuntassa.[20]

Scribal Influence in the Kingdom

We can hardly overestimate the power and influence which the Chief of the Scribes and indeed other high-ranking members of the scribal hierarchy must have exercised within the kingdom. These men were amongst the king's closest confidants and advisers. Their positions could not have failed to give them considerable influence in the king's dealings with his vassal rulers and with foreign kings, for no doubt it was they who drafted the treaties which the king contracted with vassal and foreign rulers—documents of fundamental importance to the maintenance of Hittite influence and authority in the Near East.

We have drafts, often fragmentary, of a number of treaties, and final versions of others. Particularly from the surviving drafts, we can piece together something of the process involved in the composition of a treaty. It was probably along the following lines: A new ruler has been set up on a vassal throne, his elevation due to the death or deposition of his predecessor. In Hattusa the king's scribe carries out some research on the history of the vassal kingdom and on other pertinent facts preserved on tablets in the foreign office department of the state archives. From the archives in the Temple of the Storm God he retrieves copies of treaties with former rulers of the kingdom. He may also retrieve from other locations copies of correspondence with them. Together with information relating to the current situation in the kingdom, this material provides the basis for a draft treaty which the scribe draws up, perhaps after initial consultation with the king. Standard clauses and formulas relating to vassal's and overlord's obligations to each other, and to the conditions under which these obligations will become null and void, provide a template for the treaty. The scribe adds a long list of the deities of both the homeland and the vassal state who will serve as witnesses to the pact between overlord and vassal. Then he includes a series of clauses referring to the blessings or the curses that will follow respectively from the vassal's observance or violation of the treaty's provisions. Specific provisions contained in treaties with earlier rulers of the kingdom are incorporated into the new treaty, if still of relevance. The scribe may also include tentative new provisions relating, for example, to newly defined territorial boundaries.

On completion, the draft is read out to the king. As he listens, the king dictates various emendations or additions, which the scribe notes in the margins of the draft. Or he requires some words or phrases to be deleted as irrelevant or out of date. The scribe crosses them out in his draft. Obviously the draft tablet would have to be soft when the corrections were made, before the clay had dried and hardened. It may thus have been brought to the king for his consideration shortly after its completion. If there were some delay before he was able to deal with the matter, the tablet could still have been kept soft, and even re-softened if necessary, by wrapping it in damp cloths. There is discussion over a suitable preamble to the treaty. On the basis of information from the archives, the preamble may be used to stress the loyalty of the vassal king's predecessors as a model for his own behaviour. (Any past actions which contradict this can be conveniently ignored.) On the other hand if a vassal's predecessors have behaved contrary to their overlord's interests, a reminder of their fate and of the king's beneficence to the vassal throne's present incumbent may serve as a useful introduction to the treaty. A final version of the treaty is then produced by the scribe. After the king has heard it and approved it, the scribe arranges for it to be inscribed on metal—gold, silver, or bronze—validated with the king's personal seal and also the seal of his contracting partner. A number of copies of the treaty are made, under the scribe's supervision, the number often being recorded in the colophon to the treaty.

Without doubt the highest-ranking scribes of the kingdom played a major role in the kingdom's diplomatic activities. The qualities which they brought to their office must have included a high degree of political astuteness, and considerable knowledge of and sensitivity to local conditions and political issues in the various regions over which their sovereign held sway. They may also have played no small role in negotiations between the king and his royal counterparts. Mastery of the appropriate diplomatic and legal forms of expression was essential for the higher order of scribes. Many clauses in the treaties clearly reflect authorship, or at least considerable input, by a person well versed in legal terminology. So too scribes were employed in drawing up protocols, legal contracts, and the many land-grants which the king bestowed on favoured subjects. The precisely specified terms and conditions of the land-grant documents again clearly reflect their drafting by a legal expert. Scribes too had the task of reviewing and redrafting laws, recording court decisions, and very likely acting as advisers on legal matters to the king and others invested with judicial authority prior to judgements being handed down. We know that in Mesopotamia the scribal school curriculum included the learning of thousands of Sumerian and Akkadian legal terms and formulas,[21] and very likely the training of Hittite scribes at an advanced level contained a similar requirement.

Specialization in Scribal Activity

Within the scribal hierarchy, we are unaware of what degree of specialization operated at each level. We do know that scribes who reached the more elevated levels of their profession employed others to take dictation for them. Thus Mahhuzzi, who had risen to the status of chief of scribes, dictated to Duda the protocol of King Tudhaliya IV.[22] Was Duda employed purely to take dictation? And were there scribes employed purely as copyists, or did they have a broader range of functions? Were other scribes employed purely as archivists, responsible for cataloguing, shelving, maintaining, and retrieving when required the documents housed in the capital's tablet repositories?

As yet we cannot give firm answers to these questions. But that there was some degree of specialization in the scribal profession is suggested by the term 'Scribe of the Wooden Tablets'. From this title (and from other references) we know that wood as well as clay and metal was used as a writing medium in the Hittite world, and used commonly enough to have a specially designated scribe in charge of tablets of this material. For what purposes were wooden tablets used? Not surprisingly, given the perishable nature of the material, no such tablets have survived from the Hittite world. However, the discovery of a folding wooden tablet in the Late Bronze Age Ulu Burun shipwreck off the Lycian coast near Kaş, with ivory hinges and still bearing traces of wax, probably provides a good indication of what the tablets looked like. Indeed Homer's description of the wooden tablets which Bellerophon took to Lycia accords very closely with the Ulu Burun find.[23]

A significant feature of the tablets with their wax-coated surface was that they could be used repeatedly, by smoothing over the wax surface and thus erasing an earlier inscription to make way for a new one. This suggests that the wooden tablets were used for purely temporary records—information which could be deleted after a period of time when no longer applicable, or raw data which was gathered, for example by government officials, for subsequent incorporation in a permanent record. (Conceivably the statistics relating to transportees and captured livestock were first recorded in this form, as also perhaps details of a farmer's produce for taxation purposes.) That is to say, wooden tablets may have served much the same function as modern notebooks. But they apparently served other purposes as well. Hoffner notes their use, particularly in Kizzuwadna, to record the traditional rites accorded to the gods in festivals and rituals.[24] It is also possible that they were in some cases used for letters, or at least for written messages. Indeed that was the function of Bellerophon's wooden tablets. In Roman times such tablets were regularly used for this purpose. It may be, then, that amongst their other uses wooden tablets in the Hittite world served to convey informal letters or messages, with the possible advantage that after reading the message the recipient could erase it and inscribe a response on the same tablet.

All this of course is largely speculation. Until we have a better knowledge of what exactly the Hittites used their wooden tablets for, we are at a loss to explain why the Hittite chancellery saw fit to assign them a bureaucratic category of their own, with a scribe or scribes in charge.

On a Personal Note

A personal touch is added to a number of formal letters by the scribes' occasional habit of appending little messages to each other—at the very end of the letter. One scribe asks his counterpart in the recipient court to tell him his name in his next letter, and in future to write in Hittite (that is, not in Akkadian!), another asks after his counterpart's health. Others, writing from Maşat, ask the recipient scribes in Hattusa to check up on their families and belongings in the capital.[25] (This, incidentally, provides a good indication that scribes from Hattusa were expected to serve for a period on a provincial governor's staff, apparently leaving their families behind, before being allowed to continue their profession in the capital.) Whether or not their superiors approved of or condoned this exchange of notes is something we do not know. The likelihood is that they were unaware of the practice. There was really no need for a scribe to inform his master of what was after all a quite harmless custom, even if it does sometimes have the effect for the modern reader of adding a touch of bathos to a document otherwise written in a formal and, to us, sometimes pompous style.

CHAPTER 4
The Farmer

> To the king, queen, princes, and to all the land of Hatti, give life, health, strength, long years, and joy in the future! And to them give future thriving of grain, vines, fruit, cattle, sheep, goats, pigs, mules, asses—together with wild animals—and of human beings![1]

In our investigations of almost all aspects of Hittite life and society we are constantly aware of one basic fact: the prosperity and well-being and sustenance of the kingdom depended, to a critical degree, on the industry of its food-producers, the productivity of its soil, and the benevolence of the elements. That a country needs to produce sufficient quantities of food to feed its population may appear self-evident. Yet in poor-yielding years many countries have been able to supplement their own production and buffer themselves against famine by accessing stores of supplies accumulated in good years, or by importing supplies acquired through trade or war or as tribute from subject states. The Hittites too sometimes boosted local food supplies with imported grain, probably only on an occasional basis during the earlier years of the kingdom, more regularly towards its end. But to a very large extent their ability to 'keep alive the land of Hatti' depended on what they themselves could produce annually from their own resources—their own crop and orchard and grazing lands, worked by their own labour forces.

The task was a challenging one. The central Anatolian plateau provides a harsh and often hostile environment for an agriculturally based society. In summer it was, and still is, a hot, dry, thirsty land, poorly served for irrigation purposes by its meagre, unnavigable rivers. The rainfall for the whole year rarely exceeds 500 millimetres and is often considerably less. The winters can be bitterly cold, with the land often buried deep in snow and at least in ancient times often cut off totally from the outside world for months at a time. River valleys and pockets of land between mountain ranges offered the best opportunities for cultivation of the soil, but even in these areas soil fertility was often low, and in between lay rugged tracts of virtual wasteland. It was a land chronically vulnerable to the vagaries of climate and to the whims of the gods who controlled it. Drought and famine were seldom more than a poor-yielding harvest away, the result of a labour shortage or a low seasonal rainfall or a devastating storm at harvest time, or the depredations of vermin, which included mice and a wide range of insect pests. The land lacked the capacity to absorb such setbacks—which any agriculturally based society must accept as a matter of course—without serious and sometimes devastating consequences for large sections of the population. Seton Lloyd wonders why the Hittites should ever have chosen for their homeland and seat of government what he refers to as 'this unprepossessing region of Anatolia'. 'One is even tempted', he says, 'to attribute certain aspects of the Hittite character . . . to over-familiarity with the "unupholstered" virility of the plateau land-scape, or even to an ascetic appreciation of the austerities imposed on them by such an environment.'[2]

Yet for those who lived close to the land (and that applied to persons at all levels of Hittite society and in almost all occupations), who understood it and used it efficiently, there could be prosperity and good quality of life. Indeed for the Hittites it was hard to envisage any kind of life which did not have a farming or agricultural basis. Their gods—who could presumably have chosen to do otherwise if they wished—lived much of their lives on celestial pastoral estates, and their kings retired to similar estates specifically allocated to them after their deaths, well stocked for their sustenance and diversion with sheep, cattle, and game.

The Workers of the Land

Efficient use of the land meant in the first instance intensive exploitation of relatively small areas suitable for orchards and crop production. When this was done, and provided the gods were cooperative, the land was capable of producing grain crops, fruit, and vegetables in some abundance. There was little that one might find in well-stocked markets today that was missing from the Hittite range of produce. Grain crops included four kinds of wheat and two or three kinds of barley. Vegetables included a wide range of legumes (like peas, beans, broad beans, chickpeas, lentils), root and bulb vegetables (carrots, onions, leeks, garlic), cucumber and watercress and parsley, and that ubiquitous Mediterranean product the olive. Various herbs and spices such as cumin and coriander were cultivated. Orchards produced figs, apples, pears, apricots, grapes, pomegranates, and perhaps plums and tamarisks. Apiaries produced honey, dairies milk, cream, and cheese.[3]

The key unit in the agricultural economy of the Land of Hatti was almost certainly the small mixed farm, whose success depended primarily on two factors: intensive cultivation, and diversification of produce. On each farm one would expect to find a variety of fruit, vegetable, and grain crops, with perhaps some crop rotation being practised, complemented by a range of domesticated livestock—cattle, sheep, pigs, goats, donkeys, horses, and poultry, including partridges and ducks.

One such farm was worked by a man called Tiwatapara. He was a family man with a wife, Azzia, and three children, a boy Hartuwanduli and two girls Anitti and Hantawiya. A land-grant document provides us with an inventory of his assets:

> Estate of Tiwatapara: one man, Tiwapatara; one boy, Hartuwanduli; one woman, Azzia; two girls, Anitti and Hantawiya; (total) five persons; two oxen, twenty-two sheep, six draught oxen . . . eighteen ewes, and with the ewes two female lambs, and with the rams two male lambs; eighteen goats, and with the goats four kids, and with the he-goat one kid; (total) thirty-six small cattle: one house. As pasture for oxen, one acre of meadow in the town Parkalla. Three-and-a-half acres of vineyard, and in it forty apple trees, forty-two pomegranate trees, in the town Hanzusra, belonging to the estate of Hantapi.[4]

Though by no means a wealthy man, Tiwatapara and his family had sufficient resources to provide for all their material needs, so long as all the family were prepared to work hard, and they suffered no major setbacks through drought, storms, or illness. They had a small mixed herd of livestock, some of which were bred for ploughing the fields, some for their meat, and some for their milk and their wool (sheep seem to have been bred primarily for their wool). They were able to diversify their earning capacity with a small vineyard, which also contained apple and pomegranate trees. And very likely they kept a vegetable garden, within an enclosure around their mudbrick, timber-framed house, in which they grew onions, lentils, peas, beans, and the like. We do not know how large Tiwatapara's actual farm was—some farms may have been as small as 600 square metres.[5] Tiwatapara apparently had enough space to run most of the livestock listed on his inventory, but needed additional pieces of land to pasture his oxen and to cultivate his vines and fruit trees.

This was quite consistent with the general pattern of farming in the Hittite world—small pieces of land owned or leased by or allocated to the one person or family but scattered over several or more locations. Even when the king made land-grants to those who had served him well,[6] he tended to do so in small parcels rather than in single large estates. For political reasons, it has been suggested, he thought it wise to fragment the holdings even of his most trusted subjects; large landowners with consolidated land-holdings and a large labour force at their disposal might be tempted to entertain ambitions beyond their station and pose a potential threat to the stability of the regime in Hattusa.[7] But it is just as likely that there were economic reasons for the policy. Smaller land-holdings were more likely to be fully utilized for food production than large estates, where the owner might have devoted only a part of his land to productive purposes. In a later period this was amply demonstrated by the use made of *latifundia*, the large estates of the Roman world, whose under-exploitation caused serious shortfalls in food production in Italy during the later years of the Roman Republic.

Tiwatapara seems to have been in the position, probably regarded as a fairly privileged one for a small farmer, of having several plots of land available to him, including the one on which he and his family lived. No doubt this was a reflection of his industry and enterprise. He is probably a good example of the basic yeoman farmer on which Hittite society largely depended. Land could be acquired in a number of ways. It could be bought, or it could be leased—from the crown, a town or village, or a wealthy neighbour. As we have already noted, it could be bestowed on favoured individuals, and sometimes on institutions like cult centres, as a gift from the king. The grant might be quite substantial, including woods and meadows and sometimes whole villages, along with livestock, equipment, buildings, and a workforce. Lower down the scale, small farms were apparently allocated in lieu of other forms of payment to employees in the king's service, including such persons as heralds, couriers, and the king's cupbearers and table servants.

The term for such persons, 'Man of the Weapon' (LÚ ^{GIŠ}TUKUL), suggests that it once applied to soldiers in the king's service who presumably worked plots of assigned land and produced their own food during periods when they were not required for military service; the government would thus be saved the administrative difficulties of directly feeding standing army troops all year round.[8] But such an arrangement would not have been without its problems, since soldier-farmers must often have been away on campaign at precisely the time their farms most needed their attention or supervision, for example during the sowing or the harvest. Also, the unsettling effects of dividing one's time between the excitement and unpredictabilities of military campaigns on the one hand and the day-to-day and often tedious routine of farming life on the other would hardly have been conducive to the maintenance of a stable productive agricultural workforce. The use of the system for paying troops may have been abolished or considerably scaled down quite early in Hittite history, while being extended to other forms of employment in the king's service; the original term continued in use for persons paid in this way, although its military connotations may no longer have applied.

At all events the state seems to have given much attention to ensuring, through a mixture of sticks and carrots, that all land capable of cultivation was worked to its maximum capacity. All assigned land, whether bestowed as a gift or as payment for services rendered, or granted as a leasehold, imposed clear obligations on the assignee. All farming enterprises were subject to taxes, generally in the form of agricultural produce, and under the system of socage many farmers were also obliged to provide payment in the form of part-time service to their liege-lord; if they were tenants of the crown, this might involve the provision of their labour for public works or on crown estates.[9] Tax and labour exemptions might sometimes be granted in special cases or for special reasons. But to have too many exemptees could seriously impact on overall productivity and revenue for the state, and it appears that the originally long list of those routinely granted exemptions had been considerably whittled down by the beginning of the New Kingdom. The large landowner was obliged to ensure that all tax and labour requirements for his estates were fully met, whether from land directly worked by himself and his own labour force or from land which he had leased to tenant farmers. Similar obligations must have been imposed on temple establishments, which often owned extensive tracts of farm and pasture land, like the Church in more recent times, and were no doubt responsible for both the efficient use of the land and the collection of all revenues due. Small farmers who worked plots of land as lessees or tenant farmers were also obliged to demonstrate full utilization of their land or risk forfeiting it to someone else. Shortfalls at this level would ultimately affect an estate's overall productivity, for which the large landowner was responsible. It was his job to ensure maximum efficiency at all levels within his ambit of responsibility.

Grain gathered as tax from the Hittite farmlands, in addition to what may have been sent as tribute from vassal states, was stored in a number of grain depots strategically located throughout the homeland. We have important new information about the nature of some of these facilities from the recently discovered silos in Hattusa. Eleven underground grain pits have been excavated on the mountain ridge now called Büyükkaya on the city's north-eastern extremity. And behind the so-called 'postern wall' on the south-west of the Lower City, an underground storage complex consisting of two parallel rows of sixteen chambers each has come to light.[10] Dr Seeher, the excavator, has estimated a storage space ranging from a possible minimum of 128 to a possible maximum of 648 cubic metres for the individual silos on Büyükkaya, and a total storage space of up to 9,800 cubic metres for the postern wall complex. In terms of weight, the latter had a maximum holding capacity of some 5,880 tonnes of grain, a sufficient annual ration for up to 32,000 people. There were undoubtedly other grain silos, both underground and above-ground, built in the city throughout its history,[11] as also in the kingdom's regional administrative centres. We may suppose that the large silos in Hattusa and elsewhere served as redistribution centres for large areas of the homeland, and not merely for the sustenance of the immediate population.[12] None the less the considerable numbers of troops, palace and temple functionaries, administrative officials, and labourers who constituted the capital's workforce clearly made much higher demands on the state commissariat than any other parts of the homeland, necessitating substantial food storage facilities within the city simply to meet its own needs.

One of the crucial factors in agricultural productivity was the availability of an adequate labour force. For the Hittites this was a chronic problem, sometimes reaching critical proportions. Annual military expeditions imposed a constant drain on the homeland's labour forces. However often Hittite armies returned home laden with rich spoils of conquest, the fact remains that military campaigns were conducted between spring and autumn, at precisely the time the agricultural labour needs of the homeland were greatest. When on top of this the homeland population, including a substantial proportion of the labour force, was decimated by plague, the kingdom could end up on the brink of starvation—as forcefully stated by King Mursili II in a blunt address to the gods:

> What have you done, o Gods? You have allowed a plague to enter the land of Hatti and all of it is dying! Now there is no-one to prepare food and drink offerings for you! No-one reaps or sows the god's fields, for the sowers and reapers are all dead! The mill women who used to make the bread of the gods are all dead! All the corrals and sheepfolds from which cattle and sheep were chosen for sacrifice are empty, for the cowherds and shepherds are all dead![13]

The importation into the homeland each year of hundreds, sometimes thousands, of transportees from conquered territories must have contributed much to the alleviation of labour shortages. A significant proportion of the transportees were almost certainly used to swell the agricultural workforce on Hittite farms and pasturelands. Becoming in effect slaves, they were undoubtedly a valuable asset to the homeland, and well warranted the effort and the risks involved in getting them there. Probably for this reason rather than for humanitarian considerations they enjoyed a higher degree of protection at law than one generally finds in slave-owning societies.

Buying Land

As we shall see (Chapter 7), The Laws allowed slaves to accumulate property of their own, to the point where some generated sufficient wealth to attract free persons into their families through marriage. This 'enlightened' approach to slavery (as far as any slave-owning society can be called enlightened) was almost certainly pragmatically based—on the principle that the best way of maximizing human productivity is through an appropriate system of rewards and incentives. In the case of slaves this was a particularly important consideration at times when many of the able-bodied male population were absent on military campaigns, and a large proportion of those who were left to work the fields were persons who were there because they had no choice in the matter. To the Hittite way of thinking, their cooperation could best be achieved by waving carrots rather than sticks under their noses. Many such persons were apparently given the opportunity of working one or more plots of land for themselves, perhaps raising a few livestock, and keeping at least some of their earnings, in addition to performing the services required by their master. In this way they could eventually build up sufficient resources to buy property of their own.

From the various prices recorded in The Laws it is clear that this was well within an enterprising and industrious farmer's capability, however modest his starting point. Land which was suitable for farming purposes but had not been developed was very cheap. It was possible to buy a small uncultivated 1-IKU plot, around 3,600 square metres, for no more than two or three shekels of silver[14] (the IKU was a basic unit of land measurement, with larger holdings measured in multiples of it).[15] But let us suppose that a farmer wants a piece of land already under cultivation. This will cost him considerably more, up to twenty times the cost of an uncultivated plot. Initially he may not have sufficient funds to pay for it. But it is well within his reach if he is prepared to devote several years of hard work and enterprise to achieving it. Let us suppose that he has his sights set on a small vineyard. Forty shekels of silver will secure him a 1-IKU vineyard plot.[16] In working towards his goal, he starts off with a couple of sheep and goats, and breeds from them over the next few years. As his stock numbers grow, he periodically sells off some of them, or their wool, and with the proceeds buys several calves, which he also uses as breeding stock. Within a few years he has built up a small herd of cattle, some of which he sells for their meat and their hides. The list of selling prices in The Laws indicates the sort of returns he could expect; for example, 'one plough ox—twelve shekels of silver; one bull—ten shekels; one full-grown cow—seven shekels; one pregnant cow—eight shekels; one weaned calf—four shekels; one yearling plough ox or cow—four shekels; one sheep—one shekel; two lambs—one shekel; three nanny-goats—two shekels; two kids—half a shekel'.[17] The proceeds from just a few such animals would clearly put his vineyard within his grasp. As we shall see, once he has it he could expect to recoup his purchase price within about four years.

The Laws indicate many other means by which a farmer starting out with very modest means, and whether slave or free, could eventually buy or lease land of his own. In the slave's case, there might also be a further incentive beyond mere asset accumulation—the opportunity to acquire sufficient wealth to pay a 'bride-price' for a free woman, and thus ensure free status for his offspring. Everyone stood to benefit—the slave himself from the opportunities to improve his position as allowed by Hittite law, the owner from the slave's increased productivity on his master's as well as his own behalf, and the state which was the ultimate beneficiary of a productive workforce.

The Hire of Labour

We do not know how far down the rungs of Hittite society slave-owning went. But for a farmer like Tiwatapara, the costs of acquiring and maintaining a slave and securing him against escape were probably not warranted by the return he would get from him—particularly during the winter months when the slave would still have to be fed and sheltered without being fully employed. At busy times of the year Tiwatapara's own family of five could not have coped with all the work which the land he farmed generated. Small working 'households' seem to have required somewhere between seven and ten personnel.[18] Tiwatapara probably hired the labour of free persons on a contract basis for a month or two at a time as it was needed, particularly during the labour-intensive periods of the agricultural year. The basic hire rate for a male was apparently one shekel of silver per month. Female labour could also be hired, at half that rate. But the rate and method of payment probably varied, depending on the period of the year and the nature of the work required. Thus The Laws stipulate that in the harvest season: 'If a (free) man hires himself out for wages, to bind sheaves, load them on wagons, deposit them in barns, and clear the threshing floors, his wages for three months shall be 1,500 litres of barley. If a woman hires herself out for wages in the harvest season, her wages for three months shall be 600 litres of barley' (clause 158).[19]

Payment in kind was clearly the most convenient form of remuneration at this time. The labourer simply took a share of the grain harvested and stored it for consumption by his family in the period before the next harvest. Professor Hoffner has calculated that 1,500 litres of barley equates to 3.75 shekels of silver, slightly better than the standard rate of one shekel of silver per month for a male, although the woman's remuneration of 600 litres, equated to one shekel of silver, is worse than the standard rate of half a shekel for one month's hire. The difference between the male and female hire rates may well be a reflection of the different work each was required to do, with the more physically demanding tasks reserved for the male (as suggested by clause 158 above). On the other hand women shared in many of the tasks undertaken by men, particularly at times of labour shortages, whether due to plague, or absence of males on military campaigns, or redeployment of males for work on public projects. More generally we hear of women employed in a range of manual activities—as millers, cooks, weavers, and fullers as well as in more specialist occupations as doctors and ritual practitioners. Elsewhere they appear as musicians, dancers, and tavern-keepers.

The Farming Communities

The various little farmsteads were probably grouped in clusters, each of which constituted or was attached to a community or village of its own. Each had its own council and administration which was responsible for overall supervision of the territory within its jurisdiction, extending up to about five kilometres or three miles from the village centre.[20] The council had the task of ensuring effective use of the land and the payment of taxes due, as well as arbitrating on disputes between landholders and other members of the local community. Apart from the land which was owned or leased by small farmers, there was also land owned communally by the village, which might earn revenue for the village by being leased out, or by the villagers themselves apportioning a certain amount of their time to it.

The intensive cultivation of small plots of land located next to each other, and probably in many cases without clear lines of demarcation between them, must often have been a source of tension and dispute between neighbours. And indeed a number of clauses in The Laws deal with offences committed by a careless or malicious neighbour. A landholder was, for example, responsible for damage done by any of his stock which, presumably through lack of adequate supervision, strayed into an adjoining orchard or vineyard: 'If a person lets his sheep into a productive vineyard, and ruins it, if it is in fruit, he shall pay ten shekels of silver for each 3,600 square metres. But if it is bare (*i.e. already harvested*), he shall pay three shekels of silver' (clause 107). The ten shekels probably represents the estimated annual earnings of a vineyard of the specified size, which the offender must now pay to the owner as compensation for his loss of income. (On this basis our supposed vineyard purchaser, discussed above, could expect to recoup his initial outlay of forty shekels in perhaps no more than five years, allowing for a year's income to cover his labour and other recurrent costs.)

Among the hazards faced by those who lived in the closely settled farming communities, fire must have been one of the most feared, particularly in the hot dry months of the central Anatolian summer. A fire that swept through crops and orchards and farm buildings had the potential for destroying a farmer's livelihood for years to come, possibly forever. There could of course be a number of quite valid reasons for starting a fire on one's own property. But a man who did so was obliged to exercise particular care in keeping it under control, and was liable to pay substantial compensation if he was careless enough to allow the blaze to spread to his neighbour's property: 'If anyone sets a field on fire, and the fire takes hold of a fruit-bearing vineyard, in the event that a vine, an apple tree, a pear(?) tree or a plum tree is burnt up, for each tree he shall pay six shekels of silver, and he shall re-plant the plot. And he shall look to his house for it. If the offender is a slave, he shall pay three shekels of silver for each tree' (clause 105).[21]

Six shekels, even three shekels, per tree could amount to a very considerable sum, even for a small orchard or vineyard, particularly when compared with penalties imposed for other offences dealt with in The Laws. Indeed in some cases the compensation payable could well have reduced the culprit to ruin—for what was perhaps no more than a moment's carelessness—if the fire for which he was responsible not only wiped out his neighbour's current crop but also totally destroyed the trees or vines from which the crop was produced. Yet that is the nature of the compensatory principle in The Laws—the offender must bear the full cost of reparation, forfeiting everything he owns if necessary. No doubt too the size of the penalty emphasized to all the need for constant vigilance in preventing what may well have been an all too frequent occurrence in the small farming communities of the Hatti land.

Herding and Herdsmen

In the mixed farming economy of the Hittite world, probably every small Hittite farmer derived part of his livelihood from a modest assortment of livestock as well as from the soil. Indeed much of the wealth of the Hittite land depended very largely on its flocks and herds. Professor Beckman notes, for example, the vital role played by wool production and processing in the Hittite economy.[22] Goats, horses, pigs, and asses along with cattle and sheep figure among the livestock run by small landowners and large landowners alike. The latter, which included palace, temple, and royal mausoleum establishments, had substantial flocks and herds, which were regularly augmented by war booty. Cattle and sheep constituted the bulk of the booty brought home as the prizes of military conquest. Some were taken by the king for his own estates, others were distributed among the estates of the king's officers, as their share of the spoils of battle.

For pasturing these animals, extensive tracts of territory not suitable for crop cultivation were required. Central Anatolia abounded in such tracts, but many parts of the region, then as now, could not have sustained all-year-round grazing by large numbers of stock. Transhumance, the shifting of stock on a seasonal basis, from winter grazing on their owners' estates to mountain pasture in the hot summer months, must have been a regular feature of Hittite pastoral life, as indeed it is in parts of the Near Eastern and Mediterranean lands and the sub-Saharan continent today. Some stock-owners without permanent land of their own spent much of their lives on the move, nomads or semi-nomads living in 'tent villages', and moving with their cattle and sheep from one region to another wherever pasture was available.[23] Landowners used herdsmen to accompany their stock (which might include horses and goats as well as cattle and sheep) to distant grazing areas as the season demanded, and generally to act as guardians of the animals throughout the year.

In the ancient Near Eastern as well as the Classical world, the herdsman's lot was often a harsh, lonely, and dangerous one. It was certainly not one to which a free man might aspire of his own accord, no matter how humble his status, and in fact herdsmen seem generally to have been slaves, including transported prisoners-of-war. Their lowly status was hardly commensurate with the considerable responsibilities which their task entailed—ensuring above all the well-being of the herd in the harshest conditions and often for considerable parts of the year far removed from their master's estate. Presumably only the most trustworthy and most reliable of those who were legally bound to a master could be safely assigned a herdsman's role. As in many cultures, dogs assisted with herding activities.

A dog specially trained for this purpose was one of the farmer's most prized possessions, to judge from the twenty-shekel compensation payable to him if someone struck and killed his animal (clause 87). This was twenty times the penalty inflicted for similar injury done to an ordinary dog, and by far the highest of a number of penalties specified in The Laws for injury done to other farm stock, including an ox, horse, mule, ass, and pregnant cow.[24]

Some forty or so of The Laws, around 20 per cent of the entire collection, are devoted to livestock—a clear reflection of the crucial role pastoral activities played in the welfare and prosperity of the kingdom. The number also reflects the considerable potential for legal disputes and claims involving livestock and the criminal activity often associated with them. Apart from setting prices and hire rates, the pastoral laws dealing with stock are principally concerned with provisions covering grazing animals that have been stolen or injured or have strayed.

Regardless of how vigilant their herdsmen were, stock-owners almost inevitably experienced some losses, due to theft or misadventure, or to individual animals straying from the main herd or flock. Such losses may have occurred fairly frequently, particularly when stock was being grazed on open, unfenced pasture land. Very likely thieves accounted for most of these losses, and partly as a deterrent measure, The Laws imposed severe penalties for theft of stock. Thus: 'If anyone steals a plough-ox, formerly they gave fifteen cattle, but now he shall give ten cattle: three two-year-olds, three yearlings, and four weanlings, and he shall look to his house for it' (clause 59). The scaling-down of the original penalty may simply be in line with general reductions in penalties in later versions of The Laws rather than the adoption of a more lenient attitude towards stock-thieves. In any case the revised penalty still went considerably beyond simple one-for-one compensation for the victim. Here as elsewhere in determining an offender's liability, two factors were of particular relevance: first, whether the offence was deliberate or due to negligence; and secondly, the scale of the victim's loss in terms of how much his livelihood was likely to be affected.

The risks of an owner's stock going missing, or getting mixed up with someone else's, were all the greater when flocks or herds of several different owners were grazed together on common pasture land. We have no clear idea of what stipulations governed the use of such land, which legally belonged in its entirety to the king, or who precisely had access to it. But we do know from treaties or agreements made with a group of pro-Hittite Kaska peoples that the herds of a number of owners might share common pasture land, and on occasions become totally intermingled. The agreements allowed the friendly Kaska groups to graze their herds alongside Hittite herds in Hittite territory, but held them responsible for any losses of Hittite stock, and prohibited them from letting their stock mingle with those of hostile Kaska groups.[25] Clearly, each stock-owner must have had some means of identifying his own animals, some form of branding process, which enabled him to prove ownership if it was disputed with a neighbour, if allegedly stolen stock were recovered, when the time came to extricate his own animals from two intermingled herds, or if some of his animals had strayed and were recovered by someone else. In this last case, a man who found strayed stock had to follow a clear procedure: 'If anyone finds a stray ox, a horse, a mule or a donkey, he shall drive it to the king's gate. If he finds it in the country, they shall present it to the elders. The finder shall harness it (*i.e. use it while it is in his custody*). When its owner finds it, he shall take it in full value, but he shall not have him (*i.e. the finder*) arrested as a thief. But if the finder does not present it to the elders, he shall be considered a thief' (clause 71).

The procedure was obviously designed to prevent genuine thieves from avoiding a charge of theft by claiming that the animals in their possession were strays that they had found. A clear distinction is drawn in The Laws between theft on the one hand and finding stray livestock on the other. In the latter case the compensatory payment for someone who finds a stray animal and makes no effort to restore it to its rightful owner is significantly less than for an act of deliberate theft. The distinction in this case is basically between that of a premeditated and unpremeditated act; the offender is less culpable in the second instance.

Apart from the identification of individual animals, the Hittites had precise definitions for various categories of stock, from horses ('a stallion—if it is a weanling, it is not a stallion; if it is a yearling, it is not a stallion; if it is a two-year-old, it is a stallion'—clause 58), to various kinds of horned cattle, three categories of dogs,[26] different varieties of sheep and pigs, bees, and even birds, though the last may have been kept for purposes of augury rather than as poultry.

From reading The Laws, the various land-grant documents, and other texts relating to agricultural activity in the Hittite world, we have the clear impression of a highly regulated society, which stipulated forfeiture of land for failing to work it effectively, fixed penalty scales for a broad range of offences, and apparently fixed prices and wages and hire rates. The impression may well be an accurate one, given the absolute importance of ensuring that all food-producing land was worked to its maximum capacity. Those who threatened the livelihood of their neighbours, whether through deliberate criminal action or malice or simply through negligence, were also a threat to the well-being of the state as a whole. Their punishment could not be left to whim or chance. And given that many of the farming communities on which the Hittite homeland depended for its sustenance were closely settled, it was important to have in place strict regulations governing the activities of these communities—more so than in communities with farmsteads more widely spaced.

CHAPTER 5

The Merchant

> If anyone kills a Hittite merchant, he shall pay 4,000 shekels[1] of silver, and he shall look to his house for it. If it is in the lands of Luwiya (= Arzawa) or Pala, he shall pay the 4,000 shekels of silver and also replace his goods. If it is in the land of Hatti, he himself shall (also) bring the aforementioned merchant (for burial).[2]

From our study of Hittite agriculture it is clear that a great many Hittites lived off the land. Indeed the revenues of the kingdom depended to a very large extent on the land's agricultural produce and the taxes which it generated. Other sources of revenue came from the tribute of vassal states, in the form of a wide range of goods, including consignments of food, precious metals, and various other raw materials, or from war booty in the form of livestock and looted objects of gold, silver, and copper. Textile production, mining enterprises, and the output of metallurgical centres no doubt also produced some income for the king's treasury. But by and large the Hittite economy was not a significantly diversified one, nor apparently one which involved much direct interaction with international trading partners.

International trade had been the defining feature of the pre-Hittite Assyrian Colony period (twentieth to eighteenth centuries), with regular trading activity conducted between Assyria and the kingdoms and communities of eastern and central Anatolia.[3] Textiles and tin were imported into Anatolia in exchange for locally mined gold and silver. But the initiatives and risks seem all to have been on the Assyrian side, amply justifying their handsome gross profit margin (about 100 per cent on tin and 200 per cent on textiles). The Assyrians had set up merchant colonies in Anatolia to facilitate their trading enterprises, and with the abandonment of these in the first half of the eighteenth century the region which was to become the Hittite homeland lost its commercial links with the wider Near Eastern world.

With the establishment of the Hittite kingdom the constant demand for tin, used in the manufacture of bronze tools and weaponry, made it imperative for the Hittites to gain access to large sources of supply of the metal. And unless it was mined in Anatolia, or at least in far greater quantities than at present appears to be the case,[4] it had to be imported, probably along the same routes from the south-east used by the Assyrian caravaneers. This may have been one of the incentives for King Hattusili I's regular campaigns into Syria—to gain and maintain control of, or at least remove potential or actual threats to, vital supply routes from Mesopotamia and Syria to the Land of Hatti.

The Hazards of Merchant Enterprises

The Hittites acquired a range of commodities and other goods by peaceful means as well, though the texts have very little to say about trade and commerce in the Hittite world, and archaeology is if anything even less helpful. The passage from The Laws which introduces this chapter contains one of the few references we have to a merchant of the Hittite land.[5] It is a reference of some significance. In the Hittite context where criminal offences against persons or property were generally punished by fines, the penalty prescribed for killing a merchant is extremely high in comparison with penalties inflicted for other offences. This, it has been suggested, must reflect a very high status enjoyed by merchants in Hittite society.[6] If so, it is surprising that so few Hittites were apparently attracted into the profession. What, then, does the clause really signify? There is no doubt that the crime specified in this case is one of intentional homicide—a crime committed in order to rob the merchant of his goods. This is the significant point. It is the loss of the goods rather than the killing of the merchant that the penalty is intended to reflect. As we learn from a later version of the clause, if the merchant is killed in a quarrel or accidentally—that is to say, robbery is not the motive for the offence—the penalty is substantially reduced, from 100 minas, or 4,000 shekels, of silver to 240 and 80 shekels of silver respectively. The 100 minas was an amount calculated to reflect the value of the goods plus compensation, which was perhaps in the order of three times the goods' value (to judge from the later version of the clause).[7]

Merchant travel in the Near East was a hazardous business, and the situation presented in The Laws was a far from hypothetical one. The Amarna letters exchanged between Akhenaten and his foreign counterparts and vassal rulers contain a number of references to merchants waylaid and murdered as they were going about their business. In one of them Burna-Buriyash (II), king of Babylon, complains to Akhenaten that Babylonian merchants have been murdered in Canaan by subjects of the pharaoh, and demands that they be apprehended and executed.[8] Even caravans under royal escort were not secure from brigands. Again Burna-Buriyash writes to Akhenaten complaining that a royal caravan with gifts for the pharaoh has been robbed by the pharaoh's own subjects in Egyptian territory.[9]

Merchants seem to have been particularly prone to attack in the Syrian region. And as we have seen, a good deal of the litigation in the courts of the region presided over by the local viceroy had to do with crimes against merchants, including cases of murder, robbery, and hijacking. Even if they managed to avoid or had a strong enough guard to resist the local banditry, merchants were still subject to the depredations of the local rulers through whose territories they passed. Taxes and tolls might be legally imposed, as we know from a letter to Akhenaten from the king of Alasiya (= Cyprus or part thereof) requesting tax exemptions for his merchants while they were in Egyptian territory,[10] and also from references in a letter by Queen Puduhepa to Niqmaddu III, king of Ugarit, who had apparently complained that merchants were bypassing his territory and thus avoiding customs duties on their goods.[11] But sometimes local rulers proved unduly rapacious, as we have seen in the case of the merchant Mashanda, who had been forced to hand over to the king of Ugarit 400 donkeys, worth 4,000 shekels of silver, from his caravan (Chapter 2).

The chances of bringing to justice the actual perpetrators of crimes against travelling merchants must often have been extremely remote, particularly in countries like Amurru and Ugarit. The mountainous regions of these countries were infested with bandits (like the Habiru) who no doubt had perfected the art of swooping on merchant caravans and then rapidly disappearing with their loot back into their mountain fastnesses before any effective action could be taken against them. Presumably in the hope of encouraging greater efforts by the locals in protecting travelling merchants against crime, the Hittite king held citizens or authorities of the districts where the crimes were committed responsible for the merchants' safe conduct. When they failed to discharge this responsibility, they were forced to pay substantial compensation. For example, in an accord set up by Ini-Teshub, viceroy at Carchemish, the citizens of Carchemish were obliged to pay to Ugarit compensation of three minas of silver for each Ugaritic merchant killed while travelling in their territory. A similar obligation was imposed on the citizens of Ugarit with respect to merchants from Carchemish.[12] There were in fact a number of occasions on which Ugarit was obliged to make substantial payouts to compensate for the death of a merchant or the robbery of his merchandise. The perils of travel in Ugarit, Dr Singer comments, must have cost its treasury a fortune. As he notes, Ini-Teshub played a very active role in establishing a supportive legal framework for trade in Syria, with appropriate compensation to be paid to the families and business associates of merchants killed in the course of their business.[13] Thus the merchant Talimmu received the enormous sum of a talent of silver from the citizens of Apsuna, in whose territory his business associates had fallen victims to foul play.[14] A merchant might also claim compensation for damage to his cargo or equipment, whether caused accidentally or through negligence, as in the case of a man called Sukku who was found guilty of damaging the ship and cargo of a citizen of Ugarit and ordered by the court to provide reimbursement.[15]

The efforts made to protect merchant activities, even if often unsuccessful, serve to highlight the importance attached to their role in the network of international trade during the Late Bronze Age. The standard currency used in the Near East was generally silver, or occasionally lead—in the form of bars or rings whose value depended on their weight in shekels or minas. But no doubt there was also some degree of trading carried out by exchanging goods in kind.

The Trading Emporia

The cities of the eastern Mediterranean littoral were of central importance to the international trading network. Those of Ugarit in particular served as major trading emporia, providing both outlets for the products and raw materials from the inland regions of Egypt, Syria, Mesopotamia, and Anatolia, and markets for incoming goods and the exchange of merchandise from all countries, as far west as the Mycenaean kingdoms of the Greek mainland, and perhaps even further afield. To the north-west, Ura, on the coast of Classical Cilicia, served also as a major redistribution centre, playing an important role in the provisioning of the Hittite world, particularly in its final decades.

We can readily imagine the scene in one of the international trading emporia. An enormous array of goods is on display or available for inspection along the waterfront and in the streets leading to it. There are closely guarded consignments of precious and semi-precious materials, much in demand in the Aegean and Near Eastern worlds: lapis lazuli brought by Mesopotamian merchants from Afghanistan; gold from a number of regions, including Hatti and Egypt; amethyst, jasper, and turquoise from the deserts of the Nile valley; figurines, finger-rings, earrings, and bracelets, exquisitely wrought in all these materials by craftsmen from Minoan Crete. Large two-handled vessels of olive oil and wine are being unloaded from a merchantman recently arrived from Crete; the vessels themselves with their beautifully shaped contours and marine and floral motifs will be retained as collectors' items in their own right after their contents have been consumed; so too the rows of little ceramic containers of salves and perfumes, also the work of Minoan craftsmen and also much sought after as *objets d'art*. Dyed woollen textiles and fine linen garments from Egypt are on display, expensive items but eagerly sought out by the merchants, for there is always a high demand for them amongst the wealthy classes of Mesopotamian and Hittite society. Depots have been constructed to house the large consignments of raw materials, particularly commodity-metals like tin, copper, lead, and bronze, often shaped into the form of oxhide ingots to facilitate transport and storage. There are standing orders for such goods from a number of kings and merchantmen both in the Near East and across the sea. The caravaneers have been contracted, and the consignments will soon be loaded for the journey to the metallurgical centres at their final destinations.

Nearby, representatives of a Great King are inspecting horses from Babylon and Egypt. Careful selection is essential, for the animals must have the strength and build to endure the rigours of a long journey through harsh terrain and be fit enough at the end of it to pull a manned chariot at high speed into battle. Agents for the Hittite king are checking out the animals for age, sturdiness, and length of limb.[16] A crowd has gathered around a platform at the end of the harbour where a group of fine-looking dark-skinned men, women, and children are having their merits loudly proclaimed. They are a long way from their home in Nubia, and the crowd presses in eagerly, to see more clearly and to touch this exotic human merchandise, for their dark skins are still something of a novelty amongst the paler-complexioned northerners. The slave-trade itself is by no means a novelty of the commercial activity of this age.

One can imagine the bustle, the dust, the noise, the babel of languages, and the combination of smells, both fragrant and foul, of these centres at the height of the trading season. Caravaneers from the interior, their cargoes safely unloaded, are making a brief round of the markets before selecting goods for their return journey. Ships from across the sea and smaller coast-hugging vessels from places closer to hand jostle one another for space in the crowded harbours. The captains of two of them are having a heated argument over damage mutually inflicted on their vessels from being anchored too close to each other. Each threatens the other with legal action, and worse. Street vendors loudly proclaim the merits of their wares and the exotic places whence they came. Taverns and wine-bars are doing a roaring trade. So too are other establishments, catering for patrons in search of more horizontal forms of refreshment.

Sea Trade

Meanwhile the merchantmen are being loaded with consignments destined for the ports of the Aegean lands. Some of the vessels are of local Syrian origin, others hail from Cyprus and the Mycenaean world. During the sailing season they are in constant service, plying their trade along the sea routes which take them from mainland Greece to Crete, and from there south to Egypt, then to the ports of the Syro-Palestine coast, from there to Cyprus[17] and along the southern and perhaps up the western Anatolian coast back to the Greek mainland.[18] Their cargo is always a varied one, and might be made up of gold, ivory, faience, glass, amber, silver, jars of frankincense, orpiment, fig-medicine, in addition to their consignments of copper and tin ingots;[19] for as some of their goods are discharged at their various ports of call, new goods are taken on to replace them. Large quantities of metals, some originally brought to collecting depots in Mesopotamia from further east and conveyed to coastal ports along the established trade routes passing through Babylon and Mari, are carried westwards and replaced for the return journey with tools and weapons and jewellery, often made from these same metals, and wine and oil and perfumes.

There are handsome profits to be made in these sea-trade enterprises, but the hazards of travel by sea are if anything greater than those of merchant travel by land. Sea pirates are a constant menace, in spite of sporadic efforts by the kings of the region to keep their activities in check. There are natural hazards to be faced as well, particularly in the waters off the long and frequent harbourless stretches of the southern Anatolian coastline. The recently discovered wrecks off Cape Gelidonya and Ulu Burun on the Lycian coast,[20] part of the Lukka Lands in the Late Bronze Age, provide material evidence of the fate of ships suddenly caught at sea by a violent storm and failing to make the safety of the first available harbour.

Hatti's Commercial Contacts

Almost certainly the Hittites' commercial dealings with foreign countries were conducted largely if not exclusively through the trading centres on the Levantine and Cilician coasts. Already in the Hittite Old Kingdom the Syrian campaigns of Hattusili I may have been partly intended to facilitate Hittite access to the international merchandise which found its way into Syrian markets. Products from the Aegean world were no doubt included amongst this merchandise. But they were just one component of a multiplicity of goods coming from all parts of the Near Eastern world and Egypt as well as from regions further to the west. Through their access to these markets, purveyors of merchandise for the Hittite world had a wide range of international goods from which to choose. Suppiluliuma I's campaigns in northern Syria in the fourteenth century and the establishment of a network of Hittite vassal kingdoms throughout the region in the wake of these campaigns must have greatly facilitated merchant travel between the ports of the Levantine coast, most notably those of the kingdom of Ugarit, and the Hittite homeland. Ugarit's relatively extensive coastline contained four or more major seaports, making it an important link between the Mediterranean world and the lands stretching to the Euphrates and beyond.

Our texts indicate trading contacts between Hatti and a range of other countries, including Babylon, Assyria, Mitanni, Syro-Palestine,

Egypt, and Cyprus, though we generally have little indication either from these texts or from the archaeological record of what goods the Hittites imported and what they exchanged for them. A few pieces of pottery from northern Syria and Cyprus, a couple of Babylonian cylinder seals, and the odd Egyptian scarab and alabaster vase have turned up at various central Anatolian sites,[21] but hardly in sufficient quantities, particularly given the indestructible nature of such materials, to suggest that there was anything like regular trading activity between these countries and the Hittite homeland. One must fall back—and it is probably quite legitimate to do so in this case—on the old standby of trade in items which leave little or no trace in the archaeological record. Perishable and consumable items such as oil, perfume, grain, and textiles belong to this category. Large ceramic vessels might initially have been used for the transport of commodities like oil and grain by sea, but then very likely these items were transferred to other containers of a perishable nature, like the saddle- and side-packs used in the donkey caravans of the Assyrian Colony period, which were more practical for overland transport.

As we shall see, professional expertise was imported—doctors from Egypt and Babylon (at least as visiting consultants), and scribes and quite possibly a range of other experts, like practitioners in the fields of ritual and divination, from Babylon. Horses were certainly imported from time to time, from Babylon, Mitanni, and Egypt, and perhaps also from western Anatolia which may well have been, as Homer suggests, a major horse-breeding region around the time of the Trojan War. Grain too was imported, on an increasingly regular basis in the final century or so of the empire, in amounts corresponding to shortfalls in home production. Shipments of grain came from Syro-Palestine, and Egypt had also become an important source of supply shortly after King Hattusili III drew up his 'eternal treaty' with Ramesses II. Indeed declining homeland production may well have been one of a number of considerations which prompted Hattusili to come to terms with the pharaoh. Puduhepa claimed in one of her letters to Ramesses that there was no grain in her lands, a claim designed to persuade him to collect as soon as possible the horses, cattle, and sheep provided as a dowry for the Hittite princess sent to be his bride.[22] The pharaoh may already have been aware of Hatti's grain-shortage, since it was around the same time that a high-ranking Hittite official was sent to Egypt to arrange the prompt shipment of a consignment of wheat and barley to the Hittite land.[23]

Such imports probably became increasingly regular, and near the kingdom's very end the pharaoh Merneptah's statement that he sent shipments of grain to Hatti 'to keep the land alive'[24] may have been much closer to the truth than many a rhetorically exaggerated Egyptian claim. It is consistent with the strong sense of urgency in a letter dispatched from the Hittite court during the reign of Tudhaliya IV, the second last king of Hattusa. The letter was written to the king of Ugarit, either Niqmaddu III or Ammurapi (his name is not preserved in the text), demanding a ship and crew for the transport of 2,000 *kor* of grain (*c.*450 tonnes) from Mukis to Ura. It stresses the need for its recipient to act without delay.[25]

The letter also indicates the route by which grain shipments reached the homeland. The consignments obtained in Egypt and Canaan were transported by ship along the coastal sea-route to Ugarit. From here they continued their journey by ship through coastal waters to Ura on Anatolia's southern coast, and were thence transported overland to Hatti. Coast-hugging by the transport vessels avoided the need for open sea travel, an important consideration given the risks a vessel constantly faced from either pirates operating from the harbours of Alasiya[26] or the forces of nature. Even coastal travel was not free of these perils, as we learn in a letter sent from Tyre which describes a storm in which grain ships from Egypt were caught off the coast of Tyre.[27]

The transport of merchandise from the coast to the Hittite homeland seems to have been largely in the hands of merchants of Ura, who acted as agents of the Hittite king in organizing the shipping of goods from Ugarit to Ura, and the subsequent conveyance of these goods into the Hittite homeland.[28] In spite of the risks which his occupation entailed, an enterprising merchant well equipped to deal with the hazards of his journeys could make a lucrative living. His vital role in the provisioning of the Hittite world was no doubt reflected in the substantial rewards for his services—sufficient for him to engage in some property speculation on the side. While waiting to pick up a new consignment of goods in Ugarit, a number of merchants from Ura took the opportunity to invest in the local property market. That led to considerable social tensions. Local resentment at choice pieces of real estate falling into the hands of foreigners was intensified when some of the locals were forced to hand over their own properties to these foreigners in order to discharge a debt. The situation became so serious that the Ugaritic king

Niqmepa wrote to his overlord Hattusili III asking him to sort the problem out. That provided Hattusili with something of a dilemma. He was concerned at the prospect of social unrest in his vassal kingdom, but at the same time he was anxious not to alienate the group of men whose professional services were becoming increasingly indispensable to the kingdom. So in response to his vassal ruler's plea, he issued a decree which was in the nature of a compromise: the merchants of Ura were to be allowed to continue their business activities in Ugarit during the summer months, provided they returned home for the winter (when most trading activity came to an end anyhow). They were to cease their speculations in Ugaritic real estate and were forbidden to take property from locals to discharge a debt. However, a debtor unable to repay his debt by other means was obliged to work off the debt in the merchant's service.[29]

By and large, then, it appears that much of the trading activity of the Hittite world, particularly international trade, was in the hands of foreign intermediaries and entrepreneurs. The Hittites' apparently minor role in international mercantile activity must be to some extent a feature of their geography. In contrast to Cyprus, Egypt, the countries of the Aegean, and the states of the Syro-Palestine littoral, the territory of Hatti was landlocked. The Hittites had no seagoing capacity of their own, for either military or commercial purposes. Any naval activities in which they did engage, and those attested are very rare,[30] required the use of ships from one of their maritime vassal states, such as Ugarit.

Generally the great trading civilizations were those which had direct sea access, like Cyprus and Minoan Crete and Mycenaean Greece in the second millennium BC and Phoenicia in a later age. But that is not the whole story. To be active and successful in international trade a country must not only have safe, reliable travel routes and a good trading infrastructure (port facilities etc.) but must also be able to provide in substantial quantities goods and materials for which there is a demand in other countries and which cannot be obtained from more accessible sources of supply. Now that the myth that the Hittites were an iron-producing people has been laid to rest, it is difficult to identify any items produced in the heartland of the Hittite world, whether raw materials or manufactured goods, which might have attracted substantial and constant international trading interest. Minerals like gold and silver, copper and lead were mined in central Anatolia and other areas under Hittite control, and significant quantities of at least the precious metals could well have been exported, but probably less as export items in their own right than as payment for goods received from international sources.

Like their Assyrian Colony predecessors in central and eastern Anatolia, the Hittites seem to have been relatively passive participants in the world of Late Bronze Age trade and commerce.[31] Much of the international trading activity in which they did engage was very largely conducted on their behalf by intermediaries. It is to other fields of human endeavour that we must look for instances where Hittite initiative and enterprise come to the fore.

CHAPTER 6
The Warrior

> I held up my hand to My Lady, the Sun Goddess of Arinna, and thus I spoke: 'My Lady, Sun Goddess of Arinna, the neighbouring enemy lands which called me a child and humiliated me, and were forever striving to take your territory—O My Lady, Sun Goddess of Arinna, come to my support and smite those neighbouring enemy lands before me!'
>
> (from the Annals of King Mursili II)

Someone has recently come up with the estimate that since the beginning of recorded history scarcely more than three hundred years have been free of major wars. To put this another way, if we were to take at random any period of a hundred years in the last five thousand, we could expect ninety-four of them on average to be occupied with large-scale conflicts in one or more parts of the globe. The immediate causes of these conflicts have varied. But Thucydides' statement in relation to Athenian imperialism, echoed by Aristotle in his justification of slavery, serves to highlight a fundamental *casus belli* throughout history: 'There has always been a fixed principle that the weaker should be subject to the stronger,' Thucydides declares. 'Considerations of justice have never yet diverted anyone from establishing his superiority by the exercise of force, whenever the opportunity has offered.'[1] 'That one should rule and others be ruled', says Aristotle, 'is both necessary and expedient.'[2] Throughout history it has been almost axiomatic that a nation seeking to avoid subjection to a foreign overlord must itself achieve and exercise the powers of an overlord, and will succeed in doing so only by having at its disposal substantial military capabilities—and using them. One must rule or be ruled; there is no middle course.

In this general context, and specifically within the turbulent centuries of the Late Bronze Age, it is hardly surprising that the history of the Hittite world is by and large a history of military conflict—a chronicle of wars fought regionally and internationally by Hittite kings in their efforts to extend their kingdom's territories and political and commercial interests, and to defend their frontiers against their enemies. In so doing, they were generally no more ruthless than their Near Eastern contemporaries, predecessors, or successors, and often rather less bloodthirsty in the aftermath of conquest. Whereas an Assyrian king might seek to cow his enemies into submission by exemplary acts of brutality, in similar circumstances a Hittite king often portrayed himself as a magnanimous victor, making a display of clemency even towards an allegedly treacherous enemy who little warranted such treatment. In fact such displays had less to do with compassion and humanity than with hard-nosed pragmatism, as when King Mursili II called off at the last minute the siege of a rebellious vassal's city—in response to an appeal from the vassal's aged mother:

> I would certainly have marched against him (the disloyal vassal) and destroyed him utterly, but he sent forth his mother to meet me. She came and fell at my knees and spoke to me as follows: 'My Lord, do not destroy us. Take us, My Lord, into subjection.' And since a woman came to meet me and fell at my knees, I gave way to the woman and thereupon I did not march to the Seha River Land. And I took Manapa-Tarhunda and the Seha River Land into subjection.[3]

This apparent act of chivalry was almost certainly dictated by practical, strategic considerations.[4] Yet we should not miss the significance of the image which the king sought to convey—of a merciful, compassionate overlord in contrast to a ruthless butcher prepared to give no quarter to those who defied him.

Attitudes to War

Fighting one's enemies was as regular and natural an activity amongst the Hittites as cultivating the soil and worshipping the gods. The king regularly led his people in war, just as he led them in the celebration of state festivals and in the dispensing of justice. With few exceptions he could expect to spend a substantial part of each year away from his capital on military campaigns. These might take him to the north, to restore Hittite authority in regions under constant threat from the Kaska tribes. Or to the west or south-west to deal with rebellious Arzawan states. Or to the south-east, on expeditions against Mitannian, Egyptian, or Assyrian forces, or rebellious vassals in the Syrian region.

Warfare was by and large a business. It provided an important source of revenue, from the plunder and spoil of conquered cities and territories and the subsequent flow of tribute from these territories. It helped secure against enemy depredations food-producing land and supply routes for essential goods. And it provided the kingdom with a regular source of manpower, in the form of prisoners-of-war or 'booty-people' (NAM.RA.MEŠ) transported back to the homeland. The transportees were used as a labour force on farming estates, as recruits in the royal militia, as temple personnel, and many may also have been assigned to populate or repopulate sparsely inhabited areas of the kingdom.[5]

In a world where lasting peace was the exception rather than the rule, there is hardly a word spoken of the horrors and carnage of war, of its innocent victims, of the destruction of property and the catastrophic waste of human effort and resources. War, not peace, was the normal state of affairs. There was no ideology of peace.[6] The very existence of important deities with a predominantly military role, like the goddess Ishtar/Shaushka, indicates that warfare was seen as a natural and inevitable and divinely sanctioned condition of human existence. Yet there are relatively few instances where Hittite kings appear to take pleasure in war or glory in its outcome. We have no reliefs from the Hittite world depicting a king destroying his enemies in the field of battle or exulting over the corpses of the slain, as in Egyptian and Assyrian reliefs. Even the written records of a king's exploits present military successes in bald, matter-of-fact terms, briefly stating the events leading up to the conquest followed by a summary of its results, including the numbers of prisoners-of-war and other plunder taken as spoils of battle. There are occasional exceptions. Hattusili I seems to have delighted in the carnage and destruction of military conquest for its own sake, revelling in the image of the lion which destroys its prey without mercy. But his apparent pride in slaughter and destruction *per se* finds few echoes in the records of his successors. Indeed later kings sometimes devote more space to recording their attempts to avoid conflict with an enemy or rebellious vassal than to a description of military triumphs.

There is an ideological as well as a practical dimension to this. Though his kingdom was geared to a state of constant military preparedness, the king himself was never the instigator of aggression, at least to his way of thinking. He sought to represent himself as one who took the field only *in reaction to* unprovoked aggression by his enemies or rebellion by disloyal vassals, or against states or communities who provided asylum for his fugitive subjects. Ultimately the object of his military campaigns was to restore peace, order, and stability to a world which had been plunged into turmoil and disorder by his enemies, to bring about a state of *eunomia*. The rightness of his cause was never in doubt, for his gods went by his side or ran before him as he marched into battle—'My Lady, the Sun Goddess of Arinna, and My Lord, the mighty Storm God, and Mezzulla and all the gods went before me'—just as the image of a glowing cross preceded Constantine into battle at the Milvian bridge. This somewhat paradoxical ideology which represents war as the instrument for the restoration of order and harmony underpins much of the propaganda associated with warfare, particularly so-called wars of liberation, throughout history. It goes back at least to the tradition of Marduk's brutal, bloody triumph over the forces of chaos and disorder, represented by Tiamat and her monstrous brood, in the Babylonian Myth of Creation.

In the Hittite as in other worlds, this basic ideology had to be reconciled with the expectation that a king would demonstrate his fitness to rule by his prowess as a military leader, by doing great deeds which emulated or surpassed the achievements of his predecessors. This was reflected in the parade of titles in his nomenclature—'My Sun, the Great King, King of the Land of Hatti, the Labarna, the Hero'—like the array of medals emblazoned across a modern war hero's chest. War provided the opportunity for this. And the distribution of the material rewards gained from military successes was undoubtedly important in ensuring for the king the loyalty of his leading subjects.

Logistics and Strategies

Yet there were not a few occasions when Hittite kings were genuinely reluctant to take the field against their enemies, for very practical reasons. Above all, there was the question of manpower. The forces available to the king for military enterprises were far from unlimited. The Hittite homeland itself seems to have been chronically underpopulated, a problem which at times assumed crisis proportions, as when the homeland was ravaged, allegedly for twenty years, by the virulent plague which broke out at the end of Suppiluliuma I's reign. A major military campaign conducted away from the homeland probably involved a force of up to 10,000 men.[7] Considerably more in the case of the famous battle of Kadesh, in which the Hittite king Muwatalli II put some 47,500 troops into the field against the pharaoh Ramesses II.[8] The core Hittite force might on occasions have been reinforced by auxiliaries from a vassal state in the campaign region, and perhaps sometimes by mercenaries. None the less the departure of a Hittite army on campaign seriously weakened the homeland's defence capabilities, leaving it vulnerable to attack by hostile neighbours. Indeed on a number of occasions a king had to return promptly to the homeland after a victorious campaign abroad in order to flush out enemy forces who had invaded the heart of his kingdom in his absence. It seems that kings seldom had sufficient forces at their disposal to ensure that the homeland remained secure while they conducted campaigns away from it. And as we might expect, homeland security became even more problematical when the need arose to mount campaigns in two different regions simultaneously.

A campaigning season could extend from spring to early autumn—through the period, from sowing to harvest, when demands on the homeland's agricultural workforce were at their highest. As we have seen (Chapter 4), a substantial proportion of Hatti's able-bodied population worked the land in one capacity or another. The importance of their contribution to the maintenance of the kingdom can hardly be overestimated, given the predominantly agricultural basis of Hittite society. Yet large numbers of the male workers were probably required on a regular basis for military service, taking them from essential food-producing activity for weeks, perhaps months, during crucial periods of the agricultural year. To some extent manpower deficiencies were made good by the regular importation of transportees into the homeland and their allocation to farming estates, temple service, underpopulated frontier regions, and to the king's militia. But the supply of manpower must frequently have fallen short of demand, requiring the king to make hard decisions as to whether or not he could afford the commitment of his manpower resources to a particular campaign. Would the rewards of such a campaign be worth it? Would the consequences of *not* taking action outweigh the costs of doing so?

Hittite kings were often particularly reluctant to commit themselves to military campaigns in western Anatolia. The dangers of the Hittites not maintaining an effective presence in the west, through their overlordship of vassal states in the region, were made very evident to them several times in their history. Left unchecked, the kingdoms of western Anatolia could pose serious threats to the security of the Hittites' southern buffer territory, the Lower Land, and other subject territories in the region, and ultimately to the homeland itself. But as far as possible the kings sought to resolve military and political crises in their western territories by diplomatic means. Hence the remarkable forbearance which Tudhaliya I/II and Arnuwanda I showed towards their treacherous western vassal Madduwatta.[9] Hence Hattusili III's repeated attempts to negotiate a settlement with the renegade Piyamaradu who had stirred up anti-Hittite insurrection in the west, even while the Hittites were on the march against him. Hence Hattusili's subsequent attempts to win the cooperation of the Ahhiyawan king, who had almost certainly backed Piyamaradu's enterprises, in restoring peace to the region without the need for further military intervention.[10]

Each military campaign in the west took the Hittites in precisely the opposite direction to that in which their interests—political, strategic, cultural, commercial—primarily lay; in particular the region extending from south-eastern Anatolia, through Kizzuwadna, into northern Syria and for a time across the Euphrates. In Syria lay their most valuable and most profitable vassal kingdoms, like Ugarit and Amurru. Here they established viceregal kingdoms at Aleppo and Carchemish, under the direct rule of sons of the Great King. Through this region lay the major trade and communication land-routes of the Near Eastern world. Here was the international arena where Hittite kings came most closely into contact, and conflict, with the other Great Kings of the Near East. Here they had won their most illustrious victories and gained their richest spoils—in Hattusili I's campaigns of plunder across northern Syria and beyond the Euphrates, in Mursili I's sack of Babylon, in Suppiluliuma I's conquest of the heartland and subject territories of Mitanni, in Muwatalli II's victory (in terms of its long-term consequences) over Ramesses II at Kadesh. A strong, permanent military and political presence in this region was vital to Hatti's status as one of the great international powers of the Late Bronze Age.

But while maintaining this status, it could not afford to ignore other regions, particularly the west. That was a lesson which Suppiluliuma I had failed to learn. When crises did occur in two or more regions at the same time, priorities had to be established. Only rarely were campaigns mounted in more than one region simultaneously—and then only under dire necessity.[11] Risks of taking action in one region at the expense of not taking it in another had to be carefully assessed. So too all costs and likely consequences of such action. The relatively small reservoir of military resources available to the Hittites, for policing and protecting a vast expanse of territory, from the Aegean coast of Anatolia in the west through to the Euphrates river in the east, had to be used as sparingly as a particular situation allowed, especially when the prospects of rewards were small. And when committed to conflict, troops had to be used with maximum efficiency, in as brief a campaign as possible, and extracting the maximum rewards from victory, in both manpower and *matériel*.

We need also to bear in mind that military operations had to be completed before the onset of the winter snows. That in itself imposed a limit upon the time available for a campaign, particularly if the year was well advanced when it began. Only rarely did the king and his troops spend the winter in the campaigning region or its vicinity.[12] And there were times when a king was forced to break off military operations *in medias res*, returning home for the winter and starting all over again the following year. Yet even when he had completed a campaign in a single season, there was inevitably some delay before he and his army could begin their homeward trek. A political settlement might need to be made in the wake of a military victory; and in the case of a city that had refused surrender, time was needed to loot it and load the spoils for the journey back to the homeland. A basic 'rule' of warfare was that a city which submitted without resistance and pledged allegiance to the victor was spared despoliation. But one which proved defiant and had to be taken by force could legitimately be looted and plundered once its defences were breached. There are many earlier precedents for the fate suffered by Constantinople in 1453 after it rejected the terms offered by Mehmet II, sultan and commander of the Turkish force laying siege to the city.

The Spoils of War

When encumbered with booty, the army's return to their homeland may well have taken a great deal longer than their outward journey. Carts stacked with the glittering trophies of victory, including the images wrought in precious metals of the vanquished cities' gods, life-size bulls of gold, chariots of silver, boats with silver-plated prows, must in themselves have substantially slowed each day's progress. But in many campaigns by far the greatest part of the spoils consisted of human booty and livestock. Military texts particularly from Mursili II's time onwards refer repeatedly to the transportation of booty-people and sheep and cattle from the conquered territories back to the homeland. The number of transportees ran sometimes to the hundreds, sometimes to the thousands; sometimes the prisoners and captured livestock were too numerous to count. 'The transportees I brought to the palace numbered 15,000. However, the transportees, the cattle and the sheep which the generals, the infantry, and the chariotry of Hattusa brought were beyond count.' So Mursili records in the aftermath of one of his victories.

Such bald, matter-of-fact statements provide a recurring refrain to the litany of conquests. Yet they give little indication of the enormous logistical operation involved in conveying masses of unwilling humanity, and livestock 'beyond count', back to the homeland, sometimes over hundreds of kilometres of inhospitable terrain. Able-bodied men, women, and children were culled from the conquered population and forced to undertake the trek under close military guard to the land of their conquerors. For a number of these transportees, the prospect of spending the rest of their lives deprived of their freedom in a strange enemy country was a compelling incentive to try to escape back to their homelands, or to find refuge in other lands. Effective measures in preventing this must have been one of the Hittites' chronic problems, especially when the numbers of their prisoners were large and their route took them through unfamiliar and hostile territory. Efforts were made to discourage would-be escapees by trying to ensure that they had nowhere to go. Dire threats were uttered against local rulers likely to provide asylum to escaped transportees. But while this may have discouraged, it did not always prevent the flight of prisoners *en route* to Hatti. And the refusal of certain local kings to return to Hittite authority those transportees who had escaped from it and sought refuge with them often led to prompt and severe military reprisals.

Apart from its custodial responsibilities—maintaining strict control over the prisoners and preventing their escape—the Hittite expeditionary force had the task of ensuring that the captive population and their livestock were adequately provisioned and protected during the march. On their outward journey the army carried supplies from Hattusa, replenished perhaps from food-storage depots at strategically located intervals along the campaign route, and supplemented by provisions made available by local rulers in vassal states through which the army passed. But on the journey home, in addition to providing food for themselves and their animals, the army had to ensure that there was sufficient food and water to sustain hundreds and sometimes thousands of captive men, women, and children, and sheep and cattle in greater numbers, for the duration of the journey. Even if care were taken to select the healthiest of the conquered population as transportees, many were unlikely to have had the stamina necessary to cope with the journey. The rigours of travel often extending over many weeks in often harsh environmental conditions must have taken its toll. Yet for the army to arrive home with a booty contingent severely reduced in numbers and in a seriously weakened state would rather have defeated the purpose of the whole undertaking. Casualties on the march had to be kept to a minimum. This must have slowed the journey even more than did the carts of inanimate spoils, and required a considerable escort force to ensure the safe conveyance of the live booty to the homeland. It is quite likely that at the end of a campaign the king returned to Hattusa as quickly as possible with as many of his troops as he could afford to take with him, particularly if their presence was urgently required there. But the supervision and provisioning and protection of thousands of prisoners and livestock on the march undoubtedly meant the commitment of a large part of the army to ensuring that they eventually reached their destination.

Nevertheless the prizes of conquest clearly outweighed the costs, risks, time, and effort involved in getting them all back home. The sacking and despoliation of cities whose palaces and temples were richly adorned with objects of precious metals and other valuable items, like the plunder Hattusili I brought back from his south-eastern campaigns, made for a dazzling display of spoils by the conqueror on his return, and surely won him considerable goodwill from his country's gods to whom such loot was often dedicated. But it was the live booty which in practical terms provided the most valuable outcome of many campaigns. We have already referred to the uses to which booty-people were put. Not the least of these was their incorporation into the agricultural workforce, which no doubt went a long way towards meeting, or at least reducing, shortfalls in home-grown sources of labour. The constant influx of transportees may have played no small role in the agriculture-based economy of the Hatti land. And the fact that many of the transportees were allocated as a labour force to the king's landowning military officers undoubtedly helped ensure the ongoing support and allegiance which the king expected from those so rewarded.

Rebellion and Civil War

There was one category of warfare where the costs could be substantial, with none of the usual rewards to compensate. If warfare was a business, then civil war was a bad business, a very bad business indeed. Already in the earliest years of its recorded history, the Hittite land was plagued with internal rebellions against the authority of the king. Hattusili I tells us of an uprising against his grandfather, then of rebellions in his own reign by his sons and his daughter, apparently over the matter of the royal succession. These rebellions were quashed, and Hattusili's grandson Mursili eventually succeeded peacefully to the throne, in accordance with his grandfather's wishes. But his distinguished career, which included the conquest of Aleppo and Babylon, was cut short when he was assassinated and replaced by his brother-in-law Hantili. That set a pattern. Each of the succeeding four kings occupied the throne by violently dislodging his predecessor. It was virtually open season on whoever happened to be king at the time until the last in the series of usurpers, Telipinu, tried to sort the whole mess out by formalizing rules for the succession, as recorded in his famous decree.

The most serious consequences of these bloody internecine conflicts was that they divided the kingdom against itself and made it easy prey for its enemies—to the point where on Telipinu's accession it had been reduced to little more than the capital and the region immediately surrounding it. Faced with the task of winning back as much of the kingdom's former territories as was practicable (which he did with no little success), Telipinu expounded at length in the preamble of his decree on the disastrous consequences of a country at war with itself. It was not merely its human enemies that the fractured kingdom had to worry about. The gods themselves intervened, according to Telipinu, punishing the usurping kings and their subjects with drought and enemy invasion.

We cannot be sure how far these dynastic disputes and rebellions involved the people of Hatti as a whole. Yet even if they scarcely reached the status of full-scale civil wars, their consequences may have been just as devastating for the homeland. Telipinu's succession rules did give some added stability to the monarchy, even though on a number of later occasions blood was shed over the matter of who had the right to sit on the throne in Hattusa. But undoubtedly the most notorious of the royal coups was the one which did plunge the Hittite state into full-scale civil war. This was around the year 1267 when Hattusili III, uncle of the reigning king Urhi-Teshub, seized the throne from his nephew. In the document commonly referred to as *The Apology*, Hattusili sought to defend his action. The arguments he mounts are specious in the extreme. There was no doubt that Urhi-Teshub was the rightful king, even though not the son of a first-rank wife, and that Hattusili had turned against him out of anger and humiliation at being stripped of the high offices he had held since the reign of Urhi-Teshub's father (and Hattusili's brother) Muwatalli II. This personal affront precipitated a conflict which assumed the proportions of a major civil war, one which extended beyond the homeland and included fighting and looting in Hattusa itself. It caused serious and lasting divisions in the allegiances of both the homeland population and the vassal states.

We have only Hattusili's record of events, which amply illustrates the oft-quoted adage that history is written by the victor. The victor in this case considerably downplayed the scale of the conflict and the devastation which it caused, and indeed the strong support which Urhi-Teshub undoubtedly had. We can assess these only through passing references in the *Apology* and in a proclamation which Hattusili subsequently delivered to the people of Hattusa. A victory by Urhi-Teshub would very likely have provided us with a dramatically different version of events. How did Hattusili defend his actions? A military leader can readily find justifications for taking the field against a foreign enemy. But how can he justify taking up arms against his own people? In Hattusili's case by representing the conflict which he had initiated as a legal contest between two adversaries. The usurper claimed divine endorsement for his coup. It was the gods who gave judgement on the rightness of his cause.[13] In such a way the political or military upstart/pretender seeks to conceal blatantly illegal conduct beneath a veneer of pseudo-legality. The gods, like the judge in a court of law, will assess the validity of the opposing claims, and give judgement, in the form of military victory, to whichever party is in the right. 'Let us go in judgement before the Storm God My Lord and Shaushka of Samuha My Lady,' says Hattusili. 'If you prevail in the trial, they will raise you; but if I prevail in the trial they will raise me.'[14] So too Hattusili's grandfather King Mursili II had declared to the Arzawan king Uhhaziti, who had defied Mursili's demand for the return of his prisoners: 'Come then! We shall join battle. Let the Storm God My Lord judge our dispute!'[15] So too Henry V sought to justify his war with Charles, king of France. Such has been the specious justification for many a 'holy war'. In such a way the victor demonstrates, so he believes, that God is on his side.

The Composition of the Army

The king was commander-in-chief of the Hittite army and on major campaigns regularly led his troops in person.[16] Indeed, he could be expected to spend a good deal of each year, between spring and late autumn, away from the homeland in wars against his enemies. A prospective king's military training, as probably also that of his brothers, began in the first years of adolescence and sometimes involved actual battle experience at this early age. The future king Tudhaliya IV, for example, seems to have been no more than twelve when he participated in campaigns in the Kaska region. But while many Hittite kings were no doubt well trained in the arts of war, they almost certainly directed most of their military operations from a vantage-point safely removed from the thick of the battle, or if ever participating in the battle itself, well protected by their bodyguards. The hero of Greek epic might be expected to put his life on the line every minute of a battle. But Hittite pragmatism would surely have seen to it that His Majesty was not too closely exposed to the hazards of war. For all his military prowess, the possibility that a well-directed enemy shaft, or a lucky sword thrust, could in an instant plunge the whole kingdom into crisis was an unacceptable risk. In all Hittite history, and in spite of the fact that many kings spent part of almost every year of their lives on the battlefield, there was not one king, as far as we know, who died on the field (though battle-wounds might have contributed to Hattusili I's death). This is much more likely to have been a case of prudence and good management rather than remarkably good luck.

On a number of occasions, when the king was occupied with

another campaign, or attending to pressing matters elsewhere, or felt obliged to remain in or return to his capital, or was indisposed, or felt that a campaign was not of sufficient significance to warrant his presence, he entrusted military command to a deputy. Sometimes with outstanding success, as in the commands King Suppiluliuma I assigned to his sons Arnuwanda and Sharri-Kushuh. Sometimes with disastrous consequences, as in the command Tudhaliya I/II assigned to Kisnapili in south-western Anatolia. Kisnapili's army was ambushed and routed, and its commander and his deputy were killed. Alternatively the king could assign to a deputy the command of a division within an army under his general command. His chief deputy was generally the son he had designated as crown prince. Thus Arnuwanda I, (adopted?) son of Tudhaliya I/II and later his co-regent and eventual successor, became during his father's reign a military commander in his own right. So too Suppiluliuma I's son Arnuwanda II came to the throne as a battle-hardened warrior who as crown prince had commanded Hittite armies in both Mitannian and Syrian territory. Other sons of the king were also given military commands, notably Arnuwanda II's brother Piyassili (Sharri-Kushuh), the viceroy at Carchemish who had substantial military responsibilities in the region on both sides of the Euphrates. Suppiluliuma himself before his accession undertook military commands on behalf of his ailing father Tudhaliya III, though not in this case as crown prince, an office to which another son (the luckless Tudhaliya the Younger) had been appointed.

The king's brothers seem often to have been appointed to high military commands immediately below the king and the crown prince, particularly if they held the highly prestigious post of GAL *MEŠEDI* (Chief of the Bodyguards). Those appointed to this post were sometimes given independent military commands. The later king Hattusili III had held the post while his brother Muwatalli was on the throne. His tenure of it brought him considerable military distinction—both in the battle of Kadesh and as commander-in-chief of the troops stationed in the northern half of the homeland—and no doubt helped nurture his ambition to occupy the throne himself. Another prestigious post, that of GAL GEŠTIN (whose literal meaning 'Chief of the Wine (Stewards)' belies its exalted status), was also generally held by a brother of the king or another close member of his family. This too was an office with which an independent military command was sometimes associated.[17]

Officers of lower status within the military hierarchy, though still often members of the royal family, included the commanders of the chariot and infantry contingents, generally one officer for each thousand men. Beneath these were a range of other officers, at the higher levels landowning nobles and dignitaries of the land of Hatti. In terms of their status and responsibility, their ranks extended downwards from the ancient equivalent of colonels to sergeants.[18]

The army itself was made up of infantry and chariotry. Riders on horseback are also depicted in Egyptian reliefs. But these were very likely used only for reconnaissance or as dispatch riders. We have no clear evidence of cavalry contingents in the army, though it is possible that as in Egypt and the Mycenaean world, cavalry played a small part in Hittite military operations.[19] The infantry, who served in the army as spearmen, provided the bulk of the king's forces, something over 90 per cent of the total. Its core consisted of a permanent body of troops, the king's own militia, recruited from the free male population of Hatti supplemented by levies from the appanage kingdoms and districts on the empire's fringes.[20] The standing army wintered in military barracks in Hattusa, and when not engaged on military activities could also be used as a police force, as a labour force for building projects, and also occasionally as participants in rituals and festivals.[21]

For major campaigns the permanent army was reinforced by levies from the general population, perhaps including significant numbers from the estates of the king's landowning nobility. On rare occasions the army might have been further supplemented by mercenaries from states outside Hittite control—as in the battle of Kadesh, to judge from Ramesses' jibe that the Hittite king Muwatalli stripped all his land of silver to swell his ranks with hired troops.

The chariotry constituted the elite force of the army. The horse and light chariot were introduced into the Hittite world, as elsewhere in the Near East, probably around 1600, and henceforth became the most powerful element in a kingdom's fighting capacity. Originally the Hittite chariot had a crew of two—a driver and a fighter armed with bow and arrow. By the time of the battle of Kadesh in 1274, this number had been increased to three, as depicted in Egyptian relief scenes of the battle. The third member of the crew carried a shield to protect the archer. Pulled by two stallions, the chariot was built for speed and manoeuvrability. Its frame was of

Fig. 2. Hittite charioteers at Kadesh

wood with a leather covering and it ran on two wooden spoked wheels, set wide apart to ensure stability—particularly necessary with a crew of three on board.[22]

Effective use of chariots required a rigorous training programme, both of men and horses, a fact which, as Professor Goetze comments, created a professional class with its own ethos.[23] The importation, breeding, and training of horses was a costly and time-consuming exercise, but one which was vital to the kingdom's defence. The horses had to be trained not only for speed, strength, and stamina within the battle itself, but also to withstand the rigours of a journey of perhaps hundreds of kilometres and still be in a fit state to perform at maximum capacity when battle was finally joined. A strict training programme has been preserved in a document commonly called the Kikkuli text, a manual which provides comprehensive instruction on all aspects of the training of chariot horses, including a culling process and detailed advice on a diet and exercise regimen.[24] Almost certainly the horse and chariot were introduced into the Hittite world via the Hurrians, as were the training techniques contained in the Kikkuli text, a further example of the impact of Hurrian civilization on the kingdom of Hatti.

A word about the transport of chariots to the region where military operations were to be conducted. It is inconceivable that chariots were actually driven to the battlefield, particularly if this lay a significant distance from the departure point. As we have noted, the chariots were lightly constructed, built for speed and manoeuvrability in battle. They would have been totally unfit for this purpose if driven hundreds of kilometres prior to battle over frequently rough terrain—even if they did manage to survive the journey in one piece! On the other hand vehicles built to withstand the rigours of a long journey would have had to compromise on speed and manoeuvrability to such an extent that they would have been more of a liability than an asset in battle. But even if chariots which combined both functions could have been miraculously produced, they would have needed horses to pull them, and at least one person in each to drive them. The journey itself would have been taxing enough for horses who may have had no time for recuperation before being plunged into battle. The added burden of hauling a manned chariot hundreds of kilometres immediately prior to this would have been unthinkable. Hittite armies on campaign were accompanied by large baggage trains; supplies and small items of equipment were carried by donkeys, larger items by four-wheeled ox-drawn carts (as depicted in Egyptian relief scenes of the battle of Kadesh). These larger items must have included the chariots. Even then, chariots may well have required regular repairs and maintenance throughout a campaigning season, and presumably large numbers of spare parts were also taken on the campaign, to replace irreparable breakages or to avoid the need for lengthy repairs for which there might be little or no time.

An oath-taking ceremony marked the induction of the lower order of officers and the rank-and-file troops into the army. The accompanying ritual threatened grave consequences for those who violated the oath. In the course of the ritual:

> They bring the garments of a woman, a distaff and a mirror, they break an arrow and you speak as follows: 'Is not this that you see here garments of a woman? We have them here for (the ceremony of taking) the oath. Whoever breaks these oaths and does evil to the king and the queen and the princes, let these oaths change him from a man into a woman! Let them change his troops into women, let them dress them in the fashion of women and cover their heads with a length of cloth! Let them break the bows, arrows, and clubs in their hands and let them put in their hands distaff and mirror!'[25]

Military Success Rates

To judge from the surviving records, set battles with rebellious vassal states or hostile local independent kingdoms almost invariably resulted in Hittite victories, due no doubt to a combination of superior training, weaponry, and tactics. In the occasional confrontation with the armies of other Great Kings, battle honours were more evenly shared. Suppiluliuma had probably suffered a military reverse at the hands of the Mitannian king Tushratta not long before his brilliant one-year campaign which marked the first stage in the final collapse of the Mitannian kingdom. Tudhaliya IV's army was soundly defeated in battle by the Assyrian king Tukulti-Ninurta, and Muwatalli II's qualified success over Ramesses II at Kadesh in 1274 had come just a few years after his troops had been thoroughly trounced on the same field by Ramesses' father Seti I.

Even in conflicts with the smaller states the Hittites experienced the occasional humiliating defeat, the occasional failure to achieve a military objective. And quite frequently an enemy city which had allegedly been thoroughly sacked after the rout of its army rose remarkably quickly from the ashes of its defeat, and began afresh to threaten Hittite interests in its region. Most difficult to deal with were the Kaska people from the Pontic zone, who took every opportunity to sweep across the frontiers of Hatti, and occupy territory within the Hatti land, on one occasion capturing and sacking the capital itself. When they did venture to commit themselves to pitched battle, they were generally no match for a Hittite army. But a total conquest of the Kaska people forever eluded their Hittite adversaries. Like the Germanic tribes who constantly harassed, invaded, and occupied the frontier regions of the Roman empire, the Kaskans had no overall political organization and lived and fought as independent tribes. They could not be conquered *en masse*. Further, the rough mountainous terrain in which they lived made it virtually impossible for any army, no matter how large, well equipped, or well trained, to find and flush them out of their mountain fastnesses and establish permanent authority over the region.

Siege Warfare

Quite apart from this, victory in the battlefield did not necessarily mean a successful conclusion to a campaign. If the defeated enemy troops refused to surrender and had a strongly fortified city in which they could take refuge, their conqueror in the field might be faced with the prospect of a long siege, without any certainty that the city would eventually fall to him. By the Late Bronze Age, fortification architecture had reached a high level of sophistication and effectiveness, as illustrated by the walls of Hattusa, built in the city's last decades, the fortifications of Troy VIh, and the citadels of Mycenaean Greece. The solid towering defences, sometimes supplemented with curtain walls, postern gates and subterranean passages designed to give the city's inhabitants secret access to and exit from the city or access to subterranean water-sources, made the task of breaching the defences with a sudden attack or starving it into surrender by a lengthy blockade a formidable and often frustrating one.[26]

Basically there were four main options open to a Hittite king who sought to round off a successful military campaign with the capture of a strongly fortified enemy city:

(a) He could try for a bloodless takeover, ordering the city's ruler to throw open its gates as a token of surrender, with the assurance that the city would not be sacked or looted if he complied.

(b) In the event of a refusal, he could confine his post-battle operations to ravaging the city's peripheral territory, primarily its food-land, with the intention of returning in a later campaign to attack the city itself. This might particularly apply if he had other campaigns to complete before the end of a campaigning season,[27] or if the campaigning season was already close to an end.

(c) He could try to take the city by direct assault, sometimes attacking at night to maximize the element of surprise. Both infantry and chariotry were trained for night manoeuvres.[28] The attack was concentrated primarily on the main gate. Battering rams might be used to try to force entry into the city. And here very likely the most intense fighting took place as the defenders came forth to meet their assailants. In this way the city of Hahha on the Euphrates finally succumbed to Hattusili I, but only after its defenders had courageously rallied three times against the Hittites—just like the heroic but ultimately futile resistance of the citizens of Xanthos in Lycia against Brutus in 42 BC.

(d) He might prepare for a protracted siege. There was always the hope of a quick result. Indeed Carchemish, the final Mitannian stronghold, fell to Suppiluliuma in a furious battle only eight days after the siege of the city began. But siege operations could occupy many months. They involved the construction of towers and earth ramps for getting across the walls, the digging of tunnels for getting underneath them and repeated use of battering rams in an attempt to break them down. Starvation might succeed where brute force failed. A siege involved a blockade of the city, in the hope that if nothing else worked its inhabitants would eventually be starved into surrender. Yet to judge from the famous 'Siege of Urshu' text,[29] it could prove extremely difficult to prevent passage to and from a besieged city, both by the city's inhabitants and their allies. Though the value of the text as a historical record is open to question, it very likely does reflect the Hittites' reluctance to engage in protracted siege warfare, as well as the fact that they were really not very good at it.

Without doubt a protracted siege was the least favoured of the above options, both because it tied up valuable manpower resources which might be urgently needed elsewhere, and because if a siege continued for too long, the besieging force might be obliged to call it off before the onset of winter and thus have to begin all over again the following year; that might sometimes entail the distinctly unpleasant prospect of wintering nearby until the beginning of the next campaigning season.

Lords of the Watch-Towers

To protect the homeland from foreign incursion in regions where the frontiers were considered to be vulnerable, Hittite kings established a number of frontier settlements, basically military outposts defended by a garrison and placed under the command of an official called the *BĒL MADGALTI*, an Akkadian expression which as we have noted means 'Lord of the Watch-Tower'. The term applied to border commanders or district governors, officials in charge of outlying regions of the kingdom, particularly where the frontiers were most vulnerable. Watch-towers were spaced at regular intervals between the towns, and were manned by lookouts ready to report suspicious enemy movements. Patrols were sent out to scout enemy territory to increase the vigilance over the frontiers. The officer's prime responsibilities were the protection of the frontiers, maintenance of the fortresses, regular inspections of the local garrison, and constant surveillance of neighbouring enemy territories. We have seen (Chapters 1 and 2) that he also had religious and judicial responsibilities throughout the district under his authority. From the range of the king's instructions to his Lords of the Watch-Towers it is clear that the frontier settlements were not merely military fortresses but townships with temples and a significant civilian population—no doubt in line with the policy of repopulating underpopulated areas of the homeland, attested in the reigns of Mursili II and Hattusili III, as a means of keeping in check enemy encroachment on homeland territory.

Sites Accursed

We have already referred to the frequency with which cities allegedly wiped out by Hittite military action were restored and became militarily active again within a very short space of time. In a few cases a city's or kingdom's persistent defiance of Hittite authority resulted in harsher measures. For example, Mursili II seems to have solved the problem of the repeated uprisings of the kingdom of Arzawa Minor by evacuating its entire population, men, women, and children, relocating them in the homeland as transportees, and dividing up the kingdom's territory among neighbouring states who had shown a greater willingness to toe the Hittite line. Very occasionally in the aftermath of conquest, a city was razed and declared accursed (literally 'sacrosanct (to the god)'), its site sown with weeds, and a ban placed on its resettlement. Thus Anitta, king of Nesa, conquered and destroyed Hattusa, and declared its site accursed during the Assyrian Colony period. But his ban on its resettlement proved to be short-lived—as also did Mursili II's ban on the resettlement of the Kaskan settlement Timmuhala: 'Since the town of Timuhala was loathsome to me, and furthermore because it was an inaccessible place I offered Timuhala to the Storm God, My Lord, and I made it sacrosanct. I established its borders and no man will settle it again!'[30] Whatever the reason for the ban on its resettlement—persistent defiance of Hittite authority, or the site's difficulty of access—it was occupied again shortly afterwards and before long was provoking Mursili into another campaign against it. Hattusili I's destruction and banned resettlement of Ul(lam)ma, a city already active in the

Colony period and a stubborn enemy of Hattusili in his campaigns against his rebel vassal states, may have had more effect since we no longer hear of Ulma after this time. But overall, banning resettlement of destroyed enemy or rebel towns proved an ineffective means of controlling difficult areas, and Hittite kings hardly ever adopted the practice.

CHAPTER 7

Marriage

> A man and his wife who love each other and carry their love to fulfilment:
> That has been decreed by you, Ishtar.
> He who seduces a woman and carries the seduction to fulfilment:
> That has been decreed by you, Ishtar.[1]

In a number of respects, the Hittites adopted a quite liberal and pragmatic approach to the institution of marriage. De facto as well as formal marriages were recognized. There were regulations to ensure that marriage contracts were fulfilled, and due compensation paid to the aggrieved party when they were not. Pre-nuptial agreements were entered into which envisaged the possibility of a marriage breaking down. Divorce was apparently not uncommon, and divorce proceedings could as easily be initiated by a woman as by a man. Particular concern was given to the disposition of the children of the marriage and to inheritance rights in the event of a divorce. Slaves as well as free persons were covered by this provision. And there were provisions to ensure that a widow was adequately provided for after her husband's death. Amongst other things, she had the legal right to disinherit her sons if they failed to take care of her.[2]

Contractual Arrangements

Marriage entailed the all-important matter of the bestowal or transfer of property, and formal marriages at least were very much in the nature of business contracts between two parties, the bride's parents and the groom (or his family). The Laws contain a number of clauses which spell out the rights and obligations of each of the parties. Quite possibly the relevant provisions were inserted into documents specifically drawn up at the time a marriage was contracted. When a girl had been promised to a man, but prior to the actual betrothal, it

Fig. 3. Probable wedding scene, from vessel found at Bitik (near Ankara)

was customary for the man to make a gift to his prospective bride or her family. Subsequently, when the girl was formally betrothed, her intended provided a further and probably much more substantial 'gift' to the bride's family, a *kusata*, generally translated as 'brideprice'—though as we shall see 'spouseprice', or perhaps even 'spousegift', might be a more appropriate term.[3]

The bride herself was presented with a dowry by her father—very likely a quite valuable gift, representing her share of her father's estate. It was to remain her property throughout her married life. Her husband became custodian of the dowry, but only acquired ownership of it if she predeceased him. That was the situation if the marriage were *patrilocal*—that is, if the wife became a member of her husband's family. But if the wife were to die in her *father's* house (that is, if the marriage were *matrilocal*) and she had children, her husband did not receive the dowry. Such is the stipulation in clause 27 of The Laws: 'If a man takes his wife and leads her away to his house, he shall carry her dowry to his house. If the woman dies there, they shall burn her possessions, and the man shall take her dowry. If she dies in her father's house, and there are children, the man shall not take her dowry.'[4] The interpretation of parts of this clause is not entirely clear,[5] but its chief concern appears to be to ensure that the inheritance rights of any children of the marriage—and the dowry becomes a part of this inheritance—are fully protected. Very likely the dowry passed to the children after their mother's death, as in Babylonian law.

From the prominence given to the 'gifts' in the marriage clauses it is clear that these were not merely token offerings, particularly as the recipients were obliged to return them in the event of their not fulfilling their side of the bargain. As in other societies where gifts are exchanged as part of a marriage settlement, their value could be quite substantial, often to the point of imposing a considerable financial burden on the giver. Hence, very likely, the importance attached to keeping track of them once they were given and retrieving them if the arrangement of which they were a part broke down. Quite possibly the nature and value of the gifts were not decided on purely by the giver but were matters for negotiation between giver and recipient as part of an overall marriage settlement. The quality and value of the gifts were as much a reflection of the perceived status and importance of the recipient as of the giver.

Marriages between Slave and Free

The acceptance of a *kusata* became in effect a formal acceptance of a contract by the recipient—in much the same way as the acceptance of a deposit by a vendor on a property he has for sale binds him to the deal. But there was a further important aspect to gift-payment. The handing over of a *kusata* to the bride's family clearly conferred on the marriage a status which more informal unions lacked. This was a matter of particular concern in marriages between free persons and slaves. Such marriages were legally sanctioned, and obviously raised the question of the subsequent status of each of the marriage partners. Did a marriage between slave and free formalized by a *kusata* confer free status on the slave partner? And if not, did it confer free status on the offspring of the union? This was clearly an area on which the court was required to rule, and indeed The Laws contain several clauses which do just that. We may compare the following:

1. If a male slave gives a brideprice for a woman and takes her as his wife, no one shall change her social status. (clause 34)

2. If a herdsman takes a free woman in marriage, she will become a slave for three years (less likely: *after* three years). (clause 35, Old Hittite version)
3. If an overseer or a herdsman elopes with a free woman and does not give a brideprice for her, she will become a slave for three years. (clause 35, New Hittite version)

The interpretation of the first of these clauses is uncertain. Some scholars believe it means that even if a slave did pay a brideprice for a (free) woman, she would none the less become a slave. Other scholars take the view that the payment of the brideprice ensured that the woman retained her free status.[6] I am inclined to the latter view, which fits better with what else we know of mixed marriages. The clause appears to make an implicit contrast between simple cohabitation between male slave and free woman and a more regular marriage formalized by payment of a *kusata*. This may indicate that in the latter case the free person suffered no loss of status. By implication a liaison of the former kind did involve such loss. Although common law mixed marriages were recognized, a free woman was apparently discouraged from such a liaison with a slave, by the threat of reduction to slave status. What was the rationale behind this? It may have been one of practical economic incentive. A slave was probably bound to slave status for the rest of his life, but there were opportunities for at least some slaves to accumulate wealth of their own, to the point where they were able to pay a *kusata*—which presumably only a person with reasonably substantial material assets could do. Wealth accumulation provided an incentive in its own right, but for a slave there was a further important incentive—the prospect of using his wealth to obtain a wife of free birth and thus producing with her children who would be free. A woman of free birth might be persuaded to marry a slave of some means, if the nature of the marriage was such that she retained her free status. On the other hand, it is doubtful that any free woman would have been prepared to enter a common law marriage with a poor slave and be thereby reduced to slavery herself. A slave who wanted to marry a free woman might have to work hard to achieve this. The state as well as the slave himself would benefit from his labour and presumably increased productivity.

The obvious way for a slave to obtain wealth was through acquiring land, perhaps as a tenant farmer if not outright, and making it productive. The emphasis which The Laws place on working land to its maximum capacity, and the likelihood of frequent if not chronic labour shortages in the agricultural workforce (see Chapter 4), may well have led to a series of measures designed to encourage maximum effort and enterprise in the kingdom's agricultural activities—with rewards for those who succeeded and penalties for those who failed. Quite conceivably the state in its own interests offered strong incentives for slaves to acquire wealth, particularly through working the land. A slave who had accumulated sufficient funds could use them to buy a marriage with a free woman and thus free status for his descendants.

Throughout the ages the two greatest aspirations of slaves have been to die free, and to have children who are born free. The Hittite Laws made at least the second of these distinctly achievable.[7]

Matrilocal Marriages

Clause 36 of The Laws presents a somewhat different picture: 'If a slave gives a brideprice for a free young man and acquires him as a son-in-law-who-enters-his-family (^{LÚ}*antiyant-*), no-one shall change his (*i.e. the son-in-law's*) social status.' Here again the marriage settlement involves a *kusata*, the implication being that its payment is a necessary condition of the young man's retaining his free status after marrying a slave. We also have the unusual situation of the father of the bride *paying* the *kusata*, a complete reversal of the normal practice. The likelihood is that the father, though a slave, was a man of some means who wanted to ensure that his grandchildren were born free. The law allowed for this, provided that at least one of the parents was of free status, and that a *kusata*-marriage had taken place. Therein could lie a problem. The sort of free young man who might be induced to marry into a materially comfortable slave family could well have been one who lacked resources of his own. If so, he would have been in no position to pay the *kusata*. But without doing so, he would have forfeited his own free status, on marriage, with no benefit to his new slave family. Hence the reversal of the normal process, made perfectly legal by The Laws, whereby the father of the bride handed over the *kusata* to the young man or his family. Obviously, perhaps for the reasons already suggested above, the state was quite happy to condone such a procedure, on the understanding that the state as well as the individuals concerned would ultimately benefit from it.

It may be that the young man in question handed the *kusata* back to his wife's family after the marriage, to satisfy the precise letter of the law, or that the *kusata* paid by his father-in-law actually remained in the father-in-law's or his family's possession. Indeed that was probably the situation *whenever* a man married into his wife's family. We know that a number of Hittite marriages were *matrilocal* in character. That is to say, the husband became a member of his wife's family, as reflected in the Hittite term *antiyant-* 'son-in-law', literally 'one-entering-into (his wife's family)'.[8] The very existence of this term suggests that although Hittite society was predominantly patrilocal, matrilocal marriages were not altogether uncommon and were to be found at all levels of the social scale. In most if not all cases they probably arose out of practical considerations, with benefits for both parties, as in the case we have just considered.[9]

At the highest level, a man could enter the king's family as husband of the king's daughter, sometimes as a prelude to being adopted as the king's son and heir to the throne.[10] At a much lower level, we have considered the possibility that matrilocality may have had the purpose of elevating a family's eventual status from slave to free. But more generally matrilocal marriages probably served to import husbands into families which had a shortage of male members, to ensure the continuance of the family line, for the purpose of managing or working family estates, or undertaking other responsibilities normally carried out by a natural son. Such shortages may not have been uncommon, as a result of an attrition rate among young males due to the hazards of military campaigns, to the siphoning off of such males into the king's standing army, temple service, the scribal service or the state bureaucracy in general. And periodic outbreaks of disease, such as that which ravaged the homeland for many years from the end of King Suppiluliuma I's reign, must have threatened the extinction of many families, unless propped up by new marriages with the importation of either sons- or daughters-in-law as the situation required.

Arranged Marriages

In general terms marriages in the Hittite world were often, perhaps in the majority of cases, contracted for practical reasons, probably with little or no regard for the personal feelings of those directly involved. At the highest level, the king's daughters were regularly married off to vassal rulers or foreign kings, or to their sons, for reasons of state.[11] In this respect a royal princess was little better than a chattel slave, subject to her father's authority, a portable asset to be disposed of when and in whatever manner her father saw fit. Such of course has been the fate of many a princess in monarchical societies throughout the ages. When these societies were also polygamous, the prospects for the princess must have been particularly daunting. In the royal courts of the ancient Near East an imported royal bride became but one of a multitude of her new husband's official bed-partners. Unless they were given a special status, such wives were no more than high-class nonentities. With their freedoms highly restricted, they were used first as tools of royal diplomacy, and then as breeding machines or instruments for His Majesty's occasional pleasure.

Extensive negotiations and elaborate preparations preceded the wedding of the daughter of King Hattusili III to the pharaoh Ramesses II, and the princess's arrival in Egypt was greeted with much fanfare. But once all this had died down and the celebrations had come to an end, we might wonder how the young bride really fared in her new country, in a culture and environment quite alien to her own, and confronted with a language of which perhaps she knew not one word. Though there may have been some pre-nuptial agreement that she be recognized as Ramesses' principal wife, she apparently ended up living in obscurity in the pharaoh's harem at Fayum.[12] If so, she would not have been the first foreign princess virtually to disappear without trace after marriage to one of the kings of the land of the Nile.[13]

Love and Marriage

At other levels of society we have seen that marriages were contracted for a number of reasons other than the free choice of the actual marriage partners. This must have limited the opportunities for genuine love-matches as the foundation of wedded bliss. The very terminology of marriage clearly reflects this, belonging as it does within the context of transference of property. There is no special word in Hittite for 'marry'; a new husband is said to 'take' his wife (as in clause 27 of The Laws) and henceforth to 'possess' her. Of course it is only to be expected that texts and clauses relating to marriage arrangements, which are by and large property contracts, should be couched in formal, dispassionate, business-like language;

the context is hardly one in which we should expect to find more personal expressions of human relationships.[14] But even in the preserved mythological and legendary traditions of the Hittite world, traditions which in other civilizations abound with lovers' tales, we find scarcely a trace of the theme of romantic love.

Yet no doubt the Hittite world had its fair share of passionate young swains, and no doubt many of these formed emotional attachments with persons other than those selected by their families as marriage partners. That is only to be expected in a society in which arranged marriages were common. In such cases there will inevitably be a number of prospective brides and grooms willing to defy family authority and upset family marriage plans because their hearts lie elsewhere. Such is the prime ingredient of Greek New Comedy and its various derivatives. Throughout the ages many young lovers who have sought to marry against their families' wishes have resorted to elopement. Very likely this situation is covered by several of the Hittite Laws:

1. If a daughter (or: young woman) has been promised to a man, but another man runs off with her, as soon as he runs off with her, he shall compensate the first man for whatever he gave. The father and mother of the woman shall not make compensation. (clause 28a)
2. If anyone runs off with a woman, and a group of supporters goes after them, if three men or two men are killed there shall be no compensation: 'You (singular) have become a wolf'. (clause 37)
3. If an overseer or a herdsman elopes with a free woman and does not give a brideprice for her, she will become a slave for three years. (clause 35, New Hittite version)

In the first case, a girl has been promised in marriage and the prospective husband has given gifts to his bride's family. As yet no formal agreement has been entered into and no *kusata* has been paid. Subsequently, and apparently before the girl has been formally betrothed, another man 'runs off' with her. It is not clear from this verb (Hittite *pittenu-*) whether the girl has gone willingly or unwillingly, but the former seems much more likely since the man's action is apparently not in itself an illegal one—as it surely would have been if he were forcibly abducting her. The law is not concerned with his action *per se*, in contrast to the Laws of Eshnunna (Tell Asmar) which prescribe the death penalty for just such an action,[15] nor does it insist that the former marriage arrangement be restored. Its concern is only with ensuring that the girl's former prospective husband receives full compensation for the gifts he has given to her family—from the second man. Presumably more substantial compensation would have been required if the 'elopement' had occurred after the girl had become formally betrothed to the first man and he had paid the *kusata* to her family. But The Laws make no provision for this—which *may* indicate that it was a matter for negotiation between the contracting parties when the marriage contract was drawn up.

At all events, it seems that although arranged marriages were apparently a common feature of Hittite society, the family, or more specifically the family head, had no legal means of compelling his daughter, or presumably his son, to enter into such an arrangement against her or his will. The Laws' only concern was to ensure that in a breach of promise situation the innocent party suffered no material loss, and to determine who was responsible for reimbursement. Ultimately, then, sons and daughters could not be compelled to accept marriage partners chosen for them by their family, provided they were prepared to accept the consequences of rejecting the choice. It may well be that the family itself sought to impose sanctions on those who upset family marriage plans, and to take some form of punitive action against the third party. If so, that was a family matter—an area into which the state had no desire to intrude. There does, however, seem to be a warning in the second of the above clauses that if a family decided to pursue the runaway couple, it was putting itself beyond the protection of the law, and could expect no legal redress in the event of the death of any members of the pursuing party.[16]

The third of the three passages cited above states that if an overseer or herdsman runs off (elopes?) with a free woman without paying the *kusata* for her, she will become a slave for three years. Her reduction in status would not, however, appear to be due to the elopement as such, but rather to the regular stipulation that in marriage between slave man and free woman, the latter loses her free status if no *kusata* has been paid.

Adultery

If Hittite law treated with relative leniency breaches of promise before marriage, it took a somewhat sterner view of infidelity after marriage. As in biblical law and other Near Eastern law codes, adultery was prescribed as a capital offence, at least in theory. Two clauses in the Hittite Laws deal with this offence:

1. If a man seizes a woman in the mountains (and rapes her), the man is guilty and shall die, but if he seizes her in her house, the woman is guilty and shall die. If the woman's husband catches them (in the act) and kills them, he has committed no offence. (clause 197)
2. If he brings them to the palace gate (*i.e. to the royal court*) and says: 'My wife shall not die', he can spare his wife's life, but must also spare the lover. Then he may veil her (*i.e. his wife*).[17] But if he says, 'Both of them shall die', and they 'roll the wheel', the king may have them both killed or he may spare them. (clause 198)

The first of these clauses concerns itself with what is still today one of the most problematical types of cases brought before the courts. Was the woman a willing or unwilling party to a sexual union? Rape or sex by consent? The distinction between the two particular locations as a means of determining the woman's guilt or innocence[18] should probably not be too narrowly interpreted. Rather it serves to illustrate the general principle that a woman claiming rape needs to demonstrate that she had not the opportunity, or was rendered incapable, of calling for assistance when the alleged offence took place.

In any case action against an adulterous wife and her lover was apparently taken only if initiated by the wronged party, that is, the cuckolded husband. If on discovering the lovers *in flagrante delicto*, he killed them on the spot, he was guilty of no offence. The implication is that he had acted in a fit of passion, and in this case his *crime passionnel* was not punishable. This is consistent with the spirit of other laws which distinguished between (for example) premeditated homicide and unintended homicide committed in anger on the spur of the moment. But if the moment of anger passed and left the lovers intact, the husband could still seek legal redress from the king's court. He had now reached the point where he could no longer take the law into his own hands. The likelihood is that he was not obliged to take any action at all, and the court, with its apparent reluctance to intervene more than necessary in family affairs, might often have preferred it that way. It is possible too that the husband was prepared to come to some other arrangement with his wife's lover in the form of damages. Such an arrangement may be referred to in the frustratingly fragmentary provisions of clauses 26b and c, which appear to indicate that a man divorcing his wife 'sells' her to another man for a sum of twelve shekels of silver. The mention of a third party *may* indicate that this party was responsible for the divorce. If so, the compensation which he pays the husband by 'buying' his wife seems very modest indeed, certainly in comparison with the death penalty. It was no more than the price of a plough-ox (clause 178). Of course an aggrieved husband might well have felt that money to buy a plough-ox in exchange for a faithless wife was a good bargain.

But if the husband wanted his full pound of flesh, he was obliged to seek it from the court. Even in this context, he could not ask the death penalty for the lover and not for his wife. While that no doubt is an illustration of the principle that those who are equally guilty should suffer equal punishment, there may also have been a practical consideration—that of substantially reducing the number of cases of this kind brought before the court with a demand for the death penalty. The court process may also have had the effect of bringing about a reconciliation between husband and wife, if we can so interpret the words 'Then he may veil her'.[19] Only when the husband asks the death penalty for both parties does the court judge the matter, with the king reserving the right, presumably on the evidence and the pleas presented, to pronounce the death sentence or to spare them.

Divorce

It is possible that divorce was another avenue open to a wronged husband. Several clauses in The Laws deal with divorce, but unfortunately these are largely fragmentary. In any case they appear to be concerned with property settlement and allocation of children when a divorce takes place, and give little information on the grounds for divorce. It may well be that this was spelt out in the marriage contract, along with the property provisions in the event of a divorce. To judge from clause 31, estrangement or finding another partner may have been sufficient grounds for divorce; in this case, however, the union to be dissolved is between slave and free, and appears to have been based on simple cohabitation. We do not know whether divorce proceedings were more complex for formal marriages or marriages between two free persons.

Divorce proceedings could apparently be initiated as freely by women as by men, and The Laws indicate what was regarded as an equitable allocation of property and children on the separation of a couple. This applied regardless of the status of the estranged partners and regardless of the type of union, whether a formal *kusata*-type marriage or simple cohabitation. In general the couple's property seems to have been equally divided, though presumably in the dissolution of formal marriages special provision was made for any property the wife brought with her by way of dowry, and the *kusata* may also have come into consideration. As for the children of the union, when partners were of equal status all but one child went with the wife, the remaining child with the husband. The reverse of that situation applied when the husband was of free status and his partner a slave.

Very likely regulations such as these were not intended to be prescriptive, since individual cases may well have required variations to what the relevant sections of The Laws actually specified. Here as elsewhere The Laws provided a set of guidelines and precedents to assist parties, in what were essentially business negotiations, to reach agreements which were fair to and protected the interests of all concerned.

We occasionally hear of divorces at the highest levels of society; for example, the divorce in the kingdom's final years of the Hittite princess Ehli-Nikkal by Ammurapi, the king of Ugarit.[20] In this case the divorce settlement was determined by Talmi-Teshub, the viceroy at Carchemish. The grounds for the divorce are unknown. One of the most notorious divorces of the period was that of Ammistamru, king of Ugarit, from the daughter (unnamed) of Benteshina, king of Amurru. Both kings were vassals of the king of Hatti. The marriage union which had been intended to strengthen relations between the two vassal states had precisely the opposite effect. Whatever the reasons for the divorce, perhaps adultery on the part of the Amurrite princess, it was a particularly messy, acrimonious affair. The princess returned to her homeland in disgrace, but at the insistence of her former husband was returned to him, and very likely to her death.[21]

Marriages which went wrong and the various provisions in The Laws which deal with this possibility should not of course distort our perceptions of love and marriage in the Hittite world. However much marriages were arranged affairs based on practical family rather than personal considerations, such marriages no doubt often resulted in stable, loving relationships. Indeed King Hattusili III explicitly links love and marriage when he tells us that the goddess Ishtar not only selected his bride Puduhepa for him but gave the pair 'the love of husband and wife'. And the abject misery which King

Mursili II, father of Hattusili, suffered on the death of his wife reflected a love for her which went far beyond a purely political alliance. The passage from Ishtar's hymn which begins this chapter clearly indicates that a deep, abiding love between husband and wife might well form the basis of a successful marriage.

Levirate Marriage

As we have seen, The Laws contain a number of clauses forbidding a wide range of sexual unions, including what it defines as incestuous relationships. But there are some exemptions to the prohibitions, notably in the event of the death of a marriage partner. Thus a man is forbidden sexual relations with his sister-in-law (clause 195), but is permitted to marry his wife's sister in the event of his wife's death (clause 192). Indeed one clause gives the impression that in the event of a husband's death, one of his surviving male relatives is *obliged* to marry his widow: 'If a man has a wife, and the man dies, his brother shall take his widow as wife. (If the brother dies,) his father shall take her. When afterwards his father dies, his (*i.e. the father's*) brother shall take the woman whom he had' (clause 193).[22]

This recalls the system of levirate marriage (from the Latin *levir*, 'brother-in-law') well known from the Old Testament. The biblical law seems to apply particularly to cases where a husband dies without leaving offspring, its purpose being to ensure continuation of the family line. Thus Deuteronomy 25: 5–6: 'If brothers dwell together, and one of them dies and has no son, the wife of the dead shall not be married outside the family to a stranger: her husband's brother shall go in to her, and take her as his wife, and perform the duty of a husband's brother to her. And the first son whom she bears shall succeed to the name of his brother who is dead, that his name may not be blotted out of Israel' (RSV).[23]

It has been suggested that the Hittite law had a similar purpose—to perpetuate the name and family of the dead man, and also to preserve his estate within his family.[24] But this was surely a matter for the family itself to deal with, and in the Hittite context it is difficult to see why the state should seek to be prescriptive—if the purpose of the law was indeed as suggested. In any case the law contains no indication that it refers only to a man who has died childless, which is of course the essential feature of the biblical prescription. It seems more likely that the Hittite law's chief concern here, as elsewhere, is to ensure that the widow is adequately provided for after her husband's death. Special provisions were made in various Mesopotamian laws for the protection by the state of widows and orphans. In Hittite society such responsibility was largely shifted to the extended family. Here the onus is on the dead husband's family to provide for the widow. And perhaps the main reason for inserting the clause at this point is to emphasize that this responsibility may be fulfilled without violating the list of prohibited sexual relationships.

Polygamy

We might here briefly address the obvious question to which the clause on levirate marriage gives rise. Does it imply that polygamous marriages were legally sanctioned in the Hittite world?

At the highest level of Hittite society we have seen that a king was expected to have an establishment of secondary wives and concubines in addition to his chief wife. This was at least as much for reasons of state as for any other considerations. As yet we have no clear evidence to indicate whether polygamy extended to other members of the royal family, or indeed beyond the immediate royal circle. The strong likelihood is that for the members of Hittite society in general marriages were very largely if not exclusively monogamous.

The one possibly attested exception to this is the provision made in The Laws for levirate marriage. Since the relevant clause does not specify that the family member taking on the widow has to be wifeless to begin with, and almost certainly was not in the case of the older members, then it may provide a rare instance where polygamous marriage was not merely sanctioned but actually stipulated—in the interests of the bereaved wife. Presumably if the family member on whom the obligation was imposed already had a wife, the new wife was relegated to the status of a secondary spouse or concubine. Of course we are merely speculating. That the clause on levirate marriage indicates polygamy in Hittite society is no more than an assumption. Neither this nor any other clause in The Laws gives any unequivocal evidence of marriage unions involving more than two partners.

Given the relatively large number of Hittite laws devoted to marriage provisions, including property and inheritance rights and the status of the marriage and the marriage partners, the lack of any reference to multiple marriage partners very likely indicates that only monogamous unions were officially recognized—with just one possible exception. Indeed there seems to have been a strong emphasis on monogamous marital fidelity, to judge from the penalties to which a faithless wife and her lover could be liable—though the lack of equivalent sanctions against a faithless husband would suggest that such fidelity was a one-sided obligation. As in many societies ancient and modern, pre-marital or extra-marital liaisons on the part of the male were probably condoned in Hittite society, or at least not seriously censured. However, Hittite wives did have the right of divorcing their husbands, and it is quite possible that adultery may have been one of the grounds for them to do so. In any case, the rights and obligations of marriage as specified in The Laws clearly applied only to monogamous relationships, whether formalized by a spouse-price or of the more informal cohabitation type. Liaisons formed outside these categories were not legally recognized, and presumably neither the partners to such a liaison, nor the children who may have resulted from it, had any claim at law to the rights and obligations which monogamous partnerships entailed.

CHAPTER 8
The Gods

> Divine Lords, lend me your ear, and listen to these my pleas! And the words which I will make into a plea to the Divine Lords, these words, Divine Lords, accept and listen to them![1]

Quite apart from other considerations, monotheistic religions like Christianity, Judaism, and Islam have one great advantage over their polytheistic counterparts: communication with one's god is generally a much simpler, more straightforward process. Worshippers in a multi-godded world have to deal with a plethora of deities, and constantly run the risk of incurring divine wrath by failing to identify which specific one needs supplicating or placating on a particular occasion. And when appeal is made to a number of gods, there is always the danger of inadvertently leaving out one or two, who will certainly take offence. Nor is there any clearly developed sense of divine omnipresence. In the Hittite religious milieu the worshipper had to be sure that a deity was on hand and actually listening when a prayer was offered up to him or her, so that the prayer would not go astray. The deity's current whereabouts might be unknown. Elaborate rituals might be necessary to entice him or her to the place where his or her services were required. Special priests or ritualists were often employed for the task of divine *evocatio*[2]—god-botherers in the true sense of the word. Sometimes extensive, time-consuming oracular enquiry was needed to determine which god's wrath was being vented on the community, and why.

Further, a multitude of gods require a multitude of temples and temple personnel, and a constant flow of gifts and sacrifices as rewards for services rendered or promised, or to ensure that services are not withheld. Monotheistic worshippers are spared much of this. Their god is both omnipresent and omniscient. Prayers can be offered to him at any place and at any time. Churches or synagogues or mosques may be built and rituals performed in his honour. But these are non-essential trappings, for the omniscient god can see into the minds and hearts of all his creatures, and for this reason the true believer does not need to make tangible demonstration of his devotion with gifts or other material goods in order to secure the god's favours.

'An Extreme Form of Polytheism'

In place of a single omnipresent, all-knowing deity, the Hittites believed that the world was populated by a multitude, indeed a plenitude, of spirits and divine forces. The whole cosmos throbbed with supernatural life. Gods inhabited the realms above and below the earth. And on the earth every rock, mountain, tree, spring, and river had its resident god or spirit. These were not mere abstractions, but vital living entities. Even substances like silver and fire were regarded as conscious living forces endowed with human emotions: 'The fire, the son of the Sun God, bore ill will, and it came to the point that he went forth into the dark night, he slid into the dark night, and he coiled himself together like a serpent.'[3]

The Hittites were polytheists in the fullest possible sense. By the time of the New Kingdom they practised what has been referred to as an extreme form of polytheism.[4] To begin with, local Hattic deities predominated, but with the political and military expansion of the Hittite world, the divine ranks of the pantheon were swelled by new members, many of whom were the gods of the city states and kingdoms that had succumbed to the military might of Hatti. The act of removing the statues of the local gods and relocating them in the temples of the conqueror physically marked the transference of these gods to the conqueror's pantheon.[5] No longer could they be summoned by the conquered, for the material casings into which they entered had now been removed to another land. In effecting this transfer, the conqueror showed all due respect and deference to his newly acquired gods, and perhaps it was regular practice for him to go through a process of seeking the gods' consent for their transference.[6] For their goodwill had to be secured if henceforth they were to extend their protection over, and generally act in the interests of, the land of their new worshippers.

In this land they retained their individual identities, even if they were identical in function and character and name with the gods of other conquered territories, or gods already long established in the conqueror's homeland. Thus there were a plethora of Storm

Gods, of Sun Gods, of Ishtars or Ishtar-equivalents.[7] All were or became members of the Hittite divine assemblage and were differentiated merely by adding to their names their local places of origin. The result was an enormously complex, unsystematic, and sometimes thoroughly confusing agglomeration of deities making up the pantheon.[8] In this respect the Hittites went far beyond the relatively systematic pantheons of the Egyptian and Mesopotamian worlds. And they took great pride in doing so. Their boast that Hatti was 'the land of a thousand gods' was hardly an exaggerated one. Palaic gods from northern Anatolia, gods from the Luwian regions of western and southern Anatolia,[9] Hurrian gods, gods taken from a whole range of cult centres in Mesopotamia and Syria were all added into the Hittite pantheon, so that eventually the majority of the pantheon was of foreign origin. Liturgies to foreign gods were often sung or recited in the native language of their place of origin.

Leaving aside theological considerations, the Hittites' unfiltered reception of ever more deities from all regions of their expanding realm was not without its advantages. In the first place it provided another dimension to the high degree of tolerance—political, social, cultural—which Hittite kings were at pains to cultivate in their dealings with their subject peoples. It reflected a policy of what Professor Akurgal has referred to as 'conscious politically conditioned religious tolerance'.[10] To boast of a thousand gods was on the one hand to demonstrate how far and over how many peoples the Hittites' conquests extended. On the other hand it demonstrated their policy not merely of tolerating but of absorbing and assimilating within the fabric of their own culture and society elements of the cultures and societies of the peoples who made up their realm. The lack of an official religious doctrine or of any form of theological dogma enshrined in sacred texts like the Bible, the Koran, or the Torah, ensured that there were no obstacles to the reception of foreign cults and deities from anywhere the Hittites wished, whether for political or other reasons.

Religious Reforms

In the final decades of the empire, attempts were made at the highest levels to bring some order to the vast array of gods who were crowding the pantheon. In her role as chief priestess, the indefatigable

Puduhepa, wife of Hattusili III, embarked on a major review of religious practices and traditions throughout the Hittite world, and began rationalizing the pantheon by establishing syncretisms between some of its chief deities, in particular identifying Hittite gods with their Hurrian counterparts. Thus the great Storm God of Hatti was now formally equated with Teshub. His consort (as recognized in the official state cult) the Sun Goddess of Arinna, chief female deity of the Hittite world, was equated with Hurrian Hepat, as reflected in the opening lines of the queen's prayer to the goddess: 'O Sun Goddess of Arinna, My Lady, Queen of all countries! You are called "Sun Goddess of Arinna" in the Land of Hatti, but in the country which you have made the cedar land you are called "Hepat".'[11]

In her purely Hurrian milieu Hepat, who was in origin a kind of Syrian mother-goddess figure,[12] had never actually had the character of a solar deity. But her prime position alongside her consort Teshub in the Hurrian pantheon and in numerous individual cult centres in Syria and eastern Anatolia made quite natural the syncretism with the most important divine couple in the Hittite pantheon. The couple's offspring were now reduced essentially to one prominent son Sharruma, a southern Anatolian Hurrian god who was equated with the Storm God of Nerik, and a daughter Allanzu, who had a particularly close association with the cult centre Kummanni. Sharruma achieved high prominence in the last decades of the empire as the personal deity of King Tudhaliya IV. At Yazılıkaya he appeared in both the male and female files of deities, in each case immediately behind his respective parent. He is symbolized in Hittite art as a pair of human legs.

On one level these syncretisms were obviously aimed at reducing the multiplicity of like gods in the pantheon. But they also clearly reflect the progressive Hurrianization of Hittite culture. This had become particularly marked in Hattusili's reign, no doubt partly under his Hurrian wife's influence. The syncretizing process seems not to have extended, at least officially, below the highest level of divine society. But further efforts were made to give some sort of system to the divine ranks of the pantheon by new groupings of male and female deities into *kaluti* or 'circles', as depicted in the separate male and female files at Yazılıkaya[13] (with one exception on each side).

Such reforms were not just a matter of theological housekeeping.

They must also have been intended to promote a greater sense of coherence and unity, both cultural and political, within the empire as a whole. Not a plethora of different gods of different regions, but the same gods for all peoples and all regions of the empire. In theory the advantages are obvious, if one takes the overlord's point of view. But care had to be taken that the promotion of imperial unity, on a cultural and political level, and official attempts to rationalize and systematize the gods of the realm, did not run contrary to the spirit of tolerance in which the Hittites obviously took such pride, and to the preservation and maintenance of local traditions, local beliefs, local gods. Theological rationalization, abstract concepts of cultural homogeneity and unity count for little with local communities if they believe that the individuality and the very 'localness' and distinctiveness of the gods whom they worship are in danger of being lost to a broader, more impersonal unity.

Such considerations must have been taken into account in the comprehensive programme of religious reform, including a census of local cults, undertaken by Tudhaliya IV, perhaps in continuation of the initiative taken by his mother Puduhepa.[14] Indeed the programme may well have been a collaborative one between mother and son, at least in the early years of Tudhaliya's reign. To begin with, Tudhaliya sent officials to all parts of the realm to inspect the condition of the temples and sanctuaries, their personnel and equipment. Temples that had fallen into disrepair were renovated or rebuilt, old cult equipment, old divine images were replaced with new, often of precious metals in place of original wood or stone, the numbers of temple personnel were increased, land-grants were made for the upkeep of temples and sanctuaries.

There were no doubt several reasons for this burst of religious activity. On the one level, Tudhaliya obviously sought to build up as much credit as he could with the divine powers in the ever-darkening final years of the empire. But perhaps just as importantly he was seeking to assure the peoples of his kingdom that far from threatening to destroy their cherished religious traditions, or showing indifference to them, he was in fact intent on strengthening them beyond all previous measure. This too as a demonstration that in spite of the mounting threats which were beleaguering him from many different quarters, his hands were still firmly on the reins of empire, and his concerns were still very much with the welfare of his subjects.

The Nature of the Gods

To the adherents of a religion whose god epitomizes perfect goodness, the gods of the Hittites, and for that matter those of the Near Eastern world in general, may appear to have offered little that was either morally or spiritually uplifting. By and large the gods of the ancient Near East, as indeed those of ancient Greece and Rome, were human beings on a grand scale. They were subject to the same range of emotions, like love, anger, fear, jealousy, they sometimes neglected their responsibilities, they could deceive and be deceived, they enjoyed the pleasures of the flesh, and they liked a variety of entertainment—dancing and music, horse races, comedy acts, mock battles, and athletics contests. 'Are the desires of gods and men different? In no way! Do their natures differ? In no way!'[15]

The gods' relationship with their mortal worshippers is like that of a king with his subjects, a master of a household with his servants. And like kings on earth the great gods lived in magnificent palaces, with a staff of subordinate gods to assist them in their duties and tend to their every need. Just as subjects and servants are dependent on their king or master for their welfare and well-being, so too are the worshippers of a god. And just as a master is dependent on the labours of his servants for his physical sustenance and well-being, so too a god is dependent on his worshippers. A god who neglects his responsibilities to his subordinates can become the victim of his own negligence, just like a bad master. Prayers to such a god can contain rebukes and direct appeals to his self-interest, in the hope that he will be shamed into resuming his responsibilities.

Yet prone though the gods were to the frailties of humankind, they none the less were concerned to ensure the exercise of justice, morality, and right conduct amongst their mortal worshippers. Again an element of self-interest was involved. For without such things law and order break down within society, and it was the gods as beneficiaries of the fruits of organized human endeavour who would ultimately bear the consequences of this. A life lived in obedience to the gods in which a mortal pursued no evil course ensured that the mortal would enjoy the protection and blessings of divine favour, reflected in the concept of *para handantatar*. But those who offended the gods, either through neglecting due observance of their ceremonies or through sinful conduct, would surely incur the full weight of divine wrath. A violated oath, an act of parricide or fratricide, illegal seizure of another's rightful authority, other crimes committed by mortals against their fellow creatures would be adjudged and punished by their divine overlords.

Vengeance might sometimes be slow in coming. But sooner or later the penalty for sinful conduct must be paid—even by a subsequent generation, for the Hittites firmly believed in the notion of the sins of the fathers being visited upon their sons. Thus in King Mursili II's Second Plague Prayer: 'It is indeed true that man is sinful. My father sinned and offended against the word of the Storm God, My Lord. Though I myself have in no way sinned, it is indeed true that the father's sin falls upon his son, and my father's sin has fallen upon me.'[16] More comprehensive still are the threats of divine vengeance directed at temple officials: 'When someone arouses a god's anger, is it only on him that the god takes revenge? Does he not also take vengeance on his wife, his children, his descendants, his family, his male and female slaves, his cattle and sheep together with his crop? Will he not destroy him utterly? Be sure to show special reverence for the word of a god!'[17]

Any god could be invoked as a defender of justice and punisher of wrongdoing. Thus Hattusili III proclaimed that his patron deity Ishtar had acknowledged the justice of his cause in his conflict with Urhi-Teshub and guaranteed his final victory. The Storm God too was sometimes invoked as a god of justice. When vassal and international treaties were drawn up, all the gods of both treaty-partners were called upon to witness and protect the terms of the treaty, and to punish violation of these terms. They alone had the power and the right to do so, for such agreements once divinely endorsed became sacrosanct and inviolable.

Hittite prayers often have the character of a defence made before a judge in a lawcourt, a concept common to many religious systems both ancient and modern. In the Hittite world, the most frequent type of prayer was the *arkuwar* (cognate with English 'argument' from the Latin *argumentum*) in which the worshipper pleaded his case before a divine judge, defending himself against an accusation, or justifying an action of which he stood accused, and perhaps confessing to some wrongdoing in the hope that the god would deal more leniently with him.[18] Considerations of right and justice rather than grace and mercy generally determined how gods judged and dealt with those who appeared before the divine tribunal. Yet they might be prevailed upon to discard their hostility and to show a quality of unstrained mercy, by prayers and rituals of a type designated by the term *mugawar*: 'O Sun God, My Lord, Just Lord of Judgement, King of the Universe. You rule constantly over the lands. You alone bestow victory. You alone in your justice always have mercy. You alone are just, you alone always have mercy, you alone respond to prayers of supplication. You alone are a merciful Sun God. You alone always show mercy.'[19] Just as a master may forgive a slave who confesses to having done wrong so, one may hope, a god will treat kindly a sinful but contrite suppliant.

Solar Gods

In the introductory lines of the Hittite Appu myth (see Chapter 12), reference is made to a deity 'who always vindicates just men, but chops down evil men like trees'. The deity, unnamed, is almost certainly the Sun God, supreme Lord of Justice in the Hittite world and a close counterpart to the Babylonian Shamash. He is the god who appears first (almost invariably) in the list of deities invoked in treaties,[20] he who as the all-seeing divine power presides over justice and right conduct on earth. 'O Sun God of Heaven, My Lord, Shepherd of Mankind!' prays King Muwatalli, 'You rise, O Sun God of Heaven, from the sea and go up to heaven. O Sun God of Heaven, daily you sit in judgement upon man, dog, pig, and the wild beasts of the field.'[21]

Of all the surviving Hittite royal prayers, more than half are addressed to solar deities. The obvious reason, comments Dr Singer, is the Sun's central function as the 'shepherd of mankind', a Mesopotamian concept in origin. 'A suppliant who is uncertain of the reason for which he is being punished by the gods naturally directs his prayer to the all-seeing Sun, who can reveal his sin and can soften his punishment. The Sun is best informed not only on "terrestrial" matters, but, as the "Sun God of the Gods", he is also aware of all that happens up in heaven and can reveal the cause of the anger of other gods.'[22] This concept of a supreme Lord of Justice, an all-seeing Sun God of the Gods, a god who appears to all humankind as a universal celestial disc shedding light and warmth on all lands, might seem to indicate that here at least was a deity who was everywhere recognized as a single, indivisible, divine omnipresence. Yet neither here nor anywhere else is such a notion to be found in Hittite religious tradition. As other gods appeared in multiples, so too there were a number of solar deities—and of both sexes.

The concept of a female sun deity was adopted initially from the indigenous Hattic culture. By the Hittite period, if not earlier, there were dual aspects to the deity's role, for she was both a goddess of heaven and a goddess of the underworld; she was honoured as 'Queen of Heaven' and 'Torch of the Hatti-Land', while her chthonic associations were indicated by her epithets 'Mother-Earth', 'Queen of the Earth'.[23] The concept of duality may have arisen out of attempts to explain the sun's disappearance below the western horizon in the evening and its reappearance on the eastern horizon the following day. What happened to it in between times? It must have passed the night in the netherworld regions—as Sun Goddess of the Earth, Mistress of the Underworld. But why a female deity? Was the nature of the sun sexually transformed according to the hours of the day?[24] Did the duality arise from two separate traditions which were never properly reconciled—that of a predominantly male-oriented sky-god cult representing an intrusive Indo-European element into central Anatolia, and that of an earth-goddess cult originating with the autochthonous population of the region? Something similar has been postulated for the early development of Greek religion in the second millennium. But this is all very speculative, and we should remember that the Hittites were quite comfortable with the notion of a deity who had both male and female aspects, reflecting the different roles which the deity fulfilled in different contexts.

In her chthonic role the Sun Goddess was commonly identified with the Hattic goddess Lelwani, Queen of the Gods of the Infernal Regions.[25] Lelwani's cult had been established in Hattusa during the Old Kingdom, and already at that time she had a temple or cult centre within the palace complex on Büyükkale. But it was in the last century of the New Kingdom, in the reign of King Hattusili III, that she came into particular prominence. This was due primarily to Queen Puduhepa, who considerably raised the goddess's profile by praying constantly to her for the restoration of the health of her forever ailing husband, and rewarding her handsomely whenever His Majesty's condition took a turn for the better (see Chapter 9).

Of the divine circle (*kaluti*) of solar deities to which Lelwani belonged one figure stands out conspicuously from the rest—the great Sun Goddess of Arinna (Hattic name Wuru(n)semu). The goddess was so named from her close links with the city of Arinna, one of Hatti's most important cult centres lying a short day's journey from the capital. This Sun Goddess, consort of the mighty Storm God, and highest-ranking female deity in the Hittite pantheon, was regarded as patron and protector of the Hittite state and monarchy: 'Queen of the Land of Hatti, Queen of Heaven and Earth, Mistress of the kings and queens of the Land of Hatti, directing the government of the King and Queen of Hatti.'[26] It was to her above all that the prayers to solar deities were addressed.

In a prayer spoken by King Mursili, she is addressed as though she were male: 'You alone are the Lord (EN-*as*) of just judgement.'[27] One explanation offered for this form of address is that the passage in question was taken from a hymn to the Babylonian Sun God Shamash, addressed as 'Sun God, My Lord, Just Lord of Judgement', without adapting the words to make them consistent with an invocation to a female deity.[28] Yet as we have noted, the Hittites had no difficulty with the notion that deities who performed both male and female roles had both male and female sides to their persona, and it was appropriate to address and depict them as male or female according to the particular role in which they were engaged at the time. This is particularly evident in Hittite concepts of the goddess Ishtar, as we shall see below.

The Storm God

From the very beginning the Storm God held the most exalted place among the gods of the Hittites.[29] He was the preserver of order in the cosmos, and the supreme overlord and protector of the Land of Hatti. The king was his deputy on earth. The maintenance of life itself depended on his benevolence; the most cataclysmic natural disasters were due to his wrath. He personified the forces which brought thunder and lightning and storms to the land; he also came in the form of the soothing, gentle rain of heaven that brought new life and growth to fields and meadows. To an agriculturally based society like the Land of Hatti his favour and goodwill were indispensable. If he withheld his life-giving rain, the land was plunged into drought and famine; his wrath in the form of devastating storms destroyed the land's crops and orchards and gardens—and again there was famine. He dwelt amongst mountain-tops close to the heavens, his natural sphere, and travelled across the mountains in a chariot pulled by a pair of bulls. In art he is depicted with axe and lightning flash. The bull is his sacred animal, the symbol of his strength and his powers of fertility.

As we might expect, the cult of a powerful sky-god who controlled and unleashed mighty elemental forces and who in benevolent mood made the lands fertile and prosperous was well nigh a universal one in the ancient Near East. He was particularly prominent in those lands that suffered much from the ravages and were greatly dependent on the blessings of such forces. In his overall concept and functions, he was essentially the same god wherever he was worshipped, though there were some regional variations in his titles and trappings. In Anatolia his pre-Hittite Hattic name was Taru, his Luwian name Tarhunt-. In the Hurrian religious milieu, particularly in south-eastern Anatolia and northern Syria, he was known by his Hurrian name Teshub. He was the Akkadian Adad (west Semitic Hadad). In the Ugaritic script he was called Ba'lu, 'Lord'. Old Testament Yahweh had much in common with him, and his chief powers and functions were also those exercised by the Greek god Zeus, Roman Jupiter. Yet in each region where he held sway his worshippers thought of him not as a universal god, a god of all peoples, but as a god specific to them. *They* were his special people. *Their* enemies were his enemies, against whom his protection might be sought. He shared with them in the spoils of their victories, he suffered with them the consequences of their defeats.

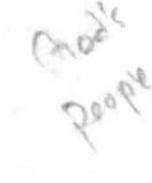

Even within regions he was conceived of as very function- and location-specific. The texts provide us with a bewildering multitude of Storm Gods. There are Storm Gods of the army, the military camp, the palace, the door-bolt of the palace, the rains, the fields and the meadows. Specific individual Storm Gods are associated with the dozens of sub-regions, districts, communities making up the Hittite kingdom, each god anchored to his location by the label applied to him: the Storm God of Nerik, of Samuha, of Zippalanda, of Manuzziya, etc. These may all have begun their existence as independent local deities of independent small communities—deities who coincidentally had many features in common, as one might expect in agricultural societies whose life and livelihood centred upon the productivity of the soil and the benevolence of the elements. With the absorption of the communities into the Hittite kingdom and the adoption by the Hittite bureaucracy of the cuneiform script, the local gods were labelled with the common

Mesopotamian ideogram for Storm God, but retained their own individual local identities.

Whether or not they really were no more than local versions of the one god was a question to which the Hittites probably gave little thought, at least before the reform programme instigated by Puduhepa. Hittite religion was not much bothered with theological speculation and contemplation. It was much more oriented to the practical, the pragmatic, the functional, the expedient. And even if one suspected that all Storm Gods were really one and the same (similarly all other deities labelled with the same name and/or having similar characteristics), why take the risk of being wrong and gravely offending a local deity whose favour and good will might be urgently needed? Thus King Mursili II went to great lengths to identify a specific local Storm God as the cause of his speech affliction, in order to undertake the rites of appeasement which were the necessary preliminary to his cure. Simplistic and unsophisticated as Hittite theology may appear to be, one has only to reflect on the bloody conflicts which repeatedly plagued the Byzantine world, the result so often of disputes over abstruse theological issues, to appreciate the practical wisdom of a policy of absolute tolerance which the Hittites demonstrated in dealing with the multitude of religious beliefs and activities of the peoples making up their world.

From Old Kingdom times the Storm God of Hatti and the Sun Goddess of Arinna were the paramount couple in the Hittite pantheon, and presided over what might loosely be called a divine royal family. Their numerous offspring include lesser Storm Gods, notably those of Nerik and Zippalanda, a daughter Mezzulla (a Hattic name in origin), whose chief cult place was also Arinna and who like her mother was worshipped in the form of a sun disc, and a granddaughter Zintuhi. Also prominent amongst their children is the vegetation and grain god Telipinu, 'who harrows and ploughs and irrigates and makes the grain grow'. Again a Hattic deity in origin (whose cult had spread into southern Anatolia by the fourteenth century BC), he is best known for his close association with the mythological tradition of the Vanishing God (see Chapter 12).

Thus already from the beginning of recorded Hittite history there was a belief in some sort of hierarchical ranking within divine society, with a broad distinction between a small number of deities occupying the first rank in the pantheon and deities of lesser status down to the very localized spirits of trees, rivers, and springs. The lower-ranking deities might sometimes serve as intermediaries for conveying prayers or requests of mortal worshippers to their colleagues on the more exalted levels of the hierarchy, just as one might appeal to the king of Hatti through lower levels of the royal bureaucracy. Thus Puduhepa asked both Mezzulla and Zintuhi to act as messenger gods on her behalf, to convey her prayers to the Storm God and Sun Goddess, their divine parents and grandparents respectively.

In the reign of King Muwatalli II (*c*.1295–1272), barely a century before the end of the Hittites' Bronze Age kingdom, a new version of the great god of elemental forces made his appearance in the divine assembly—the Storm God of Lightning (*pihassassi*). We have no earlier record of this god in our sources, and he may in fact have been a newcomer, introduced into the pantheon by Muwatalli and given high prominence as His Majesty's personal deity and intermediary with the rest of the assembly: 'The gods whom I have invoked with my tongue and have pleaded to them, intercede for me with these gods, with all of them!' Muwatalli prays. 'Take the words of my tongue . . . and transmit them before the gods!'[30] It may be that the newcomer's appearance in the pantheon was closely associated with Muwatalli's shift of the royal capital from Hattusa to Tarhuntassa.[31] At all events from this time on the god remained firmly linked with Tarhuntassa as its patron deity, even after the royal seat was transferred back to Hattusa following Muwatalli's death.

Ishtar

Throughout his life King Hattusili III had dedicated himself to the service of the goddess Ishtar. This sickly youngest son of Mursili II had not been expected to survive his childhood. But the goddess had appeared in a dream to his brother Muwatalli with the promise that the child would live if he were made a priest in her service. And so it came to pass. Under Ishtar's guidance and protection, Hattusili went on to achieve great things, in the process seizing the Hittite throne from its rightful incumbent, his nephew Urhi-Teshub. He was never in any doubt about the rightness of his actions (at least in his official declarations), for his patron goddess Ishtar was always by his side, bestowing upon him her divine favour, shielding him against all his enemies and granting him victory over them.

The goddess identified in our Hittite texts by the Akkadogram

ISHTAR, the Babylonian equivalent of Sumerian Inanna, makes her first attested appearance in Anatolia in the texts of the Assyrian Colony period. By the middle of the fifteenth century her worship had spread westwards from Hurrian Nineveh in northern Mesopotamia through northern Syria and from there into eastern Anatolia. Frequently appearing under her Hurrian name Shaushka,[32] she had important cult centres dedicated to her at Samuha on the Upper Euphrates and Lawazantiya in Kizzuwadna.

Like the Sun Goddess, she had both male and female aspects to her character, visually illustrated by sculptural representations of her in both male and female garb, and her appearance at Yazılıkaya in the files of both male and female deities. In her female aspect she was goddess of love and sexuality, and was often depicted without any garb at all. In her male aspect, she was god of war, god of the battlefield; her animal symbol was the lion, her weapon the mace. Her war-god aspect was by far the dominant one in her Hittite and Hurrian milieu. But it was her dual aspect which enabled her to exercise to the full her powers over human activity and behaviour. For as she chose she could move men to peace and love and harmony, or to hatred and conflict. Her dual aspect also enabled her to deprive the enemy of their manhood on the battlefield, to 'change them into women' and so render them incapable of fighting.

In any case the goddess's two aspects were not so very far apart. For Ishtar's brand of love often equated with aggressive sexuality, as in Gilgamesh's encounter with her, arousing passions closely akin to those which incite men to war. So too the similarity of the experiences and dangers, the passions and emotions, generated by love and war provide one of the favourite *topoi* of Latin erotic poetry in the Augustan age, and one of Virgil's main themes in his *Georgics*.

Other Deities

All mountains, rivers, and springs were inhabited by or identified with gods or spirits—generally male in the case of mountains, female in the case of rivers and springs. Mountains were themselves gods or sacred numinous regions where gods dwelt or assembled. The rugged Anatolian plateau and the great sweeps of mountain ranges in Anatolia and northern Syria provided a fitting environment for their activities and their worship.[33] Mountain-gods figured frequently in the state cults of Hatti and among the oath-gods in the state treaties. Some had independent status, others of more humble status appear to have functioned as servants of the Storm God. The latter had a number of mountains associated with his worship, one of the most famous being Mt Hazzi (= later Mt Kasios) in northern Syria near the mouth of the Orontes river. In mythological tradition Hazzi was well known as the setting for the conflict between Teshub and Ullikummi in the Hurrian Kumarbi myth cycle (see Chapter 12). The mountain's place in Hittite religious tradition provides a further instance of the importation of Hurrian elements into the Hittite world, particularly in the last century of the New Kingdom. It also provides a locational link between Near Eastern and Classical mythological tradition, as we shall discuss below.

The pantheon included a number of tutelary, or protective deities, both male and female, often identified by the Sumerogram LAMMA, used as a title and represented in the iconography by a hunting bag (*kursa-*) which served as a cult image.[34] These deities functioned as guardian spirits of individual persons, of places including the home, and of particular activities. A number of festivals were held in their honour, including one which was dedicated to all the tutelary deities of the Hittite world.[35]

Of the dozens, indeed hundreds, of other gods making up the Hittite pantheon, the majority scarcely ever appear in our texts, and we know little about them except their names or titles. Those who appear to have played a more significant role in Hittite religious life include[36]

(amongst the males):

A war god Wurunkatte (a Hattic name which literally means 'King of the Land'), the equivalent of Mesopotamian Zababa, who appears among the oath-gods in state treaties, and in whose honour an annual festival was celebrated by the king and queen.[37] In the iconography he is depicted standing on a lion and brandishing lance and shield.

The Moon God Arma (Hurrian Kushuh), who appears among the oath-gods invoked in rituals and treaties, but otherwise keeps a low profile amongst his fellow gods. His Hattic equivalent Kasku features in the Hattic myth of the moon who fell from the sky.[38]

(amongst the females):

Inar(a), a Hattic goddess in origin, and an important female member of the Hittite pantheon in the Old Kingdom, when she was honoured as patron goddess of Hattusa. She was also patron and protectress of wildlife, roughly equivalent to Greek Artemis.[39]

Halmasuit, also a Hattic goddess in origin, who was worshipped as the deified Hittite throne. Her initial association with Hattusa dates back to the Assyrian Colony period when she had been the deity responsible for delivering the city to the Nesite king Anitta.[40]

Kamrusepa (Hattic Katahzipuri), the goddess of magic who served as midwife in birth-rituals[41] and acted as guardian of herds and households.

Kubaba was another minor deity in the Hittite pantheon. From at least the Old Babylonian period she had been the city goddess of Carchemish. She was adopted into the Hittite pantheon when King Suppiluliuma I conquered Carchemish and made it a viceregal kingdom. But it was only after the fall of Hattusa, in the neo-Hittite period, that the goddess achieved high prominence, in northern Syria and south-eastern Anatolia, corresponding with the increasingly important role now assumed by Carchemish. In the course of the early first millennium BC, her influence became widespread in Anatolia. She had connections with the mother-goddess of the Phrygians, and her cult was adopted in Lydia where according to Herodotos she was called Kybebe.[42] Henceforth her worship may have spread across the Aegean, via the civilizations of western Anatolia. It is generally believed that she was the goddess who came into contact with the Greek world under the name Kybele (Cybele), the goddess whose cult was later to enjoy great popularity in many parts of the Roman empire. However, some doubt has recently been cast on the equation.[43]

Oracles

Just as the smooth management of the kingdom's affairs depended on effective communication between the king and his officials, so too the well-being of the land depended on advice and guidance which the king received in communications from his divine overlords. Sometimes messages from above might be sent by way of omens, often in the form of natural phenomena like lightning flashes, eclipses, or thunderstorms. The colour and shape of the moon could also convey a divine message. But while omens of a celestial or astronomical nature figure prominently in the Hittite collection of omen texts (which are virtually all of Babylonian origin),[44] there were many other types as well; for example, the omens observed at the time of a new-born child's birth, which provided a basis for casting the child's horoscope. Features of the birth itself, including whether it was premature, had a direct bearing on this. As did also the month of the year in which the birth took place:

If a child is born in the first month (of the year), this child will demolish his house.
If a child is born in the second month, this child will be healthy of heart.
If a child is born in the fourth month, this child will be sickly.
If a child is born in the fifth month, this child's days will be shortened.
If a child is born in the seventh month, a god will favour the child.
If a child is born in the eighth month, this child will die, and if it does not die, great distress will seize upon the father and the mother of the child.[45]

Here as in other cases knowledge of precedent must have played an important role in the interpretation of omens. Texts were consulted, including those inscribed on various models, to indicate what a particular omen or series of signs portended on the basis of what had happened in the past.

Sometimes a god sent information in the form of a dream. We know of at least two occasions when the prince Hattusili (later King Hattusili III) benefited from advice conveyed in this way by the goddess Ishtar. A king might learn in a dream that his life was in imminent danger; but the dream came in sufficient time for him to take appropriate preventative measures by arranging a substitution ritual (see Chapter 11). It was only rarely, however, that information so acquired was offered on the god's own initiative. More often than not an enquirer had to seek it out, through the process of incubation. This meant spending the night in some appropriate holy place in the hope that as the enquirer slept the god would provide an answer to his enquiry via a dream. If the enquirer was so favoured, he recounted his dream the following morning to the local seer who then provided him with an interpretation. But dream experiences seem not to have been a particularly popular way of soliciting a god's advice. Although they could be a quick and relatively inexpensive way, too much had to be left to chance. A great deal depended on how accurately the enquirer could remember the details of his dream, on how much he could trust the ability or the honesty of its interpreter,[46] or indeed on whether the dream offered for interpretation really did come from the god.

There were a range of other ways in which the divine will might be ascertained or divine advice solicited—through the process of oracular enquiry. In theory the process was quite simple. Using the services of an expert in the art of divination, the enquirer put his question to the god, an action was performed or a series of observations were made, and the outcome of the action or observations—in effect the god's response—was interpreted by the expert. But the god communicated only by means of signs, and it required extensive training to recognize, analyse, and translate the signs into an intelligible response. Even then the standard oracular response was laconic in the extreme—a simple yes or no. Which meant that to have any hope of obtaining the information he was after, the enquirer had to ask leading questions of the god: 'Are you angry because. . . . ?' 'If I take this course of action, will the outcome be. . . . ?' If the answer was negative, the whole process had to be repeated, with no hints from the god as to whether the enquirer was getting any warmer. It could be a long, drawn-out business, particularly in cases where the person seeking the information had fallen victim to divine wrath and had no idea why. The god might have been brooding over a particular offence for many years, and on the 'sins of the fathers' principle the luckless enquirer might not himself have been to blame. In fact he might eventually discover that the punishment being inflicted upon him was due to an offence committed many years earlier by his father.

The oracles were of various types. Lot- or KIN-oracles involved the use of a board with symbols drawn on it representing various aspects or activities of life. The actual procedure for seeking a divine response is unknown, though presumably it involved an action by the consultant involving the board, perhaps casting dice or some other form of token upon it. The outcome of the action was interpreted by a diviner, in this case one of the so-called 'Old Women' (see Chapter 11).

These women also conducted the enquiries associated with snake- or MUSH-oracles. In this case a basin marked out in sections, each with a special designation (e.g. 'life', 'sin', 'temple', 'house', 'prison'[47]), was filled with water and a water-snake released into it. The reptile's movement through the sections so marked provided the basis for the Old Woman's interpretation of the divine will.

Bird- or MUSEN-oracles were the province of trained augurs, sometimes apparently of slave origin. From a position in a marked-out area of land or *temenos*, often near a river, they closely scrutinized the types and behaviour of the birds who came within the bounds of the *temenos*.[48] Every detail was carefully noted. Not only were the birds' flight patterns, formations, direction of flight, and landings and take-offs carefully recorded, but also details of their individual behaviour—the sounds they made, the directions in which they twisted their beaks, the movement of their feet. Excellent eyesight and acute hearing must have been essential requirements of the job along with expertise in the interpretation of all these details.

A great deal of importance was attached to this form of enquiry. It was used, for example, in association with military enterprises. Augurs were amongst the personnel who accompanied the army on its campaigns, ready to consult the auspices whenever the field commander called upon them to do so. Indeed we hear of one occasion on which a commander delayed military action until such time as the auspices, in the quite literal sense of the word, could be taken.[49] The Romans too practised this form of oracular consultation. In fact according to one body of legendary tradition appearing in the surviving fragments of the epic poet Ennius it played a decisive role in selecting Romulus as the founder of Rome.

Extispicy was another of the oracular practices which the Hittites adopted from Babylonia. The messiest and probably the most expensive of all forms of oracular enquiry, it involved the examination of the still pulsing entrails of freshly slaughtered sheep, particularly the liver, but also the heart, gall bladder, and intestines. As was the case in the Old Babylonian period, clay models of livers were kept for consultation purposes, each marked out in sections with inscriptions identifying its individual features. Each feature had a special meaning and significance. A comparison of the freshly sacrificed animal's liver with the model provided the basis of the diviner's interpretation of the god's response.

The texts which record oracular enquiries set down the question and the god's response, and if the latter was negative, another question and another response until a positive result was obtained. These recorded processes sometimes provide us with quite sensitive information not obtainable from other sources, since in his attempts to determine the reason for divine wrath a king might be obliged to unlock some embarrassing family skeletons otherwise kept well hidden from the official records. The list of possible offences, any one of which might have offended the god, reads rather like a confessional—a breach of an oath, a murder here and there, squabbles in the royal household, trumped-up charges against an innocent man.

Even if all procedures had been meticulously carried out, there might still be some doubt as to whether a god's response had been correctly understood. That was the advantage of having a number of alternative oracular procedures. A second one could always be used to double-check the result obtained from the first. Budgetary considerations were also a factor. Liver divination, for example, must have been prohibitively expensive for all but the wealthiest classes. At the lower end of the socio-economic scale much cheaper procedures were available, all the way down to the interpretation of patterns formed by drops of oil in a vessel of water, a kind of Hittite equivalent to reading tea-leaves.

The Temples and their Divine Residents

In its overall functions the Hittite temple probably had much in common with the medieval monastery. The core function, the prime purpose of each institution, was service to the deity. Beyond that, both were landowners, both were self-contained economic and industrial units, and both were centres of learning, or at least repositories of scribal tradition. No doubt some of the larger temple establishments became, like many monasteries, rich and powerful institutions within the state. They owned extensive tracts of prime agricultural land whose income supported their personnel and cultic operations and probably left a good deal in surplus. Whether their wealth and influence led to the kind of friction between temple and palace that one observes in Early Dynastic Sumer remains unknown. But given the king's supreme authority and active role in the religious as well as the administrative life of the kingdom, this seems unlikely. In any case the substantial power which Queen Puduhepa exercised over the kingdom's religious affairs, and the extensive involvement of her son Tudhaliya in a comprehensive programme of religious reform, must have greatly minimized the possibility of temple establishments operating independently, or contrary to the wishes or interests, of the crown.

From the common person's point of view, the temples were very exclusive institutions. Unlike mosques and churches which serve primarily as places of assembly for all the god's worshippers, access to

Hittite temples was highly restricted. On festival occasions the temple became one of the venues where the king and his family and royal retinue and other participants shared in the festival celebrations. But on a day-to-day basis only authorized temple staff were generally to be found in the temple. The regulations for temple officials make allowance for certain other persons to be given access under certain conditions; but a foreigner guilty of temple trespass forfeited his life. To enter a temple without authorization and look upon the god was a serious act of desecration: 'People should not look at the Storm God; but a woman looked in at the window and a child went into the temple.'[50]

In a quite literal sense, temples were the houses of the individual gods (indeed the Hittite temple is literally called 'the house of the god') to whom they were dedicated. Lesser gods and spirits were confined to particular localities. But the great gods could leave their chief dwelling places—their celestial palaces and pastoral estates—and roam freely through the cosmos. From time to time they took up residence in their temples, which were rather like divine resort hotels, providing their residents with rest and recreation leave from their normal activities. Of course their presence in their temples was particularly required on the occasions of the festivals which were held in their honour and in which they were actual participants. There were rituals for summoning a god to his temple: 'O Cedar-gods! See! I have covered your ways with the scarf that goes with the long gown and have spread for you fine flour and fine oil. So walk you over it to this place! Let no fallen tree impede your feet, let no stones inconvenience your feet! The mountains shall be levelled before you, the rivers shall be bridged before you!'[51]

Once summoned, the god might use as his first stopping-place on earth a mountain which lay in the vicinity of the temple to which he had been summoned, and from there he came to his temple and entered into his cult image in the temple's innermost sanctuary. The image became the god's earthly casing. His physical needs now had to be attended to. On a daily basis he had to be washed, anointed, dressed in clean garments, and given food and drink. This was the task of duly appointed priests and other temple officials. Precise instructions were laid down for the services to be performed. Firstly there was insistence on absolute cleanliness of food preparation areas and those who were to prepare it:

Those who prepare the daily loaves must be clean. They must be bathed and groomed, and their hair and nails removed. They must be clothed in clean garments. They must not prepare the loaves while in an unclean state. The bakery where the loaves are baked must be swept and scrubbed. Further, no pig or dog is permitted at the door of the place where the loaves are broken.[52]

Anyone guilty of serving the god from an unclean vessel was made to drink urine and eat excrement as punishment. More severe were the penalties for those who prepared the god's food while in an unclean state, as a result of having the previous night engaged in sexual intercourse. A kitchen-hand of the god who had so indulged must bathe at the following sunrise, before having any contact with the god's food. Failure to do so incurred the death penalty—a punishment imposed upon any other servant who had knowledge of his fellow's unclean state and failed to report it.

The death penalty was also prescribed for misappropriating the food and drink that had been prepared for the god—bread, beer, and wine: 'If you ever take sacrifices which have been placed before the gods and fail to convey them to the gods themselves, and you withhold them from the gods, and keep them in your own houses, and your wives, children, or servants consume them, or if you give them to the god in several portions—you will be held responsible for dividing them. Do not divide them. He who does so shall be killed.'[53]

On a daily basis, a meal was placed on an offering table before the god's image. What happened to the food and drink which the god did not consume? The instructions to the temple officials take account of this necessary consideration by giving permission to the officials to consume, within three days, anything left over from the god's meal.

There were strict regulations regarding the nature of the offerings which were acceptable to the gods—above all the first fruits of the produce—and particularly strict regulations to prevent the misappropriation of any offerings or gifts presented to the gods. For example, no official could take for himself the silver, gold clothing, or bronze implements dedicated to the gods. Similar items might, however, be given as a gift to a man by the palace. If so, he must have certification to this effect, stating the weight, the festival where the presentation was made, and the witnesses present at the time. If the recipient of a gift subsequently wished to sell it, he must do so in public with the 'lords of Hatti' present. An inventory was to be made of what the purchaser bought. This had to be taken to the palace to receive an official seal, presumably validating the vendor's right to sell the item or items. Both vendors and recipients of such items who failed to observe these formalities were liable to the death penalty. Such measures were clearly aimed at persons who had misappropriated or illegally received items from either temple or palace and claimed that they had obtained them legitimately through either gift or sale. Illegal trafficking of this kind undoubtedly occurred, perhaps on a fairly regular basis. The insistence on certification of ownership and on obtaining licences of sale when legitimate exchanges took place, along with the severity of the penalty for those who failed to comply with the regulations, were obviously designed to limit if not prevent absolutely the theft of and black-marketeering in temple and palace property. One is reminded of the regulations which many countries have put in place today in relation to the antiquities trade.

Images of the Gods

Since the gods never physically manifested themselves to mortals, never appeared to them in the flesh so to speak, it was impossible to tell what they actually looked like.[54] But they were credited with certain physical attributes which enabled them to be visually represented, in one or more of several forms. Occasionally they were depicted in the abstract; thus in a text which presents information on the whereabouts of certain cult objects, a priest Hutarli refers to representations of the Sun Goddess of Arinna and her daughter Mezzulla as gold and silver discs respectively.[55] Occasionally they might have been depicted in animal form, though the only known instance of this is the representation of the Storm God as a bull—as on a relief panel at Alaca Höyük (discussed in Chapter 11). This is not an indication of theriomorphic worship in the Hittite world. Rather the bull symbolized one of the Storm God's most important attributes—his embodiment of the male fertility principle in nature.

Gods could also be represented by a type of cult object or totem, referred to mainly in festival texts and cult inventories by the term *huwasi*. In its basic meaning a *huwasi* was apparently a stone stele sometimes carved with a relief which was set up on an altar in a temple's sanctuary, and treated exactly the same way as a statue of the god; it was washed, anointed, clothed and given food and drink. Other *huwasi*s, probably larger than those in the temples and only roughly hewn or left in their natural state, were set upright in the open fields, in groves near springs or rivers, or on mountain-tops. Each stone represented a specific deity, and together they marked off a sacred area, signifying a place where the gods were actually present. Here in the course of the great festivals of spring and autumn came a procession of celebrants in which the statues from the gods' temples were paraded. The term *huwasi* seems also to have been used of the area itself as marked out by the individual stones.[56] We have no idea of the size or actual arrangement of these stones. It is conceivable that they differed from their temple counterparts not only by being rough-hewn or left in their natural state, but also in their size. If they were in fact of monumental proportions, their assemblage might have borne some resemblance to the earlier British henges.

In the vast majority of cases the gods were represented in human form. Which is hardly surprising, given their essentially human characteristics, needs, and frailties. In the latter part of the New Kingdom, the statues of the gods set up on bases in the sanctuaries of their temples were life-size or larger. They were made of precious and semi-precious metals—gold, silver, iron, bronze—or else of wood plated with gold, silver, or tin and sometimes decorated with precious materials like lapis lazuli. The main features of the monumental works were probably reproduced in miniature. In the context of the census of local cult centres commissioned by Tudhaliya IV, a statuette of the goddess Iyaya, chief deity of the town Lapana, is described thus: 'The divine image is a female statuette of wood, seated and veiled, one cubit (in height). Her body is plated with gold, but the body and the throne are plated with tin. Two wooden mountain sheep, plated with tin, sit beneath the deity to the right and the left. One eagle plated with tin, two copper staves, and two bronze goblets are on hand as the deity's cultic implements.'[57]

Images of deceased kings might also be found in the temples. And on at least one occasion the statue of a living king was promised to a temple, that of the goddess Lelwani. Queen Puduhepa offered Lelwani a full-size statue of her husband Hattusili, should the goddess cure him of his illnesses and grant him long life; the statue would be of silver, 'as tall as Hattusili himself, with head, hands, and feet of gold', and hung about with precious ornaments.[58]

Without these verbal descriptions, we would have little idea of the size, composition, or appearance of Hittite monumental statuary. Not a trace of any of this statuary survives, apart from a few statue bases, and we can draw only limited conclusions about it from occasional descriptions in the texts, and from a few surviving relief sculptures. From the texts we learn of a representation of the Stórm God as a seated figure plated with gold, holding a mace in his right hand, and in his left hand a golden hieroglyphic symbol—SIG, meaning 'good'. He was supported on two mountains represented by two silver-plated male figures. We have textual information about physical representations of other deities. A statue of the goddess Ishtar/Shaushka depicted the goddess seated, holding a cup in her right hand, with wings sprouting from her shoulders. A silver-plated sphinx was to be seen beneath the silver statue base. The goddess was flanked by her servant goddesses Ninatta and Kulitta, fashioned in silver with eyes encrusted with gold. The warrior god Zababa was depicted in the form of a silver statue armed with mace in his right hand and shield in his left, and beneath him a lion standing on a silver pedestal. Animals were frequent companions of divinity. Gods are described as standing on lions, leopards, and bulls. The lion appeared as a companion to Ishtar, to the warrior god Zababa, and to the Moon God Kushuh. The stag was companion to the Tutelary God of the Fields.

So much we learn of divine images from our texts. Unfortunately the monumental statues have long since disappeared, leaving us with but a few remnants of the religious iconography of the Hittite world—a small number of statuettes, a couple of impressions from Old Kingdom cylinder seals, and a few scattered reliefs, still often *in situ* and badly weathered. When we come face to face with these remnants for the first time, we may find little to impress us in these gods of the Hittites, gods who embody the mighty elemental forces which control the cosmos and everything within it, gods who lead kings to great victories, who unleash devastating storms, who in benevolent mood confer great blessings on their worshippers. Undoubtedly the loss of the great statues, gleaming with precious metals and once bathing their temple sanctuaries in the glow of their reflected light, has deprived us of the most impressive genre of Hittite religious iconography. What is left to us is a collection of miniature divine figures—short, squat, sometimes with little strutting legs, and somewhat bland, even vacuous facial expressions and bulging eyes—and rock reliefs which out of context may appear stiff, ill-proportioned, static, and impersonal. Rather more lively are scenes depicting gods on Old Hittite cylinder seal impressions—a

Fig. 4. Gold figurine of god

kilted god dispatching a fallen enemy with his sword, a hunting scene depicting a god hunting deer and standing on a lion.

Apart from the reliefs of the famous sanctuary at Yazılıkaya (see below), images of gods sculpted from living rock or from dressed stone are found at a number of locations in Anatolia. For example a set of ashlar blocks at Eflatun Pinar (near Lake Beyşehir, in the region of Classical Pisidia) depicts two enthroned figures who probably represent male and female sun deities; each is flanked by a pair of hybrid monsters holding sun discs, and the whole scene is surmounted by a large winged sun disc supported by lion-headed demons. Seated male and female deities are also depicted in a rock relief at Firaktin in Cappadocia, as recipients of libations offered by Hattusili III and Puduhepa (the former to the Storm God, the latter to the Sun Goddess). At Fasıllar in southern Anatolia an unfinished stele almost 8 metres in height depicts a god standing on a mountain-god, with right arm raised above his head and left arm extending from his shoulder.

Gods are generally (though not always) easy to recognize in these depictions, but only rarely because they are of a size or general appearance which sets them apart from their mortal worshippers. Rather they are identifiable from the dress, symbols, and various accoutrements conventionally associated with them. The basic garb of a male god is a short, sleeveless tunic which extends to just above the knees. The sword with curving blade and crescent-shaped pommel is the standard dress weapon for a god, though other weapons also appear as accoutrements of particular deities—the mace, the spear, or the bow. Male gods wear conical caps, tapering towards a peak. The caps worn by mountain-gods droop over at the peak, a little like Mr Punch's cap. A god's status in relation to his fellows is indicated by the horns attached to his cap, front and back or on either side. The greater the number of horns the higher the god's place in the divine pecking-order. Occasionally the caps are also adorned with symbols in the form of halved ellipses. Such symbols represent the divine ideogram (as we know from the hieroglyphic script) and are reserved exclusively for the most exalted of the gods. At Yazılıkaya the symbols can also be seen above the outstretched hands of the chief god and goddess, and behind the chief goddess as well, attached to a pair of human legs. Goddesses wear cylindrical hats, sometimes referred to by the term *polos* (*poloi* in the plural), and in the rock sanctuary at Yazılıkaya crenellated in the manner of the battlements of a city. Their bodies are clad in full-length garments, which have loose-fitting long sleeves, are belted at the waist, and below the waist fall in pleats to the ankles. The deities of both sexes wear another piece of typical Hittite apparel—shoes with upturned toes.

Goddesses are depicted fully in profile, male gods with head in profile, upper torso frontal, and lower torso in profile.[59] The resulting distortion and lack of perspective may in part reflect the limitations of working in very shallow relief. They may also reflect the simple transference to relief sculpture of the artistic conventions adopted in two-dimensional painted friezes or painted shallow wall reliefs, which probably adorned interior walls of palaces and other important buildings in the Hittite world as elsewhere in the Near East. Yet it is not unlikely that contacts with Egypt had the most direct influence in shaping the artistic conventions of the Hittite world. In Egyptian art the emphasis was on depicting, in explicit detail, all important features of the persons and objects the artist was instructed to record. This inevitably resulted in some distortion in the representation of human and divine figures, and a lack of overall compositional coherence since such figures do not readily relate to one another in a particular scene. But we need to judge this art on its own terms—as essentially representational rather than naturalistic. For the Egyptians, the most important requirement in visual presentations was to provide as comprehensive and as detailed a pictorial record as possible. In sepulchral art this was essential in ensuring the full materialization in the afterlife of the persons and objects so depicted. Such considerations played no small part in establishing artistic conventions in Egypt—conventions which may then have been adopted in the Hittite world, though now largely divorced from the contexts and considerations which had brought them into being.

The reliefs at Yazılıkaya are generally regarded as the pinnacle of Hittite artistic achievement. Yet in using the term 'art', we should be careful not to attempt to judge this achievement by criteria which are inapplicable to it. The sculptor's task, first and foremost, was to present in visual form a hierarchical progression of the most important deities of the by now thoroughly Hurrianized Hittite pantheon. This he undoubtedly succeeded in doing. In the main series of reliefs in Chamber A, the individual deities were clearly identified by hieroglyphic inscriptions and by attributes specifically associated with them (particular weapons, symbols of office, lesser gods, companion animals). Their importance in the divine hierarchy was made clear by their size and position in the series. Basically what we have is a pictorial counterpart to the lists of deities who figure in prayers, festival texts, and treaties.[60] The sculptor had one prime aim—to record with absolute clarity the deities whose presence at Yazılıkaya was to be invoked for the festivals and ceremonies which took place there. The impression which the reliefs may appear to convey of two processions of deities, male and female, moving towards each other is almost certainly a misleading one due largely, perhaps, to the representation of the deities' legs in profile. The figures are static, stereotypical, and compositionally unrelated to each other (except for those standing on lesser gods). On aesthetic grounds such reliefs might well be judged inferior to the artistic output of other ancient civilizations. But to criticize them on these grounds begs the question of what their purpose really was and is probably no more justified than finding fault with lists of deities in treaties and religious texts for their lack of literary merit.

Yet for all their artistic naivety, the reliefs at Yazılıkaya possess a solemn, austere dignity which contributes much to the aura of the sanctuary as a revered and holy place, perhaps the holiest place in the Hittite world. Even today one needs little imagination to sense that this was indeed a setting for an assembly of great gods, for special sacred ceremonies. But it is difficult to have a full appreciation of this without being there, in the original setting. There is a total harmony between the shallow relief panels and the rock surfaces on which they are carved. The figures conform with the contours and irregularities of the sanctuary's natural walls. They blend with rather than dominate the surface, as though in recognition of and out of respect for what nature has formed. And in places the shallowness of the reliefs, particularly those that are now much weathered, conveys the impression of figures actually in the process of emerging from the rocks on which they appear. They serve to remind us that in the Hittite world all parts of nature were the dwelling places of vital living forces.

CHAPTER 9
The Curers of Diseases

> Seeing with eyes of wholeness means recognizing that nothing occurs in isolation, that problems need to be seen within the context of whole systems. Seeing in this way, we can perceive the intrinsic web of interconnectedness underlying our experience and merge with it. Seeing in this way is healing.
>
> (Einstein, *Glimpses of Wholeness*, 1947)[1]

As elsewhere in the Near East, medicine in the Hittite world was a skilled and respected occupation. It was also an internationally shared one. Medical expertise frequently crossed national boundaries, and foreign doctors found ready acceptance in the lands of their neighbours, particularly if they came from Egypt or Babylon. On more than one occasion the kings of these countries lent doctors to Hattusa for service in the Hittite court. And to judge from their names, doctors of Luwian and Hurrian origin, probably from Kizzuwadna, also practised their profession in Hattusa.[2] Like the 'curers of diseases' in Homer's world, professional healers could expect a warm welcome in whatever lands they travelled.

In Hittite texts doctors are designated by the Sumerogram ^LÚ^A.ZU or the Akkadogram *ASÛ*. They were mostly male, to judge from the few surviving names of individuals who bore this title. But female doctors were not unknown,[3] and as we shall see, women were particularly prominent in other areas of the healing arts—notably the authors and practitioners of healing and restorative rituals known as the 'Old Women' (see Chapter 11). Another group of women participated in birthing and its associated rituals as midwives, firstly assisting with the actual birth, and subsequently uttering incantations for the well-being, health, and long life of the new-born child: 'And come! As the wind and rain cannot lift the rock sanctuary from its place—because in this (house) he was born—likewise let not an evil thing lift his life from its place! And let it likewise be protected! And let it be alive for eternity!'[4]

We have no clear picture of the terms and conditions under which doctors worked in the Hittite world, nor do we know whether they were organized into guilds or professional associations. There was, however, some sort of pecking order within the profession, as reflected in terms like 'overseer of doctors', 'head doctor', 'junior doctor'. A formal hierarchy perhaps applied to medical practitioners in the direct employ of the Hittite court, on a permanent basis or as visiting foreign consultants.[5] The latter may have been hired partly if not primarily to train and advise local members of the profession in the medical procedures of their own country. But we have no knowledge of any formal programme or medical school for the training of doctors. Many probably learnt their profession on the job, as apprentices to their senior colleagues; we hear, for example, of a 'junior apprentice doctor'. And some no doubt had the good fortune to sit at the feet of distinguished consultants from Mesopotamia and Egypt.

The remuneration payable to a doctor obviously depended on the nature of the service provided and the status of the provider. The local medico attending a patient injured in an assault could expect a fee of three shekels of silver (payable by the offender), two if the victim was a slave.[6] In terms of general hire rates, three shekels was a relatively respectable sum, amounting to not much less than the equivalent of a month's wages (paid in kind) for a hired hand at harvest time.[7] Physicians who practised by royal appointment to His Majesty no doubt received considerably higher remuneration, with additional bonuses, perhaps, for medical consultants from abroad. In one case, to which we shall return, we hear of a foreign doctor being married into the royal family and living in considerable style in Hattusa—part of a package of 'fringe benefits' which were no doubt intended to induce him to make his stay in Hatti a permanent one.

The ability to read and write was almost certainly an important part of a doctor's repertoire of professional skills (see Chapter 3). Successful diagnosis and treatment of illnesses must have required doctors to consult a wide range of texts which had a bearing on the ailments they were called in to treat. A number of texts describe the procedures to be followed in the treatment of such ailments as wounds, eye diseases, intestinal and throat problems, and in the preparation and administering of drugs. Some of these texts, which appear to have served as instruction manuals for doctors, were of Mesopotamian origin, others of local Hittite origin.[8] On the other hand, there were ritual texts to be consulted in cases where magic was needed to complement practical procedures. Doctors almost certainly had the ability to read these texts themselves. And in some cases they committed to writing their own medical experiences. Conceivably they could have used a professional scribe for this purpose. However, we have an occasional instance where a doctor indicates that he himself has actually written a particular document. The likelihood is that those embarking on a medical career underwent a period of training in the scribal schools, and may in fact have borne throughout their career the title of both scribe and doctor. In any case, training for the medical profession, whether formal or informal, must have been a lengthy and rigorous process, for doctors could not consider themselves fully qualified until they had at their disposal a wide and varied range of skills.

The Holistic Approach

Hittite medicine often involved a comprehensive, 'holistic' approach to the treatment of patients. The more straightforward ailments, like repairable physical injuries caused by assault, probably required no more than basic medical treatment and the application of the appropriate medicinal products; practical medical procedures were supported by curative salves, potions, and poultices made from various plant extracts, minerals (like lead), and animal products (like blood, bones, milk, fat, and tallow), administered orally, anally, or externally. But complex illnesses, particularly serious and chronic diseases, were in many cases attributed to malevolent forces and demons, whose influence could only be fully negated by other means. In these cases practical medical procedures were complemented or replaced by rituals, which included the application of spells and incantations, and sometimes also by direct appeals to the gods.

We should not underestimate the powerful beneficial effects that these alternative procedures could have, particularly in the treatment of what today might be classified as psychosomatic illnesses. Persons who sincerely believe that their afflictions are the result of evil malevolent forces or black magic, and who exhibit all the outward symptoms of a genuine illness, may well be restored to good health if they have strong faith in the ability of ritualists and incantation priests to cure them by dealing with these forces in an appropriate ritualistic way. In the Hittite world, medicinal preparations were often used to assist the process. Indeed it is quite possible that many of them had a good scientific basis and were quite capable of effecting a cure on their own. But in the context of the ritual in which they were used, they were seen as but one of the elements in the overall treatment of a patient, all of which were needed to achieve success.

Of course this is a feature of healing practices in many civilizations. In relation to traditional African medicine, Chief Labulo Akpata (a well known Yoruba healer) states: 'medical herbalism is divided into two branches: real treatment (i.e. treatment of physical injuries etc.) and psychological treatment. Real treatment is for those who require no incantations and other ceremonies. Psychological treatment requires incantations and other ceremonies such as sacrifices before the medicine can act—we require the services of the two together to cure the two aspects of sickness.'[9]

Physicians, priests, priestesses, and magicians clearly understood and were able to exploit the benefits of what often amounts to faith healing, even if they thought of it in a quite different way. Certain types of ailments might indeed have responded positively to their services, within the context of ritual and mimetic magic. A ritual designed to cure a man of impotence and conducted by a priestess reads in part as follows:

> I place a spindle and a distaff in the patient's hand, and he comes under the gates. When he steps forward through the gates, I take the spindle and distaff away from him. I give him a bow and arrows, and say to him all the while: 'I have just taken the femininity away from you and given you masculinity in return. You have cast off the (sexual) behaviour expected (of women); you have taken to yourself the behaviour expected of man.'[10]

In a ritual designed to restore fertility to a barren woman:

> (The Old Woman) grasps the horn of a fertile cow and says 'Sun-god, My Lord, as this cow is fertile and is in a fertile pen and is filling the pen with bulls and cows, so let this patient be fertile, let her fill her house with sons and daughters, grandchildren and great grandchildren, descendants in successive generations.'[11]

The performers of such rituals must have had genuine faith in the power of their magic to bring about the desired result. Indeed the greater their faith, the more effective their performance was likely to be. For the patients one of the most potent aspects of the ritual was its concreteness, its *sensory* character. They could actually *see, hear, feel, and smell* the various stages of their healing process taking place, via the path of ritual analogy. The mesmeric influence of the priest's or magician's chanting and gestures and movements, the sight and the smells of all the paraphernalia prescribed by the ritual—these could in themselves be powerful enough to effect a cure. So too the very process of washing, scraping, or scrubbing a patient's body to cleanse it of a pollutant inflicted by sorcery, or a curse, or even by accident[12] may well have been sufficient to convince the patient that he was undergoing a thorough spiritual cleansing as well as a physical one. He could actually see the cause of his defilement being removed by analogic magic and cast away where it could no longer do harm.

In such a context, the dividing line between doctor and priest was often a very fine one. Indeed doctor and priest frequently collaborated in the treatment of a patient, sometimes travelling together to a foreign land for this purpose. There were occasions when the doctor himself performed liver divination and other forms of oracular consultation as part of his treatment. Sometimes too he engaged in a ritual dance to the accompaniment of clashing cymbals, and pierced himself with needles. 'The presence of the physician, the "beating" character of the music, and the whirl of the dance all lead us to believe', comments Professor de Martino, 'that we are dealing with a magical shamanistic action.'[13]

Treatment involving Oracular Enquiry

Treatment for various illnesses often reflected the belief that the afflictions from which humankind suffers are divine punishments for offences committed against a particular god or the gods as a whole. Oracular enquiry was sometimes called upon to determine which doctor should be employed and which plants or herbs used to treat a particular ailment. It was also used to determine why someone was suffering from a particular disease, which god had inflicted it and what had to be done to appease the offended deity. Thus the procedure on which King Mursili II embarked, to determine the cause of a speech affliction which befell him during the course of a thunderstorm. The expression he uses to describe his affliction—'my mouth went sideways'—*may* indicate that he had suffered a minor stroke, causing partial speech paralysis[14]:

Thus speaks My Sun Mursili, the Great King: 'I travelled to Til-Kunnu. . . . A storm burst forth and the Storm God thundered terrifyingly. I was afraid. Speech withered in my mouth, and my speech came forth somewhat haltingly. I neglected this plight entirely. But as the years followed one another, the cause of my plight began to hound me in my sleep. And in my sleep the god's hand fell upon me, and my mouth went sideways. I consulted the oracles, and the Storm God of Manuzziya was ascertained (as responsible for my plight).'[15]

From a fragmentary oracle enquiry text, we learn of a (cult image of a) god sent from Ahhiyawa,[16] and another from Lazpa (= Lesbos), to make their healing powers available to this same king[17]—reflecting perhaps a further attempt to cure the illness associated with his speech affliction. The text calls to mind the dispatch, by the Mitannian king Tushratta, of a statue of the Ninevite goddess Ishtar to Egypt, on two occasions, in an attempt to heal the pharaoh Amenhotep III[18]—a significant acknowledgement of Ishtar's powers as a goddess of healing as well as a war goddess. We do not know what the pharaoh's illness was,[19] whether he was cured of his affliction, or for that matter whether Mursili was eventually cured of his. But in the latter case at least, the affliction seems to have done little to impair its victim's effectiveness as one of the Hittite world's most consistently successful rulers and military leaders, in spite of the many problems with which he had to deal during his quarter of a century on the throne. Indeed this may be an indication that through one healing process or another he did in fact make a complete recovery.

Before a patient's illness could be treated, its cause had to be determined. At a time when the physiological causes of many diseases were little understood, the diseases were generally attributed to evil forces or divine wrath. In Mursili's case, the cause and cure of his affliction were sought through oracular enquiry. This established which god had caused the affliction (the Storm God of Manuzziya) and indicated what steps had to be taken for it to be removed. All objects touched by the king on the day his symptoms had first appeared, including the garments he had worn, were to be loaded on to an ox-drawn wagon and then taken to Kummanni. There they were to be burned, along with the ox and wagon, as an offering to the offended deity.

The Transmission of Diseases

Of particular interest is the notion that a disease suffered by a person can also contaminate the objects with which he has come in contact, and that such objects should be destroyed—in this case by carrying them off and burning them. In addition, the king was forbidden to make any further use of the eating, drinking, and washing utensils which he had used up to that point. The reason for this, it seems, was to ensure that henceforth he avoided all contact with items which had been 'contaminated' by him during the period of affliction, and were likely to recontaminate him after his period of purification. (So too the implements used in cleansing a patient of the pollution which was impairing his reproductive functions were thrown into a river, along with his clothes, to ensure that they could never again affect the patient or anyone else.[20])

The Hittites had no understanding of the transmission of diseases by biological processes. None the less, the oracle had given instructions for the removal and burning of objects infected by contact with their afflicted owner. In scientific terms, Mursili's affliction was not a contagious one. Yet there was almost certainly an empirical basis to the oracle's advice: objects contaminated by contact with a diseased person can themselves become sources of ongoing contamination unless they are removed and destroyed. The ravages of plague, like the one which devastated the Hittite land before and during Mursili's reign, gave good reason to believe that disease could be spread by physical contact, even if the scientific reasons for this were not known and no distinction was made between diseases which were transmittable and those which were not: some diseases were seen to be transmitted from an object to a person or from one person to another by proximity or physical contact, and therefore all diseases, like all forms of pollution, were transmittable in this way.

There was also an appreciation of the close connection between certain types of illness (most commonly, perhaps, those of the gastro-intestinal variety) and the use of dirty eating utensils and food preparation areas. Hence, as we have noted in the previous chapter, the insistence on absolute cleanliness required both of those who prepared the gods' food and of the areas where it was prepared. Wittingly or unwittingly, the instructions issued to the relevant temple officials embody sound principles of hygiene. They would do credit to the most stringent set of modern health regulations!

Similar stringent requirements were imposed on those responsible for tending to the king's physical needs and keeping him free of contamination. Note, for example, the insistence on ensuring that water served up to His Majesty was absolutely pure, and the penalty for placing before him water that was not:

Further, you who are water-carriers, be very careful with water! Strain the water with a strainer! At some time I, the king, found a hair in the water pitcher in Sanahuitta. The king became angry and I expressed my anger to the water-carriers (saying): 'This is scandalous!' Then Arnili (said): 'Zuliya was careless.' The king said: 'Let Zuliya go to the . . . (*a kind of ordeal*). If he proves innocent, let him clean himself! If he is found guilty, he shall be killed!'[21]

The king's horror is scientifically justified. Recently a dignitary visiting a cheese factory was said to have refused to wear the regulation protective clothing, including a plastic cap. His unwillingness to do so could have resulted in a whole batch of cheese being discarded, for fear that it had been contaminated by one of his hairs or its occupants falling into it. Given the Hittite fashion adopted by both males and females for wearing the hair long, the likelihood of alien objects from a hirsute attendant ending up in the king's pitcher of water was probably far from a remote possibility. Professor Gurney has remarked that while this may appear to the modern reader as a reflection of simple rules of hygiene, to the ancient mind impurity had magical associations; when we read that the discovery of a hair in the king's washing-bowl was punishable with death, the seriousness of the crime on the part of the servant can only be understood in the light of the well-known magical properties of hairs.[22] That may be so, though one need hardly point out that in many societies apparently meaningless ritual practices and taboos often have a sound scientific basis, whether the members of those societies are immediately aware of it or not.

The Hire of Foreign Medical Expertise

We have noted that on a number of occasions the Hittite king augmented the medical services available to him from his own physicians by hiring or borrowing medical expertise from abroad. We hear of both Babylonian and Egyptian doctors at the Hittite royal court. These apparently came to Hatti as visiting consultants, per kind favour of their own king, a clear acknowledgement of the fact that medical science was rather more advanced in Mesopotamia and Egypt than it was in the land of Hatti. As we have also noted, a number of the medical texts in the archives at Hattusa describing symptoms and prognoses and methods of treatments of diseases were based directly or indirectly on original Babylonian texts.

In some cases foreign doctors were lent to the Hittite court to deal with particular cases that had baffled the local practitioners. Thus when Kurunta, cousin of the reigning king Tudhaliya IV, fell ill, and the king's own physicians were unable to effect a cure, an urgent appeal was sent to the pharaoh Ramesses II. Ramesses responded promptly: 'See, I have now dispatched the scribe and doctor Pareamahu. He has been sent to prepare medicines for Kurunta, the king of the Land of Tarhuntassa, and he will allocate all, all medicines as you have written.'[23]

This was not the first time Ramesses had received an appeal from Hattusa for medical assistance. Tudhaliya's father Hattusili had written to him requesting the services of an Egyptian doctor to enable his sister, the princess Matanazi,[24] to bear children. Ramesses' reply was blunt and to the point: 'Look, I know about Matanazi, your sister,' he said. 'The word is that she's fifty, if not sixty years old! No-one can prepare medicines to enable a fifty- or sixty-year-old woman to have children! Nevertheless I will send a competent incantation-priest and a competent doctor in case there's any way they can assist her to become pregnant.'[25]

Unchivalrous though this response was, Ramesses was speaking no more than the truth about the princess's age. In fact if anything he was being rather generous.[26] But the fact that it took a foreign king to state the obvious to Hattusili was hardly in itself a reflection on the expertise of the latter's own doctors. If the king really wanted to believe that his sister, the wife of a ruler in an extremely important vassal state in the west of his kingdom,[27] was not beyond child-bearing age, who among his own consultants would have been courageous, or foolish, enough to argue otherwise? Alternatively Hattusili might have been so desperate to have an heir of the royal blood for the vassal throne that in spite of all the advice from his local experts he was prepared to demean himself before the pharaoh to ensure that no stone was left unturned. Ramesses made the most of his opportunity!

Egyptian medical expertise was in demand elsewhere in the Near East as well. There seems to have been a dearth of such expertise in many parts of this world, which no doubt boosted the reputation of and increased the requests for doctors from the land of the Nile. Even in a relatively well developed, sophisticated, and prosperous kingdom like Ugarit, the local ruler Niqmaddu II (*c.*1350–1315) had to ask the pharaoh Akhenaten to send him an Egyptian court physician since there was not one such person in his own court.[28] Homer too speaks highly of Egyptian medical science. Egypt is so rich in medicinal plants, he declares, that everyone there is a physician, surpassing all others in medical knowledge.[29]

Yet in the Near Eastern world Babylonian medical science probably enjoyed an equally high reputation, and Babylonian medical practitioners appear to have been equally in demand in foreign courts. We know, for example, that doctors from Babylon as well as from Egypt attended Hittite royalty, and that once they were ensconced at the Hittite court, their hosts were sometimes reluctant to let them leave. This had on occasion led to tensions between the Hittite king and his Babylonian counterpart. A letter from Hattusili III to Kadashman-Enlil informs us that the latter had lent a physician and incantation priest to the Hittite court during the reign of Hattusili's brother Muwatalli, and that the loan was now overdue. Kadashman-Enlil wanted his subjects back!

When during the reign of my brother Muwatalli they received an incantation priest and a physician and detained them in Hatti, I argued with him, saying: 'Why are you detaining them? Detaining a physician is not right.' And would I now have detained the physician? Concerning the first experts whom they received here: Perhaps the incantation priest died, but the physician is alive and the proprietor of a fine household. The woman whom he married is a relative of mine. If he says: 'I want to go back to my native land,' he shall leave and go to his native land. Would I have detained the physician Raba-sha-Marduk?[30]

Did Muwatalli have a specific reason for calling in foreign medical expertise? We have seen that Hattusili was later to request Egyptian medical assistance for his sister in her attempts to bear children. And it is just possible that Muwatalli had sought foreign medical expertise on similar grounds. He is the only Hittite king *we know of* who failed to produce a son of the first rank—a son by his chief wife. He was thus obliged, as we have seen (Chapter 1), to bequeath his throne to a son of the second rank—a son by a concubine. This was perfectly legal according to the rules of succession. But it led to serious political and military upheavals in the years which followed. Could it be that Muwatalli foresaw the possibility of this happening, and that his prime reason for requesting a Babylonian doctor was to assist his efforts to produce a son of the *first* rank? He could not have applied to Egypt for this purpose, for at this time Hatti and Egypt were arch-enemies. Indeed it was Muwatalli who led the Hittite forces into the famous military showdown with Ramesses II at Kadesh. The provision of medical expertise to the Hittite royal court at this time was the last thing Ramesses was likely to be approached for, or to grant. Babylon provided the only credible alternative.

Whatever the reasons for hiring a Babylonian doctor, Muwatalli and subsequently Hattusili thought highly enough of him to induce him to take up permanent residence in their kingdom. In fact the émigré was married into the royal family—a good illustration of the high status which an eminent physician could achieve—and was otherwise rewarded in a way which enabled him to live in the Hittite capital in considerable style. This was hardly likely to endear the Hittite king to his royal brother in Babylon, who had apparently accused Muwatalli of detaining the doctor against his will. The situation was not at all helped when during Hattusili's reign a second Babylonian physician was sent to the Hittite court and had the misfortune to die there. No doubt a serious embarrassment to Hattusili, who had to use all his diplomatic skills to allay Kadashman-Enlil's deeply and now doubly held suspicions.

Calls upon Divine Assistance

In the last resort the cure of a sick person lay in the lap of the gods. Doctors and incantation priests and performers of rituals could for all their skills achieve nothing in the face of a wrathful or uncooperative deity. The most poignant example of this was the frustration and utter despair of Mursili II when despite all his efforts the plague which was ravaging his kingdom continued unabated. 'When men are dying in the Hatti land like this, the plague is in no wise over. As for me, the agony of my heart and the anguish of my soul I cannot endure any more.'[31] The reasons for the wrath of the gods responsible for the plague had been ascertained by oracle, and due restitution had been made—twentyfold. 'And yet the soul of the Hattic Storm God, My Lord, and of the other gods, My Lords, is not pacified!' If there were still other reasons for divine wrath, let the gods identify them. 'For whatever reason people are dying, let that be found out! Hattic Storm God, My Lord, save my life! Let this plague abate again in the Hatti land!' In his desperation Mursili finally tried an appeal to divine self-interest. He urged the gods to reflect that by inflicting this terrible, unrelenting punishment, they were harming themselves—by allowing all those who served their needs to be killed off—the ploughmen who worked their fields, the mill women who made their bread, the cowherds and shepherds who tended the livestock from which the beasts for sacrifice were chosen![32]

Whether or not this frank appeal to self-interest was sufficient to sway the gods, the plague did finally run its course, though it apparently took twenty years to do so. Unfortunately not the slightest indication is given of the actual nature of the disease. All we know is that it had been brought to Hatti by Egyptian prisoners-of-war towards the end of the reign of Suppiluliuma I.

Individual deities could prove more cooperative. When hope had been all but given up that King Mursili's sickly youngest son Hattusili would survive his childhood, the goddess Ishtar appeared to the child's brother Muwatalli in a dream and informed him that Hattusili would be spared if he were dedicated to her service. Muwatalli passed on the message to his father, who took the appropriate action. The goddess was as good as her word. With Ishtar as his patron deity, Hattusili not only survived his childhood but became a highly successful military commander, seized the Hittite throne from his nephew Urhi-Teshub, and lived to a ripe old age. He was, however, prone to recurrent bouts of illness in his later years, notably an eye disease and a disease referred to in a prayer as 'fire of the feet', apparently some form of chronic foot inflammation, or possibly gout. Already at the time of his famous treaty with Ramesses II we know that he was suffering from the former ailment, since the pharaoh had sent him some salves or ointments to try to cure it.[33] And the latter ailment must seriously have impaired his ability to undertake the arduous military campaigns and religious pilgrimages which were part and parcel of being a Hittite king. It may also provide one of the reasons why Hattusili apparently did not take up Ramesses' invitation to visit him in Egypt.

At all events when human endeavours failed to find lasting cures, Hattusili's wife Puduhepa sought divine assistance in a series of prayers. She begged the Sun Goddess of Arinna to appeal on her husband's behalf to the entire assembly of gods.[34] Appeals were also made to other deities, particularly the goddess Lelwani, for relieving her husband of his various afflictions. 'If my husband Hattusili is accursed and has become hateful in the eyes of you, the gods; or if anyone of the gods above or below has taken offence at him; or if anyone has made an offering to the gods to bring evil upon

Hattusili—accept not those evil words, O goddess, My Lady! Let not evil touch Hattusili, your servant!'[35]

In return she promised valuable votive gifts—on condition that the deity performed: 'And if you, Lelwani, My Lady, relay the good word to the gods, and grant life to your servant Hattusili, bestowing upon him long years, months, and days, I will go and make for Lelwani, My Lady, a silver statue of Hattusili, as tall as Hattusili himself, with head, hands, and feet of gold.' So too in a prayer to the goddess Ningal about her husband's foot problems: 'If that (disease) Fire-of-the-Feet of His Majesty will pass quickly, I shall make for Ningal ten (?) *talla* (oil flasks) of gold set with lapis lazuli!'[36]

In appeals of this kind, the suppliant sought to strike a bargain with the relevant god, offering payment in return for his, or in this case her, services—just as one might hire the services of a doctor. Deity and doctor alike could reasonably expect to benefit from their patients' indispositions. The goddess was promised payment in the form of gifts to her temple, provided she did what was asked of her. The suppliant's royal status would of course ensure that the gifts would be valuable ones. And for all their devotion to their king, the goddess's temple personnel might not have been unduly distressed when news came that one of His Majesty's ailments had flared up again—with the prospect this offered of further precious windfalls for the temple and its divine resident.

When old age, disease, the casualties of the battlefield, and the various other causes of death made their final claims, it was time for their victims to be given a suitable send-off from this world and prepared for their entry into the next. It is to this stage, the passage from life to death, that we now must turn.

CHAPTER 10

Death, Burial, and the Afterlife

> The scent of woodsmoke mingles with the early morning mists. Wraith-like wisps of steam rise here and there as the women, shivering involuntarily in the cold, crisp air of the Anatolian plateau at first light, move among the charred remains of the pyre, pouring beer and wine and walhi-drink[1] from their pitchers upon the still smouldering embers. They sift through the debris, searching for the blackened bones of the deceased. Each bone when found is carefully extracted with a pair of tongs and immersed in a bowl of oil, to cleanse it. Tongs and bowl are of silver, the metal of purity. The bones are taken from the vessel, and wrapped in linen cloth of the finest quality.

The charred remains are those of a Great King of Hatti. The gathering of them is part of the elaborate ceremonies which mark his passing from this world to the next.[2] His death is a catastrophic event, a disturbance of the cosmic order, for without the charisma of the king—the medium between gods and men—the destiny of the land, the very existence of human society, is threatened.[3] Hence the words which open the funeral ritual: 'When a great sin befalls Hattusa and the king or queen becomes a god, . . .'.

The king's death (likewise the death of a queen) sets in train fourteen days of funerary rites, in the course of which the deceased's mortal remains are duly laid to rest. The rites begin on the day of death. A plough-ox is slaughtered and placed at the feet of the king. As its throat is cut, the sacrificer addresses the corpse: 'What you have become let this become! May your soul descend into this ox!' A libation of wine is poured. Drained of its contents, the wine vessel is smashed. It is not for use again, at least not in this world. A male goat is swung to and fro over the corpse—for purificatory purposes.

Next day the corpse is taken to the place of cremation. Food offerings and libations are made, to those who will receive the king's spirit—to Allani,[4] Sun-Goddess of the Earth, to the Sun-God of

Heaven, to the spirits of the king's own ancestors, to the deceased himself, and to the Day of Death. In the evening, the body is laid on the pyre. The torch is applied and the body consumed. As the new day dawns, its bones are gathered from the pyre and after receiving due treatment placed on a chair (or a stool if the deceased is a queen) which is set before a table laden with food and drink. The funeral banquet now begins. The deceased shares in it as honoured guest. 'Before the chair on which the bones are lying they place a table and they offer hot loaves, [. . .] loaves and sweet loaves for breaking. The cooks and "tablemen" set the dishes at the first opportunity and at the first opportunity they take them up. And to all who have come to collect the bones they offer food to eat.'[5] Three toasts are drunk in honour of the deceased.

The feasting and sacrificial rites continue during the days that follow. A human figure is made from figs, olives, and raisins. The purpose of these tasty morsels seems to be to induce the spirit of the deceased to enter the image. On the sixth day the bones are taken to a building called the *hekur*-house, the 'house of stone'.[6] Here, in his tomb, the deceased is laid to rest: 'A couch is prepared in the tomb, in the funerary chamber; the bones are taken from the chair and laid out on the couch that has been prepared; a lamp with fine oil is placed before the bones. An ox and a sheep are then offered to the soul of the dead.'

Further offerings are made—to the soul of the deceased, to his ancestral spirits, to Allani, and to the Day of Death. The sounds of prayers and incantations mingle with the dirges of the musicians and the lamentations of the wailing women. The aroma of fresh-baked bread, the savoury smell of roasted meats for the funeral banquets blend with the stench of sweat, excrement, blood, and fear of the sacrificial animals. Their slaughter is an integral part of the funeral rites. Cattle and sheep, horses and asses are required for sacrifice, not only as propitiatory offerings but also to provide the deceased with livestock in his new world. A piece of turf is cut and taken to the burial site. The turf symbolizes the pastureland where the king is to take up residence. The cutting of the turf confirms this pastureland as his for eternity, by inalienable right, just as in his lifetime he bestowed gifts of land upon a favoured subject. Farming implements are also included among the grave goods. Their broken state indicates that they are no longer for use in this world. They are for their owner's use in the next.

Burials

The dead in the Hittite world were disposed of by either cremation or inhumation. Both methods are in evidence at Osmankayası, a cemetery with more than 200 burials lying between Hattusa and the rock sanctuary Yazılıkaya, *c.*500 metres from the latter.[7] Here were found a number of ceramic vessels, of varying shape and size, containing the ashes of the dead. Some of the vessels had been inserted into niches and crevices between and under rocks, others deposited in the soil beneath the rocks. For those families who preferred inhumation, the bodies of their deceased were laid intact in earth graves. The burials were often accompanied by grave gifts, generally of a modest, commonplace nature, such as shells and small pots. To judge from the quality and nature of these gifts, the cemetery at Osmankayası served the needs of the ordinary people of Hattusa. Animal bones were often included in their graves—the bones of cattle, sheep, pigs, dogs, as well as fragments of donkeys, and occasionally horses. These may be the remains of funeral banquets or sacrificial rites held in honour of the dead. But their presence in the grave could also indicate that they were intended to accompany the deceased into the next life, just as the king was provided with livestock for his royal meadows in the netherworld.

Other cemeteries, dating mostly to the period of the Old Kingdom, have been unearthed at various other locations in central Anatolia, for example at Ilica, lying some 70 kilometres west of Ankara, at Gordion, site of the later Phrygian capital, at Alişar, probably the Hittite Ankuwa, at Seydiler and Yanarlar near Afyon, and at Büget and Kazankaya, which lie close to the modern towns of Çorum and Maşat respectively, where caches of Hittite tablets have recently come to light. At some sites like Ilica both cremation and inhumation were practised, as at Osmankayası. But elsewhere, for example at Gordion, only inhumations are attested. Apart from the simple earth grave burials and stone cist grave burials used for inhumation, the remains of the deceased were often placed in large jars now called by the Greek term *pithoi*, in a contracted position with their heads facing towards the south-east. This reflects a long-standing Anatolian practice, illustrated by the *pithos* burials in the Early Bronze Age necropolis at Karataş-Semayük located in the Elmalı plain of southern Turkey. To judge from the quality of the grave goods, cist grave burials seem to indicate upper-class status, whereas *pithos* burials typified the lower classes.[8]

As a reflection of an even longer-standing practice, there are a number of cases where the dead were buried not in communal cemeteries but beneath the floors of houses. This practice, attested for example at Hattusa, is found also in early Mesopotamian societies, and in Anatolia dates back at least to the Neolithic period, as illustrated by the intramural burials beneath the so-called sleeping platforms of the houses at Çatal Höyük in the Konya Plain. Burials of this kind may indicate a belief by the deceased's family that those who have passed into the next life still continue to participate in the daily affairs of their living relatives. On the other hand, intramural burial may have had a largely symbolical significance, maintaining a sense of continuing family togetherness, like burying one's dead in a private cemetery on the family estate, or keeping the ashes of the dear departed in an urn on the mantelpiece.

Persons of lesser status apparently had some choice in the way they were disposed of after death. But the bodies of kings and queens were, it seems, invariably consigned to the pyre.[9] This in contrast to their counterparts in the Mycenaean world and Egypt. Here royalty and nobility were interred with their bodies intact, as evidenced by the Mycenaean shaft graves and tholos tombs, and the Egyptian New Kingdom cliff tombs in the Theban Valley of the Dead. The Land of Hatti had no funerary architecture on this scale. Indeed no structure has yet been discovered that can with certainty be identified as a Hittite royal tomb. Nor did the Hittite world have anything to match the elaborate procedures which characterized Egyptian preparations for the afterlife, including above all the preservation of the corpse. In Egyptian belief, the body was as important in death as it was in life. The spirit of the deceased could leave its material casing at night and roam freely from it. But the body remained the home of the spirit and needed to be preserved so that the spirit could recognize it and enter into it again after its travels in the Egyptian underworld. Cremation would have been unthinkable in such a context. But for the Hittites, the grave was merely a transitional stage between this world and the next. The spirit of the deceased was entirely independent of the body which had provided its home in this world. Once the burial rites had been performed and the spirit of the deceased duly prepared for the underworld, its mortal casing had no further use or significance.

The Afterlife

What lay in store for the deceased once he had been duly laid to rest? The Hittites clearly believed in an afterlife. And the tools, implements, and animal remains found in a number of burials and obviously intended for the deceased's use might seem to indicate that the afterlife, as they saw it, differed little from life in this world. On the other hand the world beyond the grave was for them the 'Dark Earth', a subterranean realm wherein dwelt the infernal powers and the bloodless shades of the dead. Entry to this realm was possible via a number of routes. Holes, pits, and shafts dug into the ground were common means of access. Every grave provided a point of entry, as did caves and subterranean water sources—springs, wells, rivers, and lakes. By such means one passed into the afterlife, just as gods used springs as a means of travelling to the underworld or from underworld to upper world.[10] Hittite notions of this life probably had much in common with those of other Near Eastern societies, notions no doubt reinforced or influenced by traditions from Mesopotamia, like the story of Ishtar's descent to the underworld. Such traditions had already become known in the land of Hatti during the Old Kingdom, through the medium of the scribal schools.

In Mesopotamian tradition the netherworld was a gloomy, sunless realm. It was concentric in layout—a broad wasteland in whose midst was a city, and in the city's midst a palace where Ereshkigal, Goddess of Death, presided. Seven walls ringed her palace. Each had a gate, guarded by a gatekeeper, through which one had to pass, as Ishtar did, in order to reach the innermost parts of the death goddess's domain. This seven-fold set of barriers is fleetingly reflected in the Old Hittite Telipinu myth. An appeal is made for the god's wrath to be consigned to the deepest recesses of the Dark Earth: 'The gatekeeper opened the seven doors. He drew back the seven bars. Down in the Dark Earth stand bronze *palhi*-vessels. Their lids are of lead. Their latches are of iron. That which goes into them does not come up again; it perishes therein. So may they seize Telipinu's anger, wrath, sin, and sullenness, and may they not come back (here).'[11]

We should not too readily assume that passing references to underworld concepts in rituals and mythological tales necessarily reflect firmly held convictions about what life after death really was like. Mythological constructs and ritual imagery relating to the netherworld probably indicate no more than vaguely held and sometimes inconsistent notions of the afterlife rather than a comprehensive, canonical set of beliefs about its layout, personnel, and activities. None the less the Hittites seem to have shared with their Near Eastern neighbours a generally pessimistic outlook on life after death:

One does not recognize the other. Sisters by the same mother do not recognize each other. Brothers by the same father do not recognize each other. A mother does not recognize her own child. A child does not recognize its own mother. . . . From a fine table they do not eat. From a fine stool they do not eat. From a fine cup they do not drink. They do not eat good food. They do not drink good drink. They eat bits of mud. They drink muddy waters(?).[12]

This very gloomy view of life beyond the grave is in marked contrast to attitudes to life after death in the land of the Nile. The huge commitment of human and material resources for building and equipping tombs for royalty and nobility in Egypt in preparation for the next world gave unquestionable assurance of a good life after death. For those eligible to lay claim to it, such a life free from the trials and tribulations of this mortal world, but with all its pleasures and comforts, should have been a far from unattractive prospect. Neither the iconography nor the texts of the Land of Hatti have anything comparable to this. The few references we have to life beyond the grave are mostly negative. Repeated wishes for a long life suggests that death and what lies beyond was to be avoided as long as possible. King Hattusili I, we have seen, was terrified by the prospect of his imminent death.[13] For King Mursili II, stricken with grief at the death of his wife, the Dark Earth was a region synonymous with deep melancholy, utter despair: 'Throughout the days of life my soul goes down to the dark netherworld on her account.'[14] It was the region to which evil and harmful forces, like the wrath of Telipinu, were relegated and locked up in vessels of bronze with iron latches and lids of lead.

Death might be delayed by a successful appeal to the underworld goddesses Istustaya and Papaya. Like the *Moirai* of Greek mythology these goddesses, Hattic in origin, spin the thread of a mortal's lifespan as they sit upon the shores of the Black Sea. Even the lifespan of a king lies, quite literally, in their hands: '(One) holds a spindle, they (both) hold filled mirrors (*probably reflecting pools of water*). And they are spinning the king's years. And of the years there is no limit or counting!'[15] These words belong to a ritual celebrating the building of a new palace. In the course of the ritual the priest prays that the king, the palace's owner, be kept free from all illness and afflictions. In such a context, it is appropriate to refer to the thread-spinning deities. We have noted that appeals might be made to other deities to prolong human life. And as we shall see, the king might also seek to avoid premature death via the ritual of the 'substitute king'.

However strong, however natural the desire to prolong one's mortal existence, the afterlife did have some positive aspects, at least for those at the upper end of Hittite society. For the Hittite king, and presumably for his family and the closest and most privileged members of his court, life beyond the grave was not without its compensations. In the first place, one could look forward to being united, or reunited, with one's ancestors. Admittedly some kings might not have viewed this prospect with much enthusiasm, given the methods they had used in securing the throne, and their responsibility for causing certain family members who stood in the way of their ambitions to join the ancestral ranks prematurely. But that aside, on joining his ancestors, the deceased could maintain contact with the world from which he had departed through an ancestor cult, which enabled the spirits of the dead, like the *Manes* of the Roman world, to continue to participate in the affairs of their living family, and upon entering their statues to receive offerings from the family, during the course of religious festivals.[16] If a family shifted home, the ancestral spirits went with it. Thus when Muwatalli transferred the royal capital from Hattusa to Tarhuntassa, he ensured that the spirits of his ancestors went too.

The *hekur*-house, where the king's mortal remains were laid to rest, was generally a wealthy establishment, supported by extensive land endowments and the livestock and personnel to go with them, like gatekeepers, herdsmen, domestic servants, and farm-hands. All such persons were attached to the establishment for life.[17] But the tomb itself could only be approached and entered by the deceased's immediate family. Here was the centre of the ancestor cult, the exclusive responsibility of those most closely connected with the deceased, above all his heir and successor to the throne. At regular intervals offerings of sheep and oxen were made to the spirits of dead kings, their wives, and other immediate members of their families. (We may assume that similar homage was paid to ancestral spirits at the lower levels of Hittite society. Indeed in peasant communities in particular, respect and honour for one's ancestors often play an important role in the daily life and customs of the living. In this context too we would expect regular offerings to be made to the dead, though on a more modest scale.) Offering Lists specify who the eligible recipients were, and the sacrifices to be made to them. Unfortunately they fail to provide a complete catalogue of Hittite royalty, since they end with Muwatalli II, on whose death the empire still had another century to run. And even for the period which they do cover, there are some notable and quite deliberate omissions—kings who had disgraced themselves or had been regarded as illegal occupants of the throne.

In addition to the homage he received from his own family, the king upon his death could look forward to the continuing homage of his former subjects—no longer as their earthly monarch but as a god. In this role he could continue to visit his people, and receive homage and tribute from them when, as was customary for gods, his spirit entered into the statues made in his honour. These signified his tangible presence amongst those over whom he had once ruled, now his worshippers. We know, for example, of statues erected in honour of the kings Hattusili I, Tudhaliya I/II, Suppiluliuma I, and Mursili II in the temple of the Storm God in Hattusa, and also statues of Hattusili I in the temples of the Sun Goddess of Arinna and the war god Zababa. We learn too that Suppiluliuma II set up a statue for his father Tudhaliya IV in the latter's *hekur*, quite possibly Chamber B at Yazılıkaya (see Chapter 11).

Where did the king go following his departure from this world? The afterlife offered him, and presumably those closest to him, an idyllic existence in a lush, well-stocked meadow, perhaps not unlike the asphodel meadow of Homeric tradition through which the spirit of the fleet-footed Achilles roamed[18] or the pastures, the Field of Reeds, tilled by the privileged dead in the Egyptian Coffin Texts, or the Gardens of Paradise in the Koran. Hittite funerary ritual refers to such a meadow in a prayer to the Sun God, which asks that all be in readiness for the king on his arrival: 'And have this meadow duly made for him, O Sun God! Let no one wrest it from him or contest it with him! Let cows, sheep, horses, and mules graze for him on this meadow!'[19] So too livestock graze on Homer's asphodel meadow—the animals killed by the hunter Orion during his lifetime, and now hunted afresh by him after death.[20]

This pastoral utopia is difficult to reconcile with other conceptions of the afterlife, as reflected in the kingdom of Ereshkigal, and almost certainly originates from a separate strand of netherworld tradition. It does, however, bear some resemblance to the concept of Elysium or the Islands of the Blessed in Classical tradition. Here too the privileged few enjoyed a lush, fertile land of perpetual bliss. One is reminded of the Hesiodic picture of the first age of humankind—the golden age in which men lived alongside their gods in a state of blissful ease. On the other hand a resident of Ereshkigal's kingdom might well have encountered a number of familiar landmarks if transported to the Greco-Roman Underworld, as depicted by Homer and Virgil, and parodied by the Greek comic playwright Aristophanes.[21]

Ghosts

While the living could communicate with their deceased relatives through ancestor cults, other forms of contact with spirits who had taken leave from their infernal abode could prove hazardous. 'Ghosts do exist. Death is not the end of everything. A pale shade escapes and vanquishes the pyre.' So wrote the Roman poet Propertius in his poem about Cynthia, his recently deceased mistress who haunted and harassed him for failing to give her a proper burial (as well as for his infidelity in general). A hundred years later the Younger Pliny told of the ghost of a murder victim who terrorized the occupants of a house in Athens until his bones were located and reburied with due ceremony.

A belief in earthbound spirits who interfere in the affairs of the living is common to many societies. Such spirits are generally malevolent beings who have escaped the world below, or have remained earthbound, harassing the inhabitants of the upper world until they are permanently laid to rest. So too in the Hittite world ghosts occasionally made their appearance amongst the living as malevolent and sometimes dangerous forces, like the GIDIM of Mesopotamian tradition. The living risked persecution, and also contamination by contact with spirits who returned from the land of the dead, rendering them unfit for any cultic activity until they were ritually purified.[22] Exorcism rituals might help banish a wandering ghost to where he belonged, but it was best to avoid the need for this by ensuring that the deceased was laid to rest with all due ceremony in the first place. Proper burial procedures and elaborate propitiatory rites were important not only in preparing the deceased for the next world, but also in ensuring that once there he stayed put.

There were occasions, however, when the deities of the netherworld were summoned from their infernal abode, to receive propitiatory sacrifices in the world of the living. A river bank served as a suitable location for the ritual, for rivers were important links between upper and lower worlds. In the rite of evocation, the officiating priest dug a pit with a dagger. This served as a receptacle for sacrificial offerings. A sheep was slaughtered, its blood mingling with libations of wine, beer, and other liquid offerings which were received into the pit. Bread and meal too were offered. An invocation was made to Lelwani, Queen of the Dead. She was called upon to open the portals of the Underworld, enabling the infernal deities to come forth and partake of the offerings. For these deities too shared in the homage offered to all the gods, particularly at the beginning of spring, the time of renewal of life. The goodwill of the deities of the Dark Earth was critical in ensuring fertility of the soil, new growth, new life, at the year's beginning. It was also a time for spiritual cleansing. The ritual had the further purpose of removing sin and defilement from the upper world, to be disposed of in the world below by the seer Aduntarri and the seeress Zulki.[23]

Just as the Hittite priest called forth the deities of the Underworld, so too Odysseus summons the infernal spirits in Book 11 of the *Odyssey*, the Book of the Dead. At the place where the Underworld rivers meet, and in accordance with instructions from the witch Circe, he digs a pit with his sword, and pours into it a mixture of honey and milk, wine and water. Over this he sprinkles barley and then makes his prayers to the dead. The throats of sheep are cut, and their dark blood is poured into the pit. The dead swarm forth, to drink the blood. They are like Shakespeare's bat-like ghosts who squeak and gibber in the streets of Rome. But they are held at bay until Odysseus has achieved his chief purpose—a meeting with the ghost of the blind seer Teiresias, who will advise him about his homeward journey.

In their procedures if not altogether in their overall intentions, Hittite and Homeric rituals closely parallel each other. And in both cases the chthonic rites provide the opportunity for reunion and reconciliation between inhabitants of upper and lower worlds, and for looking ahead to the future. Just as Odysseus seeks advice from Teiresias about what the future holds in store for him, so too Hittite kings could consult the spirits of their ancestors for information about future events. With similar purpose too Aeneas consults the ghost of his father Anchises during his visit to the Underworld.

Necromancy, the raising up of the spirits of the dead, is found also in Babylonian and neo-Assyrian contexts. Here too the practice was often intended to question the dead about the future. But the considerable risks involved in releasing the dead into the upper world meant that only the most skilled practitioners should engage in necromantic rites. They should do so only on rare occasions, and even then only when they were experienced in the appropriate rituals for countering the possible adverse side-effects of summoning up the dead.

In general the conduct of rituals in the Near Eastern world was a complex business requiring the skills and expertise of those specially trained in the appropriate procedures. The ritual practices of the Hittite world are well documented in our surviving texts. It is to the beliefs, procedures, and personnel associated with Hittite rituals that we shall turn our attention in the following chapter.

CHAPTER 11
Festivals and Rituals

The king's ablutions are complete, his body now cleansed of all defilement. An attendant stands by to assist him don ceremonial garb—for one festival a blue robe, for another a simple white garment, a rough shepherd's mantle, and black shoes.[1] A close-fitting skull cap and earrings of gold add the final touch. Whatever his trappings, the king is but the servant, the slave, of a higher authority in whose honour the forthcoming ceremonies and festivities will be held. Throughout the festivities he will acknowledge his subservience, by bowing or kneeling before the appropriate god, and praying to him with hands held upwards. He now enters the palace throne-room, where he is joined by his consort, high priestess of the realm. She too has undergone thorough ritual cleansing. The chief of the royal smiths presents the king with a crook and a spear—of iron, gold, or silver as the occasion warrants. The crook symbolizes the king's judicial power, delegated by the Sun God, the spear his military power. Sometimes in the course of the festival he may exchange his priestly robes for a soldier's garb.

In the palace courtyard his entourage has been assembled—the dignitaries of the realm, the royal bodyguard, the priests and other temple personnel, the singers, the instrument-players, the actors, the acrobats, the dancers. A scribe is consulting his list, checking to make sure that everyone is present. Finally, all is in readiness. A hush falls over the gathering as the doors of the palace open and the royal couple emerge into the courtyard. The king briefly surveys his entourage before leading the way through the main gate and out of the palace precincts. He and his queen mount the chariots awaiting them. Here too are the ox-drawn carriages which will convey the sacred statuettes. But pride of place is taken by the image of the god, brought from the innermost recesses of his temple for the occasion. His polished, jewel-encrusted, golden surface gleams in the spring sunlight. This is no mere inanimate object. It is occupied by the god himself. He has quite literally entered into his image, and will remain there as guest of honour in the

> ceremonies to follow. He looks forward with relish, so his worshippers believe, to the feasting and entertainment which he will share with them. The king is presented with a ceremonial axe in exchange for his spear. It is time for the procession to begin its journey.

A substantial part of the Hittite year was occupied with the celebration of religious festivals, as indicated by the large number of festival texts, far surpassing all other written sources, in the archives of the royal capital.[2] Up to 165 festivals were incorporated into the official calendar, and no doubt there were many local community and rural festivals which were never recorded in a permanent form. The state-sponsored celebrations imposed considerable demands on the kingdom's resources, in terms of time, personnel, equipment, and consumable items. Some lasted just a few hours, some several days. But the most important ones continued for several weeks, or more. Many required the king's personal participation, even if he had to cut short a military campaign to attend them, though there were certain occasions on which the queen or a prince or even a symbolic animal-hide could deputize for him.[3] Many festivals were held annually, some at more frequent intervals, and others perhaps only once every eight or nine years. Procedures had to be followed in meticulous detail, for the slightest error could invalidate the entire process.

There was no doubting that their performance at the prescribed times was essential to the welfare of the kingdom. They were the most tangible expression of the people's devotion to their gods, and in terms of the agricultural year many were strategically scheduled to maximize divine goodwill at a time when this would have the most beneficial effect. The large number of festivals was obviously a reflection of the large array of gods in the pantheon. There was some scope for rationalization, achieved by dedicating certain festivals to a number of gods all at once, or to all the gods at once. But some gods required exclusive attention, and it was always better to play it safe and avoid the risk of offending any of them—which might well occur if they were not given the recognition they thought was their due.

The Conduct of the Festivals

The crucial times of the agricultural year were spring, between September and November, and autumn, between mid-March and mid-June, the times respectively of the sowing and the reaping. Not surprisingly, these were the periods when a number of the major festivals were celebrated. So much depended on the benevolence of those in whose honour they were held—the fertility of the soil, the abundance of rain, the fruitfulness of the harvest, the increase in flocks and herds and game for hunting. Of course the gods in question could not be neglected at any time of the year. Like any master, their needs and comforts and pleasures required constant attention. But there were certain times when it was wise to ensure their benevolence by treating them and entertaining them on a more than usually lavish scale. Hence the festivals held in their honour.

The texts recording these occasions may not in themselves make riveting reading; they are full of baldly stated minutiae, sometimes repeated over and over again, with little variation from one text to another. But they were after all intended purely as reference manuals for the guidance of the participants in the ceremonies. To appreciate fully their value to us as a source of information, we must look beyond their repetitive formulaic expressions to the actual religious experiences which they reflect. Even though no complete text of any of the festivals survives, the fragments provide considerable insight into one of the central activities of the Hittite state. The detailed descriptions of the ceremonial rites, the texts of the liturgies and recitations, the inventories of the equipment and other paraphernalia to be used in the ceremonies, the food and drink to be consumed by god and worshippers, and the programme of singing, dancing, acting, and sports contests which accompanied the celebrations help us to recreate something of the colour and vigour, the sights, the sounds, the smells of Hittite religious practice in its most active, tangible form. Here indeed was a show, here indeed hospitality and entertainment, worthy of the gods.

The festivals often involved visits to many holy sites, within the capital itself, in the open countryside, and to other centres of the Hittite realm. We can retrace the path of a festival procession as it leaves the palace gate and proceeds along the ceremonial way, exiting the city through the so-called King's Gate, and passing outside the walls before again entering the city through the Lion Gate.[4] We can imagine the processional way lined with the city's inhabitants and foreign visitors, awaiting the spectacle soon to pass by them. In the distance the songs of the musicians, the sounds of the drums, cymbals, tambourines, and castanets can be heard, growing ever louder as the procession approaches.[5] The crowd catches sight of the statue of the divine guest of honour, a gleaming monumental image towering over the celebrants. This is a rare, once-a-year opportunity for the people to see the great god's image, otherwise hidden away in the recesses of his temple from all but the few specially appointed to his service. So too as the procession passes by, the onlookers may gain a passing glimpse of their king and queen, well protected and isolated from the crowd by an entourage of attendants and a phalanx of royal bodyguards. Closer at hand, acrobats, jugglers, red-robed jesters, dancers performing their steps to lute accompaniment, all in brightly coloured costume, provide entertainment for the spectators. Of course their job is primarily to entertain the god. But who among them could fail to play up to a responsive, on-the-spot, crowd in festive mood? The whole atmosphere might seem more appropriate to a carnival procession than to a religious one. But that is what a joyous celebration calls for. That is what the god himself wants.

The processional itinerary includes stops for visits to the city's temples. Here too performers and other attendants are on hand to greet the royal couple at the temple's entrance.[6] A whirling dance of welcome is performed.[7] Hymns are sung or intoned. Throughout the ceremonies to follow,[8] various cultic calls are made by designated performers and attendants—'aha!', 'kasmessa!', 'missa!'. The king enters the temple's *cella*, after thoroughly washing his hands and drying them on a perfumed towel provided by an attendant. He makes libation at the holy places within the *cella*—an offering table, a hearth, a throne, a window, even a doorbolt. A feast follows. The god is the guest of honour, the king his host. A great variety of meats and breads and pastries have been prepared—under conditions of the strictest hygiene, for the food served to god and king must be free of taint or defilement of any kind. The king again washes his hands, and then breaks one of the loaves. Some are fancily shaped to resemble a human figure or part thereof, perhaps a hand, finger, or tongue, some are shaped like animal figures, perhaps a bird, piglet, or cow, some like inanimate objects, perhaps a ball, ring, or wheel. The king is handed a silver cup brimming with wine and fashioned in the form of a bull or stag. From it he solemnly 'drinks the god'. This is a sacramental act. By it the king comes into mystical union with his divine guest, for the cup symbolizes the god himself.[9] God and king are now joined by the other guests. A herald shows them to their places at table. The king offers the god the choicest cuts of meat, grilled or roasted, from the sacrificed animals—hearts, livers, kidneys, succulent thighs, and fat (to which the gods were quite partial). The atmosphere now becomes more relaxed as the rest of the company tuck in.

The king winks at his attendants, a sign for the entertainers to appear. The dancers and acrobats have saved their best routines for the occasion, for this is not merely a royal but a divine command performance. The dancers' performance recreates a hunt, its thrills and its dangers. The performers are dressed as leopards, their actions mimicking the graceful movements of the hunters' feline prey. They always ensure that they face towards the king. The highlight of the programme is a wrestling match between two local champions. This is a form of entertainment in which the deity seems to have taken particular delight. When all is done, the meal and the entertainment concluded, the king departs, after once more washing and drying his hands.

Festival processions often took the celebrants and the images of their gods beyond the city limits to holy places in the open countryside marked off by the *huwasi* stones. Here too sacrifice was made to the god, and a feast held for him and his worshippers. Once more there was entertainment for the whole company—mock battles, including a contest between two sides representing the 'men of Hatti' and the 'men of Masa' (which the former always won[10]), more wrestling, perhaps a weight-lifting contest, foot races, horse races, and archery contests with the king acting as judge. There were prizes for the winners (tunics for first and second place-getters in a foot race) and sometimes embarrassing but light-hearted penalties for the losers.[11] All in the spirit of the fun and festivity of the occasion.

The Reliefs at Alaca Höyük

Visual representations of parts of a festival programme may feature among the reliefs at the site now called Alaca Höyük,[12] situated *c.*150 kilometres north-east of Ankara. The reliefs are carved in registers on the bases of the towers flanking the main entrance to the city, the lower register continuing into the interior face of the gatehouse on the west side. As we approach the gate we see a sacred procession depicted. The king and the queen are the dominant figures in the scene on the west tower. The king as chief celebrant wears a long priestly robe and carries the *kalmus*, his curved staff of office. Also depicted, in two registers, are the cult officials and the animals for

Fig. 5. Royal couple worship Storm God represented as bull, relief from Alaca Höyük. Photo: Feza Toker of Ekip Film

sacrifice. The royal couple face towards an altar, behind which a bull is depicted, standing on a platform. This is almost certainly a zoomorphic representation of the Storm God, one of the two deities who are the divine guests of honour in these sacred rites. His counterpart appears as the recipient of honours on the east tower, a goddess seated on a throne, no doubt the Sun Goddess of Arinna, chief female deity of the Hittite pantheon. To the left of the Storm God scene we see other figures depicted, a sword-swallower and two men associated with a ladder. The latter very likely depict the 'ladder-men' who appear amongst the entertainers in several ritual texts.[13] A lute-player is also there, perhaps even a bagpiper. Almost certainly these represent the musicians and acrobats and other entertainers who played an integral role in festival performances—though the precise significance of the 'ladder-men' has been the subject of some debate.[14]

Other reliefs, though now out of their original context, seem also to belong to the same composition. Appearing on two large blocks, each with two registers, they depict hunting scenes. There is a lion-hunt, a brilliantly conceived and executed scene in which the artist has chosen to portray the climactic moment. A lion who has reared up in pain and rage tries to grab the spear which a huntsman has

Fig. 6. Lion hunt, relief from Alaca Höyük

plunged into his neck and shoulders. The huntsman's two dogs torment the enraged and mortally wounded beast, whose fury and suffering are emphasized by his head being turned fully towards us. The dogs are barking in a frenzy of excitement at being in at the kill. One is under his belly, the other leaps on his back. Our eyes pass to another scene where a fierce bull is depicted, its head lowered ready to charge its assailants, its enormous tongue lolling from its mouth. Other scenes depict a stag-hunt, a lion pouncing upon a calf, and another huntsman who has drawn back his bow ready to fire his shaft at a wild boar bearing down upon him.

Despite the extreme flatness of the reliefs[15] and errors in anatomical detail, the hunting scenes contrast strikingly, in terms of their violence and realism and dramatic impact, with the normally tranquil and often static scenes of Hittite art. Hunting figures amongst the activities recreated by the dancers in their festival performances, and that may explain the hunting scenes here. The Anatolian countryside provided a range of game for huntsmen—lions and wild bulls, leopard, wolf, deer, hare, and wild boar.

The Major Festivals

Festivals celebrating a wide range of activities, particularly those associated with agriculture, were held at all times of the year. Some were of major national importance and necessitated the king's presence, others were more localized; some were named after seasons of the year, others after the activities which they celebrated (like the grape harvest), and others after a particular feature of the festival programme. Four major festivals provided the high spots of the festival calendar. Two were held in spring, and at least one in autumn. The spring festivals were the AN.TAH.SUM or 'crocus' festival, and the *purulli* festival. The *nuntarriyashas* festival, the 'festival of haste', was celebrated in autumn; this may also have been the season, though less certainly, of the KI.LAM or 'gate-house' festival.

Of the two spring celebrations, the AN.TAH.SUM festival was performed 'for the Sun Goddess of Arinna and the gods of the Hatti Land'. Lasting some thirty-eight days, its rites took place in Hattusa and other important religious centres of the homeland.[16] It had much in common with the *purulli* festival, which lasted for just under a month. So named from the Hattian word for 'earth', this festival belongs within the old Hattic tradition, and features the originally Hattic deities Telipinu, the Storm God, and Inar(a).[17] The king and queen were again the chief officiants. Beginning in Hattusa the festival procession passed through a number of towns, including Arinna, the city of the Sun Goddess and a day's journey from the capital, before reaching its destination.[18] Traditionally this was Nerik, the city in the northern part of the homeland dedicated particularly to the worship of the Storm God. Here the festivities reached their climax. Here there was a general assemblage of gods for the occasion, just as in Babylon all the gods gathered in deference to their chief Marduk, to celebrate the year's beginning.

In view of the peculiarly important place which Nerik claimed in Hittite religious life, its capture by the Kaskans during the reign of King Hantili II[19] was a disaster of the gravest proportions, not merely or even primarily for strategic reasons, but because it was so intrinsically important to the kingdom's religious life. We need only reflect on the emotions generated in more recent times by the loss of a holy city to an 'infidel' enemy to appreciate the full significance of the fall of the city. While Nerik was under enemy occupation, the city of Hakmis (Hakpis) in the northern part of the kingdom took over its cultic functions. But after several hundred years in enemy hands, Nerik was finally liberated by the man later to become King Hattusili III and resumed its status as one of the leading cult centres of the Hittite world.

The spring festival, which reached its climax in Nerik, celebrated the regeneration of the powers of nature. It was a time of renewals, of reconfirmation of the gods' endorsement of the king's authority, of regeneration of the life and health and vigour of the king and his consort. There was a direct connection between the king's well-being and the rhythm of nature which was essential to the growth process.[20] Two Hattic myths which have to do with the notion of death followed by new life were closely linked with the *purulli* festival: the myth of the vegetation god Telipinu and that of the dragon Illuyanka. In all likelihood both myths were performed during the course of the festival, as a ritualistic re-enactment of the process of regeneration of life at the year's beginning. We shall have more to say about this below (Chapter 12).

Like the spring festivals, the autumn *nuntarriyashas* festival, the 'festival of haste' (whatever that may mean), lasted several weeks and involved visits to holy places both within and beyond Hattusa.[21] On the other hand the KI.LAM festival, the 'festival of the gate-house', lasted only three days and was confined entirely to the capital and its immediate environs.[22] The term 'gate-house' indicates visits to a number of locations, with the procession commencing from the gate of the royal palace and passing to the gates of various temples and storehouses and apparently the city's treasury. The procession featured the Storm God, whose image was brought from his temple for the occasion and paraded through the streets in an ox-drawn carriage. But many other deities, over thirty of them, were also honoured in the festival.

The Role of Yazılıkaya in the Festival Programme

Any general discussion of Hittite festivals inevitably raises the question of the purpose and function of Yazılıkaya, the natural rock sanctuary lying a kilometre north-east of Hattusa.[23] Yazılıkaya almost certainly played an important role in the festival programme. But what precisely was this role? Human association with the site dates back to the third millennium or earlier. And from at least 1600 the site was in use by the Hittites, who initially left it in its natural state.

Fig. 7. Yazılıkaya

During Hattusili III's reign a gatehouse and temple complex with interior court and inner sanctuary was constructed across the front of the site, replacing an earlier wall and shutting off direct access into the sanctuary's two rock chambers. The archaeologist Kurt Bittel, who directed excavations at Hattusa from 1931 until succeeded by Peter Neve in 1978, remarked on the strikingly careless manner in which the complex was erected—in contrast to the very solid construction of the known Hittite temples—with foundations set on rubble and hardly anywhere going down to bedrock. He concluded that the lightly constructed buildings in front of Yazılıkaya could hardly have withstood the regular ritual usage attested for the daily cult of a normal Hittite temple, and that the sanctuary was used only on special limited occasions in the course of the year.[24]

What were these occasions? There can be little doubt that Yazılıkaya with its imposing and largely unparalleled gallery of reliefs, most notably its impressive parade of deities in 'Chamber A', was an important and revered site. Yet its full significance still eludes us. What clues do we have? Behind Chamber A is a narrow passage, guarded by a pair of winged and lion-headed demons leading to the smaller 'Chamber B'. On the right of this chamber as one enters is a sculptured frieze of twelve identical gods (indicated by their cone-shaped caps) corresponding to a similar group bringing up the rear of the procession of male deities in Chamber A, except that in this case they are carrying sickle-shaped swords. On the opposite wall are two closely linked figures. The larger one is identified by a hieroglyphic inscription as the god Sharruma, son of Teshub and Hepat, the smaller by the royal cartouche surmounted by a winged sun-disc as the god's protégé King Tudhaliya (IV). The god extends his left arm round the shoulder of the king, and also clasps his right wrist, as a symbol of divine protection.[25] Tudhaliya also appears in Chamber A, on the wall opposite the main group of deities, in a 3-metre-high relief. In both reliefs he appears in priestly garb, long robe, shoes with upturned toes, close-fitting skull cap and carrying a *kalmus*, the staff whose end curves upwards in a spiral.

On the same wall as the Sharruma–Tudhaliya relief in Chamber B the so-called 'dagger-god' relief was carved. The top part of the relief consists of a human head (evidently that of a god since it wears a conical cap), underneath which are the foreparts of two lions or lion-skins hanging head-down. All this forms the 'hilt' of the dagger. The lower part of the relief is in the form of a double-edged blade with a distinct midrib. However, the bottom half of the blade is not visible, and almost certainly the relief as a whole is intended to represent a dagger plunged into the ground. In discussing the interpretation of this relief, scholars have drawn attention to a Hittite ritual which deals with deities banished to the Underworld and describes how an incantation priest makes clay images of them in the shape of swords and fixes them into the ground.[26] Professor Bittel compared the relief with a bronze sword found in the region of Diyarbakır with an inscription dedicating it to Nergal, god of the Underworld.[27]

The twelve identical gods depicted in both chambers may also have netherworld associations, and the remains of burials, both inhumations and cremations, in the niches and crevices of rocks on either side of the path between Hattusa and Yazılıkaya add further to the impression of a site that has to do with death and the afterlife. All the figures in Chamber B face towards the north end of the chamber, and were probably intended to relate to a monument which once stood there—a statue of a god, perhaps, or of a king.

It has long been suggested that Yazılıkaya was the principal place where the Hittite New Year festival was celebrated, the Hittite 'House of the New Year', like the *bīt akītu* of Babylonian tradition. The site's apparent netherworld associations would not be inconsistent with this. Death and new life were commonly juxtaposed in the

Fig. 8. Dagger-god, relief from Yazılıkaya

ancient world, for in the cyclic pattern of things, decay and death are followed by new beginnings, new growth, new life. We can envisage that to this, perhaps the holiest of all open-country sanctuaries in the Hittite world,[28] came a procession of celebrants at the year's beginning. Here at this time perhaps all the important gods assembled, just as they are depicted and individually identified in Chamber A, and just as the statues of the Babylonian gods were assembled in the Babylonian *bīt akītu*. There was no more crucial time of the year to seek the gods' favours. There was probably no more important place where this was to be done.

Yazılıkaya may thus have served as a place for celebrating the rites

Fig. 9. The twelve gods, relief from Yazılıkaya

of spring, in the presence of all the chief deities of the land.[29] In the kingdom's last decades, it may also have served as a mortuary chapel, a place of ancestor worship where the royal family paid homage to its dead.[30] And here perhaps a Great King was interred. We have noted in Chapter 10 that after due ceremony a king's bones were finally put to rest in a *hekur*, a 'stone house'.[31] The prominence of the reliefs of Tudhaliya IV, the only human figure depicted at Yazılıkaya, suggest that Chamber B may have been his *hekur*, his tomb. We are told that his son Suppiluliuma (II) set up a statue to him in his *hekur*.[32] Conceivably, the base at the north end of Chamber B, towards which all the reliefs are oriented, once supported a monumental image of Tudhaliya, for veneration and service by that exclusive group of family members allowed entry to a king's tomb after his death.

Rituals

The Hittites drew a distinction between festivals, designated by the Sumerogram EZEN, and rituals, to which the term SISKUR applied; the former referred to 'group religious ceremonies designed to worship and provide offerings to the gods', the latter to 'magical procedures often performed by and for individuals to address specific maladies'.[33] In a broader sense, the term 'ritual' could be said to encompass any symbolic action or performance aimed at bringing about a particular outcome, or commemorating or enhancing a particular event. In any case the distinction between festival and ritual is not an absolute one since many of the procedures carried out during the course of a festival—the washing of hands, the drinking of the god, the breaking of bread, the ceremonial dances—were clearly ritualistic in character. Indeed a festival programme is to a very large extent made up of a series of rituals.

On the other hand, many of the recorded rituals from the Hittite world were clearly designed to cater for the needs of specific individuals on specific occasions. But in whatever context a ritual is performed, one of its characteristic features is that it seeks to achieve a particular result by a procedure or activity which in itself has no *direct* practical value. To till the soil and irrigate the fields may be essential to ensuring a good harvest. But these are not ritual activities. To conduct a ceremony of the plough and perform a fertility dance *are* ritual activities. They will not cultivate the ground or put seeds in it or water the seeds. But in the belief of the performers they are just as essential to the harvest's success. A midwife needs to be skilled both in practical birthing procedures as well as in the performance of the appropriate birth rituals to ensure that a baby is safely delivered. A doctor needs to be skilled both in practical medical procedures as well as in the appropriate spells and rituals and incantations in order to effect many a cure. Practical and ritualistic—the one complements and reinforces the other.

The essence of ritual is *activity*, often multi-sensory activity: the actions, gestures, movements of the participants, the sound of invocations, the herald's cries, the liturgical chanting with musical accompaniment, the fragrant odour of aromatic substances, the stench of sacrificial blood, the sight and sound and smell of fat hissing on the flames, the taste of holy wine on the tongue as one drinks the god, the physical sensation of being washed and scraped of all bodily defilement.

At the heart of much ritual activity lies the notion of sympathetic or mimetic magic—involving the belief that a desired result can be achieved by acting it out in analogy, using token symbols. Thus in a ritual designed to eliminate a source of pollution:

They make a basin . . . and from it they build a small ditch leading to the river. Into it they put a boat lined with a little silver and gold. They also make small 'oaths' and 'curses' of silver and gold and place them into the boat. Then the ditch which empties the basin carries the ship from the basin into the river. When it disappears, she[34] pours out a little fine oil and honey, and while doing so speaks as follows: 'Just as the river has carried away the ship and no trace of it can be found any more—whoever has committed evil word, oath, curse and uncleanliness in the presence of the god—even so let the river carry them away! And just as no trace of the ship can be found any more, let evil word no longer exist for my god; neither let it exist for the sacrificer's person! Let god and sacrificer be free of that matter!'[35]

Some of the most interesting rituals are those most closely associated with the lower levels of society far removed from the world of the state festivals, for these rituals, collected throughout the kingdom by royal scribes, afford us rare glimpses into the lives of the common people of the Hittite world. There were rituals for every stage in a person's development, from birth through puberty to death, to protect that person during his or her transition from one stage to the next, warding off evil forces, setting right what has gone wrong. The majority of rituals, comments Professor Beckman, have the purpose of restoring a person to his/her proper functioning within a particular sphere of life.[36] There is a ritual designed to restore a man's sexual potency, another to cure a stomach disorder, another to restore domestic bliss to a feuding household, another to purify a household from all evil influences.

The Ritualists

To ensure their effectiveness, rituals need to be carried out by properly qualified persons hired for the purpose. Prominent amongst the experts in ritual procedure, which included many males, were a group of female practitioners whom we commonly refer to as the 'Old Women',[37] misleadingly so if the term conjures for us the notion of a pack of toothless, half-crazed old crones. The Hittite term for them is *hasawa*, perhaps originally used of midwives, since it literally means not 'old woman' but rather '(she) of birth'.[38] At all events the women so designated were multi-skilled professionals who may often have collaborated with doctors, augurs, incantation priests, and other practitioners in the arts of ritual performance, healing, and divination. As was the case with scribes, many may have been continuing a family tradition, inheriting an occupation which in some cases at least appears to have been passed down through successive generations of the same family.[39] The names of fourteen of these women have survived, as authors of rituals which they practised. The women in general were almost certainly literate, and may well have been multilingual to a greater or lesser degree. A range of languages are used in the liturgical and ritual texts, including ancient Hattic, Luwian, Palaic, Hurrian, and Babylonian. These reflect the traditional languages of the particular cultic areas where the rituals originated. Many of the rituals must have required incantations to be uttered by the performers in languages other than their own native tongue, even if their knowledge of these languages was confined to the terminology of ritual. Presumably if a particular situation called for a ritual which had been composed in Hattic or Luwian or Hurrian, it would have to be performed in that language to ensure its effectiveness.

It is not unlikely that the 'Old Women' (to keep the conventional term) had a regular consultancy practice covering a wide range of situations, and presumably access to a considerable source of material on which they could draw in performing a ritual appropriate to a particular situation. Even at the humblest level rituals were complicated affairs, given all the paraphernalia required for their successful accomplishment, including foodstuffs and other consumable items of clay, wax, tallow, and wool, animals for sacrifice, and a range of ritual instruments. The slightest error could invalidate the whole procedure. Ritual texts, like records of festival programmes, have the appearance of step-by-step instruction manuals, for careful consultation by the practitioner at every stage of the process—the collection of all the materials required for the ritual, their conveyance to the place where the ritual was to be performed, the time of the performance, the words to be uttered, the chants to be sung, the procedures to be followed in meticulous detail. There was obviously a limit to how much the ritualists could commit to memory, even when they themselves had authored a particular ritual. And there may have been many cases where a situation requiring their services arose with little or no warning. Almost certainly there was a large stock of recorded material on which they could call, to ensure that they always had something ready to hand for every conceivable occasion.

Their services, conducted in the open air or in the client's own home as the situation warranted, probably did not come cheaply, especially since the client must also have been liable for the costs of the consumables required by the ritual. It does seem, however, that the cost of treatment could be tailored to meet the client's ability to pay, with less expensive items being used for a client of modest means, apparently without affecting, or at least seriously diminishing, the ritual's potency. For example, a particular ritual may have called for the sacrifice of a donkey, a not inexpensive item to judge from the prices of livestock in The Laws, which would have added considerably to the cost of the ritual. In place of a live animal, however, a poor man was permitted to substitute one of clay for the ritual's purposes.[40]

The Substitute

The concept of substitution is embodied in a great many rituals.[41] Indeed the concept is a very widespread one, occurring in many civilizations, ancient and modern, in many different forms. Basically, it involves the belief that in certain situations a substitute can take on the identity of some other person or thing. This enables it to serve as a stand-in when the original is not available, or to assume the original's burdens or afflictions, or contrarily to be used as a means of transferring burdens or afflictions to the original. Sir James Frazer in *The Golden Bough* traced the concept back to primitive humankind. The 'savage', he said, recognized that he could relieve himself of a physical burden, like a load of wood or stones, by getting someone else to carry the load for him; by extension he thought he could also transfer to someone or something else other kinds of burdens and afflictions—physical ailments, grief, and pain. In its more sophisticated forms, the substitution ritual often possessed a distinct moral and ethical element, involving the belief that not only one's physical afflictions but also the burden of one's sin or guilt could be transferred to another being. In Christian theology the martyrdom of Jesus Christ is the ultimate manifestation of the substitution concept.

From as far back as the Mesopotamian story of the goddess Ishtar's release from the Underworld and her replacement by the shepherd god Dumuzi, literature has abounded in illustrations of the substitution concept. It surfaces many times, for example, in Classical Greek literature. Thus in Euripides' play *Alcestis* the eponymous heroine volunteers herself as a substitute for her husband Admetos when he is told that his death is imminent and can only be avoided if he finds someone else willing to die in his place. In a quite different context, an example of substitution is provided by Herodotos, who records the Egyptian custom of heaping curses upon the severed head of an ox, praying that any evil likely to threaten the land may fall upon it; the ox's head is then thrown into the Nile (or else sold in a market-place if there happens to be one nearby with Greek traders present).[42] Like the scapegoat of biblical tradition (see below), the ox serves as a substitute victim, having heaped upon it and bearing away the afflictions of the people for whom it has been sacrificed.

A substitute ox was a central feature of the procedures which King Mursili II followed in order to rid himself of his speech affliction (see Chapter 9). The ox was to be sent to the temple of the Storm God in Kummanni, along with a wagon-load of the king's possessions, in particular the garments and the accoutrements he had worn on two critical days—the day when the affliction first befell him and the day when the ritual of appeasement began. Here the ox and the accompanying items were to be burned as an offering to the Storm God. In the typically pragmatic Hittite way which left nothing to chance, a second ox was also sent on the journey—a substitute for the substitute—in case the first died en route.

Animals commonly featured in rituals as substitute victims—preferably live ones, though as we have seen above, clay replicas were permissible for budget-constrained clients. Asses, oxen, birds, dogs, sheep, and pigs were all considered appropriate for substitution purposes. Thus in a ritual designed to restore harmony to a strife-torn household:

> They drive up a black sheep, the Old Woman presents it to them (*the sacrificers—i.e. the pair who have hired the Old Woman*), and speaks as follows: 'For your heads and all parts of your bodies the black sheep is a substitute. In its mouth and its tongue is the tongue of curses.' She waves it over them. The two sacrificers spit into its mouth.[43] They cut up the sheep and dismember it. They kindle the hearth and burn it. . . . The Old Woman takes a small pig, she presents it to them and speaks as follows: 'See! It has been fattened with grass and grain. Just as this one shall not see the sky and shall not see the other small pigs again, even so let the evil curses not see these sacrificers either!' She waves the small pig over them, and then they kill it. They dig a hole in the ground and put it down into it.[44]

The substitute serves as a kind of receptacle for the pollutants and evil forces which have been afflicting those for whom the ritual has been conducted, and the ritual process involves the transfer of these contaminants from sufferer to substitute. The transfer may be effected by a number of means—by verbal identification of the bodily parts of the substitute with those of the sufferer, by fashioning a substitute image in the likeness of the sufferer, on the principle that like attracts like, by the sufferer touching the substitute or spitting into its mouth, or by simply waving the substitute at or over the sufferer. Of course the process of merely transferring contaminants to a substitute does not eliminate them, any more than we solve a garbage problem by tossing our domestic waste into our neighbour's backyard. In the course of the ritual, or after it had been completed, it was essential to ensure the correct disposal of the contaminants.[45] Failure to do so could be construed as a wilful act of sorcery, liable for judgement before the king's court with possible dire consequences.[46]

Depending on their nature, the pollutants might be disposed of by incineration or burial (which thus consigned them to the Underworld), or by conveying them somewhere else. They could, for example, be set adrift on a river, like the replica silver and gold curses and oaths referred to in the pollution ritual we have dealt with above, or the ox's head thrown into the Nile. The substitute might also serve as a removalist, like the ox in King Mursili's ritual. This calls to mind Aaron's ritual with the two goats in Leviticus 16; one served as an atonement offering to the Hebrew god, the other—the 'scapegoat'—carried the people's iniquities into the wilderness. Mursili's substitute ox combined both these functions; it conveyed the affliction away from the king, and served as an atonement offering to the god. Donkeys and rams could also be used as carriers, to convey pestilence ritually transferred to them into an enemy's country. Even a mouse might serve as a carrier: 'She (the Old Woman) wraps up a small piece of tin in the bowstring and attaches it to the sacrificers' right hands and feet. She takes it off them again and attaches it to a mouse, with the words: "I have taken the evil off you and transferred it to this mouse. Let this mouse carry it on a long journey to the high mountains, hills and dales!" '[47]

Members of the royal family sometimes sought to divert their afflictions, almost invariably attributable to divine wrath, to a human substitute. Thus Mursili II's beloved and desperately ill wife Gassulawiya sent a woman of great beauty to Lelwani, supposedly responsible for her ailment, in the hope that she would be accepted as a substitute for the queen: 'If you, O God, are seeking ill of me. . . . this woman shall be my substitute. I am presenting her to you in fine attire. Compared to me she is excellent, she is pure, she is brilliant, she is white, she is decked out with everything. Now, O God, My Lord, look well on her. Let this woman stand before the god, My Lord.'[48] We cannot be sure whether the queen's substitute was to be offered up as a human sacrifice. The fragmentary nature of the text leaves this unclear. In any case the deity remained unmoved. Gassulawiya never recovered from her illness.

There was a substitution ritual designed to protect a king threatened by an outbreak of plague while returning home from a successful military campaign in enemy territory.[49] In this case the ritual prescribed that a male prisoner and a female from the enemy land be seized and brought before the king. The king removed his clothes and they were put on the male prisoner, and the female was clothed in female garb. The king uttered the words: 'If any male god of the enemy land has caused this plague, thus I have given him a man suitably attired as a substitute. May you, male god, be fully satisfied with this man thus attired, and henceforth be well disposed to the king, the lords, the army, and the land of Hatti, and may this prisoner take the plague upon himself and carry it back to the enemy land!' The procedure was repeated with the female prisoner for the benefit of a female deity. There were also animal substitutes, a bull and a female sheep decked out with earrings, and red, green, black, and white wool, to which the plague was transferred and which would also act as its carriers back to the enemy land.[50]

The stability of the kingdom depended to a very large extent on the health and well-being of its sovereign. But the sovereign was forever vulnerable to divine wrath, for he was responsible not only for offences which he himself had committed, but also for those of other members of his family, including his ancestors, or indeed for offences committed by his subjects in general. Conscientious celebration of the festivals in the religious calendar might go a long way towards keeping the gods on side. But there was no absolute guarantee of this, and it was as well to take further precautions, anticipating as far as one could any misfortune or disaster likely to overtake the king. Sometimes an omen or oracle might give warning of an imminent threat to his life. That was the signal for prompt preventative measures, with the appropriate ritual text ready to hand: 'If death is predicted for the king, whether he sees it in a dream or it is made known to him by divination from the entrails or by augury, or if some omen of death occurs in front of him, this is the ritual for it.'[51]

Thus reads the concluding statement, or colophon, to one of two recorded versions of the procedures to be followed in a substitute ritual.[52] Extending over two nights, the ritual was triggered by a sign from the Moon God and involved the use of three substitutes: a live animal, a live human being, and a life-size wooden image of a human being, decked in royal robes with eyes and earrings of gold. Although the sign had come from the Moon God, there could be no certainty that he was in fact the deity to whom the king had given offence. All possibilities had to be covered, with substitute victims appropriate to each of them. The king first addressed the Moon God: 'Since you, O Moon God, My Lord, have given an omen, if you have declared evil for me, see! I have provided substitutes in my place. Now take these and set me free!'[53]

The animal substitute, a bull, was taken to an elevated place and there, in full view of the Moon God, was sacrificed and its body burnt—thus representing the death and cremation of the king. The live human substitute was for the upper-world gods, the wooden effigy for those of the netherworld. Allowance had to be made for the possibility that either one or the other of these groups of deities had taken offence and needed to be appeased: The king says: 'This is the living supernal substitute for me, and this effigy is the infernal substitute for me. If you, heavenly gods, have afflicted me with evil or shortened my days, months, or years, this living substitute man shall stand in my place; mark him well, O heavenly gods. But if the Sun Goddess of the Underworld and the infernal gods have afflicted me, then this effigy shall stand in my place; mark it well, O infernal gods.'[54]

The ritual required that the king's substitute actually became king in his place, for the period in which he was particularly at risk. The live human substitute was a prisoner-of-war who had been selected for the occasion and anointed with 'the fine oil of kingship'. The real king stripped himself of all his regalia and presented them to the substitute: 'See, this man (is now) king! I have bestowed on this man the name of kingship, I have bestowed on him the garb of kingship, I have put on him the (royal) diadem.'[55] The substitute dismissed the real king from the palace. No longer did anyone even speak his name. His replacement was king in all respects. He was wined and dined, he slept in the royal bedroom, he was guarded by the royal officials. This continued until the seventh day. But his period of kingship was hardly one of unallayed pleasure, for it had been foretold that the king's life would be brief, and if the prophecy was fulfilled, it would be fulfilled while the substitute occupied the throne. If he survived to the seventh day, his kingship came to an end. And then he was sent back to his own land none the worse, it would appear, for his experience. Perhaps the offering of him as a substitute was atonement enough for the gods; perhaps like the scapegoat he served to convey from the palace and the kingdom all trace of the evil which had initially inspired divine wrath.

The Hittite ritual of the substitute king recalls an earlier Mesopotamian practice. In accordance with this practice a substitute was appointed at critical periods, when omens like eclipses presaged dangers for the real king. But it appears that the substitute, when his brief period of glory came to an end, was executed, to ensure that the gods were fully appeased—unless the real king happened to die at just that time. This did indeed happen when King Erra-imittī of the Isin dynasty died from quaffing a bowl of hot broth during the 'reign' of his substitute, the gardener Ellil-bāni. Clearly the gods had taken matters into their own hands. They were now satisfied, and no further atonement was needed. Ellil-bāni reaped the benefits of the situation and continued to occupy the throne—except, no doubt, for those brief periods when a substitute took his place.[56]

Magic

It is clear that the success of a ritualistic performance depended in large measure on the potent forces of magic which the ritual activated.[57] In broad terms magic has been defined as 'a reasoned system of techniques for influencing the gods and other supernatural powers that can be taught and learned . . . Magic not only manipulates occult forces but also tries to master the higher supernatural powers with which religion is concerned'.[58] Healing and purification rituals involved good magic—white magic—which had the power to cleanse an afflicted person or building or field or country of the evil forces which defiled it. This sometimes involved the use of apotropaic images; for example, figures of animals buried in the foundations of buildings—or placed at their entrance: 'They make a little dog of tallow and place it on the threshold of the house and say:

"You are the little dog on the table of the royal pair. Just as by day you do not allow other men into the courtyard, so do not let in the Evil Thing during the night." '[59] White magic was used to negate and expel the counter-influences of sorcery, black magic. These were generally not demons as they were in the Babylonian conception, but rather powerful impersonal forces, responsible for many of the misfortunes and afflictions which plagued humankind—individuals, families, communities, whole states.[60]

Their powers might be unleashed through an act of carelessness—for example, failure to dispose in the correct manner of pollutants removed from a patient or building during a ritual of purification. But more often than not, they were deliberately activated with malicious intent. To do so was an offence dealt with by the highest authority in the land. The Laws stipulate that those accused of making clay images for magical purposes will be called to account before His Majesty's court.[61] A hair from the intended victim's body, or an item of his clothing, might also be used by the practitioner of black magic. Even the act of pronouncing someone's name while killing a snake[62] resulted in a hefty fine (one mina, or forty shekels, of silver) for a free man and death for a slave.[63] If you were the victim of such an act, a ritual was necessary to remove the spell or curse from you, and to cast it back upon the perpetrator: 'Next she (the Old Woman) likewise fashions a strand out of green wool and says as follows: "Whoever has used sorcery against this person (the patient), and whoever has rendered (him or her) green—I am now removing the sorcery and the green from him/her and will give it back to its originator." Then she wraps the strand around the (magic) figures.'[64]

It was a charge of witchcraft that led to the downfall of Arma-Tarhunda, governor of the strategically important Upper Land during the reign of King Muwatalli (II). As we have noted, Arma-Tarhunda was related to the royal family, and had the misfortune to be the arch-rival of the king's brother Hattusili, later to occupy the throne as Hattusili III. Prior to this Muwatalli had made his brother governor of the Upper Land in place of Arma-Tarhunda, much to the latter's fury. It was Hattusili who had brought the charge of witchcraft, to counter an indictment which Arma-Tarhunda had brought against him: 'Furthermore he and his wife and his son began to bewitch me. He also filled Samuha, the city of the deity, with witchcraft.'[65] One cannot help suspecting that Arma-Tarhunda's charge (whatever it may have been) was not unjustified, and Hattusili's a trumped-up one; it was certainly well within the capability of the wily and ruthlessly ambitious young prince to resort to such measures to rid himself of an inconvenient rival. In any case Muwatalli found against the defendant, and handed him over to Hattusili for punishment, thus ensuring the removal of one of the chief obstacles in his brother's career path. Yet Hattusili's treatment of Arma-Tarhunda was surprisingly mild: he let him go free and returned to him half his confiscated property; subsequently he attempted a reconciliation with his family. All this, he claims, he did out of pity, for Arma-Tarhunda was now an old man. More likely he was acting out of remorse—for a charge unjustly laid.

The mere allegation of witchcraft may well have generated concerns and emotions which were almost sufficient in themselves to secure a conviction. To judge from the Proclamation of King Telipinu, even a knowledge of the black arts rendered one liable to prosecution. And persons who knew of but failed to denounce those suspected of having such knowledge were themselves liable to punishment: 'In Hattusa hereafter sorcery must be exorcized. Whoever in the (royal) family knows about sorcery, you must seize him and bring him to the gate of the palace. Whoever does not bring him here—it will come about that things will go badly for this man and his house.'[66]

This has a familiar ring about it. Note the progression: practice of the 'black arts' is an offence; then mere knowledge of the black arts becomes an offence; then knowledge of and failure to report those who practise or know the black arts becomes an offence. Herein we have an early attested example of a phenomenon of human behaviour that surfaces every so often in recorded history. It is what we call witch-hunting.

CHAPTER 12

Myth

> The god Telipinu has flown into a rage. He puts on his shoes and departs the land. Crops wither and die, sheep and cattle reject their young and become barren, men and gods starve. In great alarm the Storm God, father of Telipinu, dispatches an eagle to search for his wayward son. The search is in vain. The Storm God himself attempts to seek him out. Again to no avail. No god, great or small, can determine his whereabouts. In desperation the Storm God sends a bee to look for him. The bee searches on high mountains, in deep valleys, in the blue deep. Finally, in a meadow, it discovers Telipinu. It stings his hands and feet, bringing him smartly upright, and then soothes the pain of his stings by smearing wax on the affected parts. But the god's anger remains unabated. Indeed his fury is increased by his rude and painful awakening. In an orgy of destruction, he unleashes thunder and lightning and great floods, knocking down houses and wreaking havoc on human beings, livestock, and crops. Then Kamrusepa, goddess of magic, is sent to pacify him and bring him back. She conducts a ritual for this purpose. By the process of ritual analogy Telipinu's body is cleansed of its anger. The god's way home is made smooth by spreading oil and honey upon it. Telipinu returns and once more cares for his land. All is restored to normal. The land once more becomes fruitful.

The story of the Vanishing God is part of a small body of native Anatolian mythological tradition which has come down to us via the Hittite archives.[1] Remnants of a number of versions of the story have survived, featuring different gods (including the great Storm God himself), though it is generally the vegetation god Telipinu who has the starring role. Even his story appears in several different versions. We have parts of at least three of these, and although none are complete we can piece together from their fragments a number of elements which are probably common to all of them. Telipinu was a Hattic god in origin who retained some prominence throughout the period of the Hittite kingdom. Sired by the Storm God, he too sometimes displayed formidable Storm God characteristics, as illustrated by the destructive elemental forces unleashed by him in the Vanishing God tradition. The tradition almost certainly dates back to the early Old Kingdom, or even earlier to pre-Hittite times, though it survives only in Middle and Late Hittite texts (that is, texts of the New Kingdom).

A story recited, a tale told. This in essence is what a myth is. The notion of something *spoken* is in fact inherent in the word. 'Myth' is derived from Greek *mythos* whose prime meaning 'utterance, a thing said', was extended to refer to anything spoken or recited, particularly a story. The Vanishing God myth has all the elements of a story recited. But not merely this. In its written form it provides a script for a full-scale dramatic performance. There is a cast of characters who deliver short speeches linked by narrative:

NARRATOR: The pastures and the springs dried up, so that famine broke out in the land. Humans and gods were dying of hunger. The Great Sun God made a feast and invited the Thousand Gods. They ate but could not get enough. They drank but could not quench their thirst. The Storm God remembered his son Telipinu:

STORM GOD: My son Telipinu is not there. He became enraged and removed everything good.

NARRATOR: The great and small gods began to search for Telipinu. The Sun God sent the swift eagle:

SUN GOD: Go search the high mountains! Search the deep valleys! Search the Blue Deep!

NARRATOR: The eagle went, but did not find him. He reported back to the Sun God:

EAGLE: I could not find Telipinu, the noble god.

STORM GOD (*to Hannahanna*): How shall we act? We are going to die of hunger!

HANNAHANNA[2]: Do something, Storm God. Go search for Telipinu yourself![3]

Stage directions are inserted in the script, as much for the guidance of the actors as for their audience:

NARRATOR: Telipinu came in anger.

STAGE DIRECTION: *He thunders together with lightning. Below he strikes the Dark Earth.*

NARRATOR: Kamrusepa saw him and moved for herself [with(?)] the eagle's wing. She stopped it, namely anger. She stopped it, the wrath. She stopped sin. She stopped sullenness.

Props to be used in the performance are also indicated by stage directions:

Before Telipinu there stands an eyan-*tree* (or pole?).[4] *From the* eyan *is suspended a hunting bag made from the skin of a sheep.*

The lines spoken by narrator and actors provide but one element of a performance in which sight and sound are blended in dramatic presentation. The performance is visually enhanced by the actions and costumes of the actors, garbed as animals or gods, decked out with all their appropriate insignia and symbols, moving rhythmically in ever-changing patterns and tableaus as they mime the actions conveyed by the narrator's words, as they react and respond through gesture, facial expression, and bodily movement to each stage of the unfolding drama. There is music throughout the performance. The actors accompany their movements with singing and chanting, sometimes in unison, sometimes individually. There is also instrumental music—the rumble of drums and the clash of cymbals in the more violent scenes as the angry, wayward god vents his wrath by unleashing thunder and lightning; the soothing tones of the lute in the quieter, more solemn scenes as the god's anger is drained from him and he is finally enticed home.

At least in theory, the performance was not intended primarily for the entertainment of an assembled audience. If the audience were in fact entertained, that was a perfectly acceptable by-product; no god could take exception to that. But the myth itself merely provided the context for the performance's essential purpose—a ritual designed to induce a delinquent god through analogic magic to abandon his wrath and return to his responsibilities. The ritual passages, in their phraseology and content, and particularly in their application of analogic magic, recall many of the purificatory rituals of the Hittite land. And the leading ritual practitioner in the myth, Kamrusepa, goddess of magic, served as the divine counterpart of the 'Old Women', speaking and acting very much as they did:

Kamrusepa says to the gods: '. . . Telipinu is angry. His soul and essence were stifled like burning brushwood. Just as they burned these sticks of brushwood, may the anger, wrath, sin and sullenness of Telipinu likewise burn up. And just as malt is ineffective, so that they don't carry it to the field and use it as seed, as they don't make it into bread and deposit it in the Seal House, so may the anger, wrath, sin and sullenness of Telipinu likewise become ineffective. . . .'

The Myth–Ritual Nexus

The fact that myth and ritual have so frequently been associated through the ages has led to a widespread and long-held assumption that the two are invariably linked. This assumption goes too far, and exceptions to it can readily be found. Nevertheless, there are clearly many instances in many civilizations where a close nexus between myth and ritual does exist, as in the case of our Vanishing God. Which raises a further question. Does myth give rise to ritual, or ritual to myth? Arguably, it is possible to find examples of both. But in cases like the Vanishing God, myth almost certainly preceded ritual. The Hittite land fell frequent victim to a range of natural disasters—devastating storms, drought, plague, famine—occurring at unpredictable intervals and attributable to malevolent supernatural powers. While humankind had no practical means of controlling these powers, it could seek to influence them through other means. But in order to do so, one needed first to understand how they operated, how they behaved, how they thought. This in effect meant reducing them to human terms, and putting them into the context of human behaviour and experience. A superhuman power with human desires, failings, and vulnerabilities can more readily be dealt with than vague impersonal forces which lie beyond human conceptualization. The land is afflicted by a prolonged drought. There is some being responsible for this. It must be a being who has power over life-sustaining elements, fertility of soil and livestock, growth-inducing rain. Why has it withheld these elements? Reasons are given in terms of human emotions—and the rudiments of a myth are created. How can things be set right? By seeking to drive from the being the negative human emotions which have led to its malevolence, in this case its wrath and sullenness, as one would seek to drive out the wrath from a feuding household. How does one do this? Through the process of analogic magic. If a human being can thus be purified, so too can a god—if a god is but a human on a superhuman scale.

At first sight the Vanishing God tradition appears similar in concept to traditions from other civilizations which concern the disappearance of fertility deities and the consequent withering of life on earth. Thus in Mesopotamian tradition the abduction of the shepherd-god Dumuzi to the Underworld. In Greek tradition Persephone's abduction to the same region has similar consequences, because of the grief of her mother, the earth goddess Demeter. The Mesopotamian and Greek myths serve to explain the regularly recurring cycle of seasons, with growth and new life heralding Dumuzi's and Persephone's return to the upper world for six months in every twelve. But the Vanishing God tradition is of a different order. There is no sense here of a predictable recurrent pattern. Rather the emphasis is on the god's whimsical behaviour. Without warning, it seems, he abandons the land in a fit of pique—for reasons which the fragmentary texts have not preserved and which in any case are probably quite incidental—and his disappearance and prolonged absence are quite beyond the normal order of things, causing as much concern to his fellow gods as to his mortal worshippers.

The myth and the ritual which it incorporates have very much a reactive character. There is no sense of looking forward to the future. Rather the impression is of a response to a crisis which has already happened, is still current, and falls outside the natural cycle of the seasons. It is possible that the myth was routinely acted out at the annual *purulli* festival at the beginning of spring (as an anticipatory or precautionary measure?). But in addition, if not alternatively, it may have been performed at other times as well, in response to a critical situation, and particularly at times of imminent serious shortfalls in the land's food production, whether due to drought, or crop-destroying storms, or a decline in soil and livestock fertility. Such crises may have become ever more frequent during the kingdom's last decades.

The Illuyanka Myth

This is the text of the *Purulli* Festival. . . . When they speak thus: 'Let the land prosper and thrive, and let the land be protected'—and when it prospers and thrives, they perform the *Purulli* Festival.

So begins the earlier of two versions of the myth of Illuyanka,[5] a serpent (that is what his name means) who crawls from the bowels of the earth to engage in mortal combat with the Storm God. The myth tells of the combat, which ends with the triumph of the Storm God and the death of Illuyanka. But victory does not come easily. Initially the serpent gains the upper hand, inflicting a resounding defeat on the god, who is forced to call in outside assistance, both divine (in the earlier version) and human (in both versions). Only then, and even then only through trickery, does he succeed in overcoming his adversary and killing him.

This much do the two versions of the myth have in common. Both versions were written on a single tablet by a scribe at the dictation of a priest called Kella. Like the myths which belong to the Vanishing God tradition, the story of Illuyanka comes from native Hattic tradition. Indeed the place-names mentioned in the story, Ziggaratta and Nerik, place it firmly in the once predominantly Hattic region of central Anatolia, lying north of Hattusa and extending towards the Pontic coast. Like the Vanishing God tradition, it was probably first committed to writing during the Old Hittite period,[6] though all surviving copies date to the New Kingdom.

As the official cult-myth of the *purulli* festival, the story of Illuyanka was no doubt acted out on one or more occasions during the course of the festival—almost certainly at Nerik, where the celebrations reached their climax, and perhaps at other venues on the festival route as well. Its purpose must have been to strengthen through ritual enactment the process of regeneration of life at the year's beginning, symbolized by the Storm God's triumph over Illuyanka, who represents the forces of darkness and evil. Yet though he is vanquished and slaughtered Illuyanka will rise again to do battle, his life renewed as a snake renews itself by sloughing its skin. Like the Babylonian Marduk, who vanquishes and dismembers Tiamat but must do battle afresh with her every year, the Hittite Storm God will forever have to renew his combat with his adversary. That is in the nature of things. The struggle is a constant one; Illuyanka is never completely overthrown and the Storm God's battle with him must be fought year after year. It is appropriate that the ritual enacted to represent this is performed at the most crucial time of the year, to reactivate through sympathetic magic the powers that hold in check the destructive elemental forces hostile to civilized existence. Constant vigilance and effort are needed, by man and god alike, for whenever the dark forces represented by Illuyanka gain the upper hand, the crops will not grow, the rain will not fall.

The theme of a hero, human or divine, pitted in a fight to the death against a monster (often a serpent or dragon, or with reptilian body-parts) representing the forces of evil is typical of the mythology of many civilizations. The myths of the ancient Greeks abound in examples—Zeus and Typhon, Apollo and Python, Bellerophon and

Chimaera, Perseus and Medusa, Herakles and the Hydra—with derivatives like St George and the Dragon in more recent times. Sometimes even when the hero is a god, and despite all the weapons in his armoury, his success can only be achieved with the assistance of a mortal. In Greek tradition it was only through the services of a mortal, Herakles, that Zeus and his fellow gods finally triumphed over the Giants, the monstrous sons of the Earth sprung from the blood of the mutilated Ouranos (see below). So too in both versions of the Illuyanka myth, which differ quite markedly in many of their details, a mortal is pressed into service to help rescue the god from total and irreversible defeat. In the first version his name is Hupasiya. The Storm God's daughter seeks him out and asks him to join forces with her. He agrees to do so on condition that she sleeps with him. Which she does. The plan is put into effect:

> Inara led Hupasiya away and hid him. She dressed herself up and called the serpent up from its hole, (saying:) 'I'm preparing a feast. Come eat and drink.' So up came the serpent and his children, and they ate and drank. They drained every vessel and became drunk. Now they do not want to go back down into their hole again. Hupasiya came and bound the serpent with a rope. Then the Storm God came and slew the serpent, and the gods that were with him.[7]

In the second version of the myth, we are at the point where the serpent has defeated the Storm God and taken his heart and eyes. Again subterfuge is called for. The Storm God sires a son by a poor mortal woman, and on reaching manhood the son marries Illuyanka's daughter and becomes a member of his father-in-law's household. This is in accordance with the Storm God's plan, who now instructs his son: 'When you go and live in your wife's house, demand from them my heart and eyes (as a brideprice).' The son's new family voluntarily hands over to him the requested items, without suspecting, apparently, who the real author of the request is. The plan has worked. With his bodily parts all back in place, the Storm God once more does battle with his adversary, and this time kills him.

The tradition has a number of curious features which set it quite apart from most other monster-slaying myths. In the first place the hero can hardly be said to cover himself in glory. In both versions of the tale he is ignominiously defeated by his opponent. In the first version his ultimate success comes only after his daughter has taken the initiative and rendered the serpent utterly helpless with the aid of her mortal assistant. In both versions deception and trickery are used where the god's physical prowess has failed. Not that deception and trickery were necessarily bad things in themselves if the end warranted such means (as exemplified also in the Homeric code of heroic conduct). But the Storm God's behaviour raises other moral questions. In the first version the slaughter of the serpent and his sons grossly violates the obligations of hospitality which codes of social behaviour in almost all civilizations, ancient and modern, insist on being scrupulously observed. If, as Professor Hoffner notes, a man gives shelter and food to another, he is bound by the time-honoured obligations of a host to ensure that his guest is protected from all harm.[8] Illuyanka and his sons have been guests at the table of the Storm God's daughter and are still under her protection, according to the laws of hospitality, when they meet their deaths at the hands of her father. In the second version the Storm God's victory depends on another deliberately engineered act of betrayal. The god has produced a son for the purpose of marrying into the serpent's household, in effect becoming a member of his family. It reflects a situation familiar enough in Hittite society, where matrilocal marriages were apparently not uncommon (see Chapter 7). In such a situation the husband's first loyalty was clearly due to his new family. Yet the marriage of the Storm God's son is a perversion of this. It is to be used as a means of bringing about his father-in-law's destruction.

The involvement of a mortal in both versions of the myth has been seen as a kind of statement of the need for joint effort between god and man in ensuring that the cosmos functions properly and that evil destructive forces are kept at bay; each has his own contribution to make to the process. Given the actual role played by man and god in the myth, that interpretation is not easy to sustain. In both versions the mortals end up as the victims of their actions. In the first, Hupayasa finds himself a prisoner of the goddess to whose service he has given himself, forever denied the right of returning to his wife and children for whom he passionately longs. A punishment for his *hubris*, his arrogance, in demanding that the goddess sleep with him as a reward for his services? That is often assumed, but is certainly not evident from the text itself. Nor do we know his ultimate fate, for the text is broken at the point where it was apparently narrated. In the second version there is no doubt about the mortal's fate. The moral dilemma he faces is an understandable one; his loyalties to his natural father are in conflict with those he owes to his new family. It is the latter whom he ultimately betrays. Wracked with guilt at this betrayal and because of his part in his father-in-law's death, he begs the Storm God to kill him too. Whether as an act of mercy, an act of wrath at his son's remorse, or as an act of sheer indifference now that his son has served his purpose, the Storm God promptly obliges.

The myth may lack the sophistication of the more developed literary products of Hurrian culture. Yet the issues which it raises seem to go well beyond a simple, clear-cut conflict between the forces of good and evil. Why is the Storm God portrayed in such a negative, lacklustre way, especially in a text which was acted out in a festival in which he played a starring role? The contrast with the portrayal of Marduk in the Babylonian creation myth, to take but one example for comparison purposes, is striking. There is of course a risk of our reading more into the tale, in both its versions, than was originally intended or was apparent to those who recorded, read, or heard it, or participated in its performance. And for all we know the apparent complexities of the tale may have simply been due to its being cobbled together from several early and originally independent folk tales now lost to us. On the other hand it is difficult to believe that in a society which was closely attuned to a range of social and moral issues there were not some who pondered on the tale's moral implications. Or was the only important thing that the Storm God eventually triumphed, regardless of how his victory was achieved or who fell victim in the process? Even if this were the case, those who saw the performance must have had some sensitivity to the pathos of the mortal's plight in both versions. 'It is not too much to claim', comments Professor Hoffner, 'that the author intended the audience to feel the tragedy. Such a plot may not be "literary" in the strict sense, but it is surely evidence for good story-telling technique!'[9]

Other Anatolian Myths

The Vanishing God group of myths and the two versions of the Illuyanka myth are the most prominent examples of the small corpus of Anatolian myths and folk tales surviving in the Hattusa archives. They owe their survival in large measure to the fact that many were incorporated into rituals which were collected throughout the kingdom by royal scribes. But they can be no more than a tiny sample of what was probably a rich body of native mythological tradition, typical of pre-literate societies, extending well back before the Hittite period. Much may never have been recorded in written form. Much else may initially have been recorded during the Old Hittite period, but unlike the Vanishing God and Illuyanka tales failed to survive in the texts beyond that period. Some tales that do survive are frustratingly incomplete, like the Hattic myth which recounts how the moon (Hattic Kasku) fell from the sky, was pursued by the Storm God and other deities and finally, we may conclude (though the text is broken at this point), restored to his original place. A ritual text, also very fragmentary, accompanies the myth, thus providing the reason for its preservation in written form. Unfortunately not enough remains of either myth or ritual to indicate their full significance.

Native themes occasionally find echoes in Classical Greek tradition. The Sun God's lust for a beautiful cow whom he impregnates after turning himself into a handsome youth recalls that group of Greek tales which present variations on the theme of human–bovine couplings, Zeus and Europa, Zeus and Io, Pasiphae and the bull. (One is tempted to remark that in the Hittite context, it is somewhat surprising to find that a sexual act which is strictly forbidden in Hittite law is committed by the supreme god of justice.) In the sequel to the Hittite story the cow is horrified at the two-legged offspring, a human male child, which results from her coupling, and is only prevented from eating the child by his sire's intervention. What follows is obscured by the text's very fragmentary state at this point, and the complete loss of a passage about seventeen lines in length. When the text resumes, there is a fragmentary reference to great rivers, and apparently to some measures taken by the god for the protection of the child. Finally the god leads a fisherman, himself childless, to where the child, an apparent foundling, lies. Gathering him up, the fisherman takes him home to his wife and persuades her to feign labour pains. She does so, deluding the villagers into believing that she is delivered of a child of her own. The story ends abruptly here, but we know that it continued on another tablet now lost to us.[10]

Incomplete though it is, enough of the story survives to suggest that it may be an early example of a well known and widespread narrative tradition: A child is born in secret; its father is often (though not invariably) a god. The mother cannot rear it as her own, either because of the disgrace associated with its birth, or because reports of its birth would put it in great danger. The child is therefore entrusted to destiny by being set adrift on a river or in the sea until it is discovered, safe and sound, and reared, generally by a childless couple of humble circumstances. This in essence is the story of the origins of the Akkadian king Sargon, of the Hebrew Moses, of the Persian king Darius, of the Greek hero Perseus, of Romulus, founder of Rome.[11] In each of these cases the foundling grows to manhood and achieves great things, generally as a leader of his people and often at the expense of a king from whom his birth has been kept secret—a king forewarned that just such a person would one day overthrow him, or liberate his people from him. In the Hittite story, the role of the fisherman and references to 'great rivers' raise the possibility that in this case too the rejected infant had been set adrift on water until, under his real father's guidance, he was found and reared by his adoptive parents. If so, perhaps like his counterparts in similar stories, he grew to manhood and became a great leader of his people. Perhaps this was narrated in the final missing tablet of the story. That would make it one of the earliest surviving examples of a tradition which was to resurface constantly in a number of civilizations over at least the next thousand years.

The motif of exposing babies by setting them adrift on a river occurs again in a Hittite context in the so-called legend of Zalpa.[12] The queen of Kanes, so the story goes, gave birth to thirty sons in a single year. Horrified by this enormous brood she placed them in reed baskets caulked with mud and set them on a river (the Hittite Marrassantiya, Classical Halys, and now the Kızıl Irmak), which carried them to Zalpa on the Black Sea. After growing to manhood the sons returned to Kanes/Nesa, where their mother had subsequently given birth to thirty daughters. Unaware of the family relationship, the brothers were on the point of marrying their sisters when the youngest brother suddenly found out the truth. Realizing that they were all about to commit incest, he urgently called upon his brothers to halt proceedings. At this point the text becomes unclear and we cannot be sure whether or not his advice was taken, though the story does serve to provide a further instance of the Hittites' abhorrence of incest. With the resumption of the text, the story takes on more of a historical cast, with an account of hostilities between Hattusa and Zalpa in the reign of King Hattusili I, ending in Zalpa's destruction.

The events narrated in the first part of the tale serve to explain and justify the historical events with which the tale ends, just as the fourth book of Virgil's *Aeneid*, the Dido–Aeneas love story, provides an explanation for the eventual historical conflict between Rome and Carthage which ends in the latter's destruction. The Zalpa story's hybrid character, beginning as myth or legend, ending as genuine history, makes it virtually unique in Hittite literature. But even in the legendary-mythical episode, some scholars have seen a kernel of historical truth, with the journey of the brothers from Zalpa on the Black Sea to Kanes being a supposed reminiscence of an actual historical immigration from the north.[13] Although the earliest surviving text of the story dates to no earlier than the sixteenth or fifteenth century, it is possible that the story itself originated long before this, perhaps dating to the arrival of Indo-European elements in eastern Anatolia towards the end of the third millennium. The connection which some have sought to make between the Zalpa tradition, with its exposure of male and retention of female babies, and the Amazon tradition of Greek mythology is rather more fanciful.

Another Hittite tale which may have faint echoes elsewhere concerns the two sons of the wealthy and hitherto childless Appu. The sons are called 'Evil' and 'Just' by their father, and they live up to their names. 'Evil' attempts to cheat his brother in the division of their father's estate, just as the wastrel Perses sought to cheat his brother Hesiod of his share of their father's patrimony.[14] In both biblical and Egyptian literature we find instances of pairs of good and evil brothers, with the latter attempting to swindle the former, and as often as not receiving their come-uppance from a just god.

The Kumarbi Epic Cycle

We have noted that much of what is left of native Anatolian mythological tradition has survived because of its incorporation in rituals preserved as integral components of religious festivals. Myths of foreign origin, on the other hand, were of a somewhat different nature, and owe their preservation in Hittite texts to rather different reasons. In their written form they were introduced into the Hittite world from the culturally more sophisticated civilizations lying to their south-east, notably from Babylon and the Hurrian cultural sphere. They entered the Hittite land through the agency of professional scribes, and their preservation was in large measure due to the use made of them within the milieu of the scribal schools. Scribes learnt the skills of their profession partly by copying and recopying the 'classics' of cuneiform literature; and foreign scribes who were imported into the Hittite world brought with them and passed on not only their literacy skills but also a knowledge of the major literary traditions of their own and neighbouring lands.

These traditions are called 'literary' in the sense that they appear to have been composed and recorded primarily for their own sake, not as mere adjuncts to rituals. They obviously had entertainment value, and in the context of the extensive religious reform programme of the thirteenth century may have had a broader educative purpose which went well beyond their use as scribal school exercises. They have been described as 'rich in theological instruction needed for the Hittites to better comprehend the personalities of the gods and the organization of a pantheon that was growing increasingly complex'.[15] Yet in their earlier stages they may not have been as completely divorced from the world of ritual and analogic magic as they later appeared to be. Their world too is one of forces in conflict, of gods doing battle with and finally prevailing over monsters. And although in the form in which we find them in the Hittite texts they may lend themselves less readily to dramatic re-enactment, this would not have been impossible with effective use of symbols and conventions. It is not inconceivable that in their original form they did have ritualistic functions and were acted out accordingly. In terms of complexity of plot and structure and range of characters they may be considered more sophisticated than the homegrown Anatolian products. Yet as we have seen, the latter are not without their complexities, in terms of the questions which they raise and the issues with which they deal, even if this is sometimes belied by the relative naivety of their expression.

The most substantial and most important body of imported mythological tradition is the Hurrian cycle of myths featuring Kumarbi, 'father of the gods'.[16] The cycle consists of a series of 'songs', episodes in verse form, of which two are particularly prominent, the Song of Kingship in Heaven and the Song of Ullikummi.[17] The first relates the struggle between successive generations of gods for sovereignty in heaven: Alalu is overcome by Anu, Anu by Alalu's son Kumarbi, who bites off and swallows Anu's genitals and thereby becomes impregnated with three deities—the Storm God Teshub, the Tigris River, and Tasmisu (Hittite Suwaliyat). The precise details of what followed these events remain uncertain because of the fragmentary state of the text. But presumably the song went on to tell of the birth of Teshub (by one means or another), an ensuing struggle with his surrogate parent Kumarbi, and his eventual triumph.

The song of divine conflict is sometimes referred to as the *Theogony*, 'the Birth of the Gods', because of its similarities to the Greek poet Hesiod's poem of that name. The title is rather more apt in the latter case since like the Babylonian Myth of Creation it does deal with the procreation of gods as well as with their subsequent conflicts, whereas what we have of the Hurrian-derived composition launches almost immediately into the generation conflicts and confines its account of procreational matters to the peculiar pre-natal history of Teshub and his two siblings: 'Stop rejoicing within yourself!', the emasculated Anu tells his conqueror. 'I have placed inside you a burden. First I have impregnated you with the noble Storm God. Second I have impregnated you with the irresistible Tigris River. Third I have impregnated you with the noble Tasmisu. Three terrible gods I have placed inside you as burdens. In the future you will end up striking the boulders of Mount Tassa with your head!'[18]

It is this bizarre detail that provides one of several points of comparison with the Hesiodic composition. The gods of three successive generations in the Kumarbi myth—Anu (heaven), Kumarbi (father of the gods), and Teshub—correspond precisely to Ouranos (heaven), Kronos (Phoenician El), and Zeus in Hesiod's poem. Just as Kumarbi emasculates Anu, so too does Kronos mutilate his father Ouranos. In both cases, the dismembered genitals produce further offspring—in the Kumarbi tradition three deities who rise up against the mutilator, in the Hesiodic a race of Furies and monstrous giants who are produced when the blood of the severed parts seeps into the earth; the latter rise up against all the gods but are defeated and imprisoned in the earth. Kumarbi and Kronos are both forewarned that they face further threats—Kumarbi from the offspring, now growing within him, of his mutilated predecessor, and Kronos from one of his own conventionally produced offspring. In spite of measures taken by Kronos and presumably also by Kumarbi to forestall this (the relevant passage of the Hittite text is lost), the prophecy comes to pass. Kumarbi is overthrown and replaced by Teshub, Kronos by Teshub's Greek counterpart Zeus. In each case this marks the beginning of a new era, the Teshub-led pantheon of the Hurrian–Hittite world, the Zeus-led Olympian pantheon of the Greek world.

One difference between the Near Eastern and Greek traditions is that the former begins one generation earlier, at least as far as the male gods are concerned. Alalu has no counterpart in Hesiod's *Theogony*, which begins with Ouranos, the counterpart to Alalu's successor Anu.[19] There is a further difference. In Hesiod's version, the successive generations of gods all belong to the one family: Gaea is the mother and wife of Ouranos, who sires all her children including Kronos, later to become the father of Zeus. In the Near Eastern tradition on the other hand, the warring gods come from two separate families and appear in alternate generations: Alalu and Kumarbi represent one family line, Anu and Teshub the other.[20] Professor Hoffner remarks that these opposing families are from opposite spheres: 'Kumarbi is a netherworld god, whereas Teshub is a celestial god . . . Kumarbi's father Alalu is driven from the throne by Anu and takes refuge from Anu in the netherworld. Later, when Anu flees from Kumarbi, he heads for the sky. When one assembles a list of the deities in these myths who give allegiance to one side or the other, the opposition of netherworld and sky is confirmed.'[21]

Does this provide an indication of the myth's original purpose? In its earliest form it might have been associated with a ritual depicting a contest between forces of netherworld and upper world, and the ultimate triumph of the latter. However, with the myth's progressive development and elaboration in literary form, its links with its original ritual context became increasingly tenuous, though even by the time it reached the Hittite world these links were still detectable in the conflicts between gods from opposing families representing opposing forces or spheres of nature.

When the tradition surfaced in the Greek world, it retained the account of struggles between successive generations of gods. But a key element was now missing. No longer was the battle arena occupied by members of opposing families representing opposing forces of nature. The contestants all belonged to a single family line. That reflects a major shift in the tradition, and a major narrowing of its limits, from a cosmogonically to a generationally based conflict. It was the end of any last vestige of the tradition's ritual origins. Hesiod's poem has nothing to do with ritual. It tells a story, and in the process establishes a genealogical framework for the early generations of gods and provides a context for the emergence and triumph of the Olympians. The poet himself, Herodotos tells us, was largely responsible for the arrangement of his material, and presumably also for its selection. He may well have been aware that there were two competing divine genealogies in the original tradition on which he drew. But once the tradition had been cut adrift from its ritual origins, this became an extraneous detail. There was no longer any point in cluttering the genealogical scheme of things with two separate family lines.

A common feature of many *theomachias* is that no matter how thoroughly and comprehensively the losers are defeated, sometimes to the point of total dismemberment, they re-emerge to fight the victor another day, or else find or create a formidable monster to do this for them. From the rest of the songs in the Kumarbi cycle, fragmentary though they are, it is clear that the Storm God's ascendancy after his triumph over Kumarbi is far from secure. He may even have been replaced for a time by another god, LAMMA,[22] but he was in any case subject to further challenges from Kumarbi. These come to a head in the second major text of the song cycle, the so-called 'Song of Ullikummi'. Seeking to create a champion to act on his behalf for a final showdown with Teshub, Kumarbi mates with a mountain peak. A diorite monster results from the union. 'Henceforth let Ullikummi be his name,' says Kumarbi. 'Let him go up to heaven to kingship. Let him suppress the fine city of Kummiya (the Storm God's city). Let him strike Teshub. Let him chop him up fine like chaff. Let him grind him under foot like an ant. Let him snap off Tasmisu like a brittle reed. Let him scatter all the gods down from the sky like flour. Let him smash them like empty pottery bowls.'[23]

At Kumarbi's bidding, his son is secretly conveyed to the netherworld after his birth by the Irsirra deities and placed on the right shoulder of Ubelluri, whose feet are in the netherworld but who supports heaven and earth like the Greek Atlas. 'Let him grow higher each month, each day,' Kumarbi orders. And so it comes to pass. When he has grown so large that the sea comes only to his middle, the Sun God sees him and is greatly alarmed. He reports the news to Teshub, who resolves to do battle with the monster. But when he sees him he is filled with dismay: 'Teshub sat down on the ground and his tears flowed like streams. Tearfully Teshub said, "Who can any longer behold the struggle of such a one? Who go on fighting? Who can behold the terrors of such a one any longer?"'

Teshub is powerless against such an opponent. His sister Shaushka volunteers to approach Ullikummi and attempt to win him over by her songs and her charms. To no avail. 'For whose benefit are you singing?' a great sea-wave asks of her. 'For whose benefit are you filling your mouth with wind? Ullikummi is deaf; he cannot hear. He is blind in his eyes; he cannot see. He has no compassion. So go away, Shaushka, and find your brother before Ullikummi becomes really valiant, before the skull of his head becomes really terrifying.'

Teshub engages, unsuccessfully, in a first battle with Ullikummi. The monster continues to grow until it reaches the very gates of Teshub's city Kummiya. In desperation, and at the suggestion of his brother Tasmisu, Teshub makes a final appeal to Ea, the Mesopotamian god of wisdom, formerly a supporter of Kumarbi. Ea resolves to bring the conflict to an end. He calls for the cutting tool originally used to sever heaven from earth and uses it to cut Ullikummi from Ubelluri's shoulder. The monster's power is destroyed, and Ea urges the gods to do battle with him. They respond with alacrity, 'bellowing like cattle at Ullikummi'. Teshub mounts his war-wagon and charges to the sea. Though the end of the story is lost, Teshub must have confronted Ullikummi and perhaps also Kumarbi in a final showdown, and defeated them. Once more his sovereignty is secure.

Again, a number of parallels to the song can be found in Greek, more specifically Hesiodic, mythological tradition, in which the serpent monster Typhoeus rises up against Zeus after the latter's defeat of the Titans and tries to seize his throne from him. Closer still is the parallel between Ullikummi and Typhoeus/Typhon preserved in a later Greek tradition in which Typhon like Ullikummi grows to such a towering height that he reaches the heavens.[24] And most significantly the Teshub–Ullikummi and Zeus–Typhon conflicts are fought out in the same location, Mt Hazzi/Kasios on the coast of northern Syria.

Though clearly Hurrian in origin we cannot, in the absence of the original Hurrian text, determine how closely the Hittite version of the Kumarbi song cycle followed the original. The possibilities range from an actual translation to an essentially new composition based on an imported Hurrian tradition. The Hurrian tradition itself had clearly drawn on earlier Mesopotamian traditions, as evidenced by the Babylonian names of the deities Alalu, Anu, Enlil, Ea, and also by the very notion of gods from successive generations competing for divine sovereignty, and of vanquished gods rising up to do battle once more with their victors. In the original Mesopotamian context myth and ritual were in all probability closely integrated.

This gives rise to an obvious question. Once the myth was cut adrift from a ritual context, why was it preserved, firstly in a Hurrian milieu, then in a Hittite? Hardly because it was seen as providing a repository of spiritual or moral guidance like the canonical scriptures of a number of other religions. With the best will in the world it is very difficult to see anything at all spiritually or morally uplifting in the Kumarbi tradition. Perhaps it served to celebrate Teshub's ultimate triumph, although like his Storm God counterpart in the Illuyanka myth Teshub's own role in achieving this triumph was quite a secondary and none too glorious one; he gives way to despondency and tears on first seeing the monster, progress towards the monster's defeat is made only through the initiative of other deities, and his final victory comes only after Ea has virtually handed it to him on a plate, so to speak. None the less the song cycle had clearly become an integral part of Hurrian cultural tradition and it was this no doubt which ensured its preservation in a Hittite milieu within the context of the progressive Hurrianization of Hittite culture. Professor Lebrun comments on the educative value of the Hurrian myths: '[They] offered the Hittites a basic religious framework and defined the function as well as the kinship of certain gods; at the same time they gave explanatory shape for the hierarchy among the gods.'[25]

All this implies that the myths were not simply put on tablets and then buried away in palace archives. Rather they must often have been dusted off and recited before appropriate company. This may well have been a regular feature of the court activities of Hattusili III and probably also that of his son and successor Tudhaliya IV. The common factor in both cases was the Hurrian-originating queen Puduhepa, wife of one king, mother of the other, and a leading figure in the religious reform programme. Recitations of works like the Kumarbi song cycle may well have played a significant part in this programme, very likely with mandatory attendance at the performances by appropriate officials in the palace and temple bureaucracy. This was probably no great burden. After all the songs were not tedious litanies of repetitive formulaic phrases but exciting stories worth hearing over and over again. They had considerable entertainment value with their parade of monsters, battles, and other violent deeds, and their bizarre sexual unions, described in explicit detail—features which probably also ensured that tales from the cycle had wide currency on a popular level throughout the kingdom. Reciters of such tales were no doubt as common in the village communities of the Hittite world as they have been in non-literate communities of all ages.

CHAPTER 13
The Capital

> On its site I sowed weeds. May the Storm God strike down anyone who becomes king after me and resettles Hattusa!

In these words King Anitta condemned to oblivion the city he had just destroyed—Hattusa, the chief obstacle to his expanding empire in central Anatolia during the pre-Hittite Assyrian Colony period. It now lay in ruins, never again to be resettled! But its destroyer's curse had short-lived effect. Some 150 years later, a new city arose on the abandoned, weed-covered site. Its founder, very likely, was King Hattusili I. Whether or not he knew of the curse, it was clearly incompatible with his developing vision of a brave new world, a powerful new kingdom, of which this derelict place would be the focal point. Its natural advantages were obvious. The thickly forested surrounds provided ample quantities of timber for the predominantly wooden buildings to be constructed in the city. There was good soil for agricultural purposes in the nearby valleys. Seven springs guaranteed an abundant all-year-round water supply. The site was well located in relation to communication routes, from both north to south and east to west. And the natural rocky outcrop jutting above the site provided a ready-made, easily defensible location for a royal citadel.

Hattusa's Main Phases

There were five main phases to the city's existence. The first marked the transition between Early and Middle Bronze Age around the beginning of the second millennium. The second belonged to the Assyrian Colony period, and ended with its destruction by Anitta. The fifth belonged to the post-Hittite Phrygian period, during which the city was rebuilt, on a more modest scale, following its destruction at the end of the Bronze Age. Our concern will be with the third and fourth phases, when Hattusa was the seat of the royal Hittite dynasty, capital of the Land of Hatti.

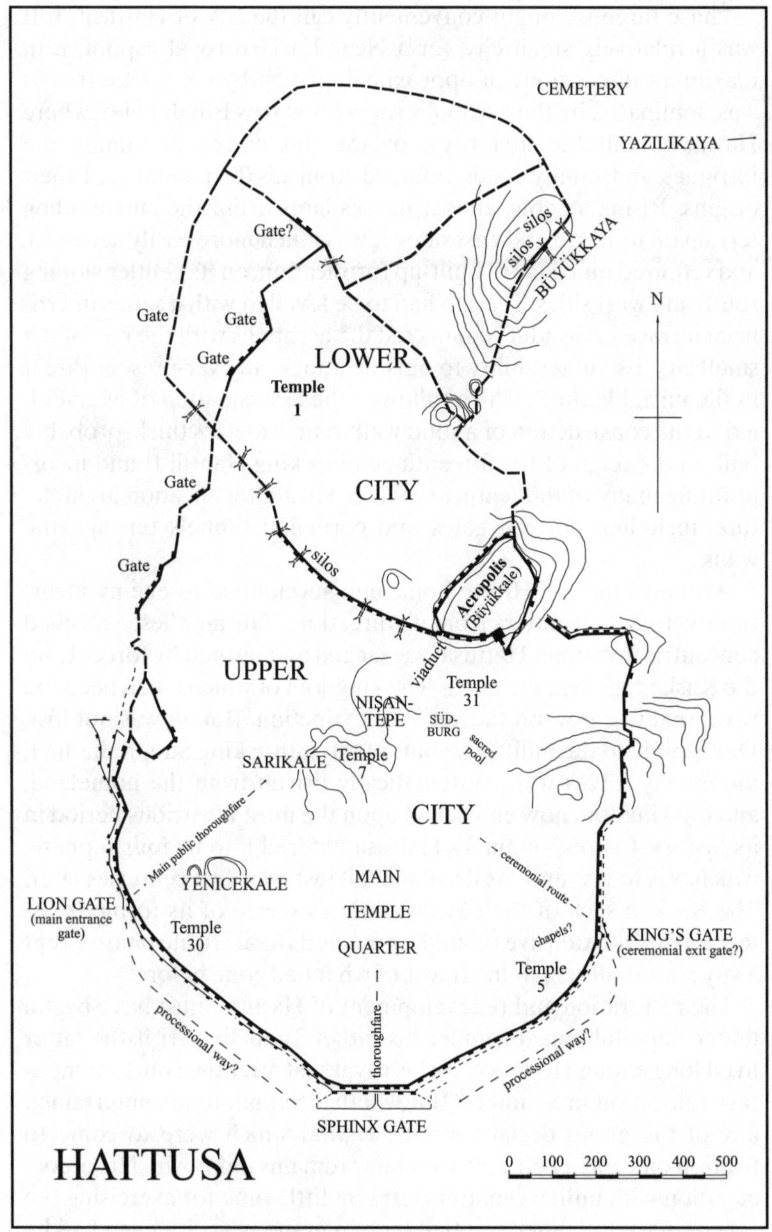

Fig. 10. Plan of Hattusa

Phase three we might conveniently call the city of Hattusili I. It was a relatively small city, for a Near Eastern royal capital, with maximum dimensions of approximately 1.25 by 0.5 kilometres. It was dominated by the acropolis (now known as Büyükkale), where Hattusili built the first royal palace and where, no doubt, the intrigues and family feuds referred to in his Testament had their origins. Rising steeply, almost unassailably, from the surrounding terrain on its north and east sides, it was much more easily accessed, and required much more built-up fortification, on its gentler sloping south and west sides. The site had to be levelled with a series of artificial terraces. A viaduct connected the acropolis with the rest of the small city. Its vulnerability to outside attack, an ever-present threat in the unstable times which followed the assassination of Mursili I, led to the construction of a solid wall some 8 metres thick, probably built in the reign of the fifteenth-century king Hantili II and incorporating many of the features of later Hittite fortification architecture, including postern gates and corbelled tunnels through the walls.

Around 1400 the Hittite homeland succumbed to enemy incursions across its frontiers from all directions. During these so-called concentric invasions, Hattusa was sacked and burned by forces from the Kaska region in the north. The kingdom of which it had been the royal seat was now on the verge of extinction. But all was not lost. Due mainly to the military genius of the future king Suppiluliuma I, the enemy forces were systematically driven from the homeland, and the kingdom now embarked upon the most illustrious period in its history. Correspondingly, Hattusa entered into its fourth phase, which was to last until its dramatic fall just over two centuries later. The Kaskan sack of the city left little evidence of its former existence. And its extensive rebuilding in this its final Hittite phase swept away almost all remaining traces of what had gone before.

The restoration and redevelopment of Hattusa must have begun under Suppiluliuma, or under his father Tudhaliya III if the latter lived long enough to reoccupy his royal seat after the court's temporary relocation in Samuha.[1] But whether Suppiluliuma entertained any of the grand designs for the capital which were to come to fruition one and a half centuries later remains unknown. His preoccupation with military matters left him little time for exercising the role of master planner and builder of a grand new city, even had he the inclination to do so. Subsequent events have left us with little knowledge of what sort of city it was that he handed to his successor on his death. If we accept at face value the claims by his son Mursili about the deplorable condition of the land at this time and the decimation of its population by the ravages of plague, the 'new' city may already have been in a state of some disrepair. If so, the situation probably did not improve much under Mursili, at least during the first part of his reign when his kingdom was still suffering from the effects of the plague. In any case Mursili like his father seems to have spent virtually every year of his reign on military campaigns; and when he was not campaigning, other urgent demands of royal office probably left him little time to devote to refurbishing his capital. Even had he embarked on a redevelopment programme, this would almost certainly have been brought to a standstill by his son and successor Muwatalli, who transferred the royal seat south to Tarhuntassa. Hattusa was not entirely abandoned, but placed under the immediate jurisdiction of the king's Chief Scribe Mittannamuwa. However, its decline in status and the redirection of resources to the new capital must inevitably have led to its further material decline.

Within a few years Hattusa was restored as the capital under Urhi-Teshub, Muwatalli's son and successor. But Urhi-Teshub's relatively short, unstable occupancy of the throne probably meant that during his reign too the city continued to languish. Indeed it is not unlikely that it suffered further substantial damage in the course of the civil war between Urhi-Teshub and his uncle Hattusili. A statement later made by Hattusili after he had seized his nephew's throne suggests that fighting between the opposing sides raged through Hattusa as well as outside it, resulting very likely in the destruction of a number of its public buildings including the royal treasury.

But finally, in what were almost the kingdom's last years, the city achieved an unprecedented magnitude and magnificence—like a firework that flares most brilliantly in the moments before it flickers out. Its concept, design, and execution are all attributed to King Tudhaliya IV, third-last king of the Bronze Age dynasty. And certainly it was in his reign that the new city took shape. But the concept at least, if not also the design, may have been inspired by his father and predecessor Hattusili III. So too the concept of the redeveloped sanctuary at Yazılıkaya was one which father and son shared. Eager as Hattusili was to establish the credentials of his own family line as provider of the legitimate occupants of the Hittite throne, he might well have seen a radical redevelopment of the capital as an important means of doing this. Henceforth this new city would forever be closely identified with *his* branch of the royal dynasty—the branch that had vigorously reasserted Hattusa's pre-eminent position in the empire after its degradation and dramatic loss of status under Hattusili's brother Muwatalli.[2] The usurper could thus assume the role of the traditionalist, the restorer of the old order of things. That would surely have won him support in many quarters, both human and divine. Moreover, the size and splendour of the redeveloped capital would leave no doubt in the minds of both foreign and vassal rulers that its chief occupant was indeed worthy of the title 'Great King'.

Layout of the City

The city had two distinct parts. The original or 'Lower City' (which we have called the city of Hattusili) occupied the northern district of the capital and was dominated in its south-east sector by the royal acropolis. To the north-west of it lay the city's largest and most important temple, the Temple of the Storm God. The palace complex on the acropolis was substantially redeveloped by Tudhaliya in the thirteenth century. But it was the massive expansion of the city to the south, more than doubling its size to a total of approximately 165 hectares, that was the most spectacular achievement of Tudhaliya's reign. It is in this region, overlooking the original city and commonly referred to as the 'Upper City' (which we have called the city of Tudhaliya), that the German excavations have been concentrated since 1978.

Up until these excavations, the extent of the city in its final Hittite phase was already known from the wall which totally enclosed it. Some 8 to 10 metres in height, it incorporated towers at 20-metre intervals and a number of tower-flanked access gates, the most notable of which are embellished with monumental relief sculptures—the so-called Lion, King's, and Sphinx Gates. Two gates in the city's north-west sector gave access to the Lower City. Four temples had also been unearthed in the Upper City (designated by the numbers 2 to 5), providing a first indication of the overall purpose and character of the new region. The excavations conducted by Professor Neve from 1978 onwards brought to light twenty-six more temples in the Upper City, covering an area of over one square

Fig. 11. Temples in Upper City

kilometre, which confirmed its sacred and ceremonial character. It was clearly built according to plan, in contrast to the 'organic growth' of the old city. But though Lower and Upper Cities are quite different in character and concept, and developed in periods some centuries apart, there is none the less a strong sense of coherence, a spiritual as well as a physical relationship, between them. The Upper City must have been deliberately planned in this way. Neve sees the layout of the whole city as symbolizing the cosmic world-form of the Hittites—with the palace as the earthly world, the temple city as the godly world, and the cult district lying in between as providing the passage from the transient to the eternal.[3]

From the three main arched, tower-flanked gates symmetrically located in the city wall's southern bend, traffic-ways led north through the environs of the temple district, converging finally on a rocky outcrop, built up as a fortress and guarded by two colossal sphinxes, now called Nişantepe.[4] Along with the nearby Südburg complex (see below), it formed a link between temple quarter and palace district. Professor Neve believes that the three gateways were integrated into a sacred, ceremonial way used on festival occasions:

the festival procession started from Temple 5, passed outside the city via the 'King's' Gate, and then progressed around the foot of the wall up a staircase to the bastion of the Sphinx Gate; from there it proceeded down a second staircase to the west side of the bastion, and thence downhill to the Lion Gate, where it again entered the city.[5]

The City's Nature and Image

By at least the last century of its existence Hattusa had developed the character of a purely sacred, ceremonial city. Thus Neve and others have concluded, from the great number of temples and other sacred buildings to which the Upper City was almost entirely devoted. But we should reflect a little on this conclusion. Many ancient cities might be categorized in this way if we were to judge them primarily on what we know of their architecture and iconography. Constantine the Great's city on the Bosporus provides a classic example. Even Periclean Athens could be so categorized on the basis of its temple-dominated archaeological remains and its sacred ceremonial route, the Panathenaic Way. The Hittite world itself may well have provided a number of examples. Indeed the homeland's most important regional cities—like Arinna, Nerik, and Zippalanda—were also predominantly 'holy cities', whose architectural features and overall layout may not have differed markedly from those of the capital, if on a smaller scale.[6]

Of course city-names need to be firmly tied to actual locations and material remains before we can be entirely sure of this. And the establishment of demonstrably correct links between names and locations may still be some time off. Even so, a number of scholars have already proposed identifying either Arinna or Zippalanda with the site now known as Alaca Höyük (approximately 30 kilometres from Hattusa), whose well-known relief scenes, on the blocks flanking the Sphinx Gate, almost certainly feature a religious festival in progress (see Chapter 11); their prominence at the very entrance to the city, along with the large palace–temple complex within, suggests that here too was a 'sacred, ceremonial city'. The representation of such festival rites on a gate which formed part of the fortification walls of a citadel would be surprising, comments Professor Mellink, if the whole complex did not bear such a sacral character.[7]

A note of caution needs to be sounded. In labelling certain cities in this way we should be aware that in a world in which religious activity permeates virtually all aspects of life, sacred and secular cannot easily be disarticulated. To identify one city as sacred and by implication others as secular is to make a distinction which would probably have had as little meaning for a Hittite as it would have had for an Egyptian or a Babylonian or indeed for a member of many another civilization, ancient or modern. In the Hittite world all towns of any size were probably dominated by temple establishments, with life revolving very largely around religious activities of one kind or another in honour of one god or another. There were after all a great many deities to be attended to, not all of whom could be accommodated in the capital and other major centres.

Hattusa's extensive redevelopment in the last decades of its existence was calculated to impress, to leave no doubt that the Hittite empire's first city was also one of the pre-eminent metropolises of the entire Late Bronze Age world. This was first made evident to the visitor as his approach to the city brought him in sight of the massive fortifications, extending over a total distance of some 5 kilometres. The main casemate wall reared up on an earth rampart to a height of 10 metres, punctuated by towers at 20-metre intervals along its entire length. Before it was a second curtain wall, also with towers built in the intervals between those of the main wall. Skilfully adapted to the rugged terrain, the fortifications not merely encompassed the new Upper City but were extended to the north-east, spanning a deep gorge and enclosing within the city limits a mountain outcrop now called Büyükkaya. Crossing the gorge twice on north and south, this north-east extension (though not entirely finished at the time of the city's final destruction) must rank as one of the most impressive engineering achievements of the Late Bronze Age world. But one must ask whether it was intended primarily to impress, rather than to serve any genuine practical purpose. Dr Singer comments similarly about the new city's fortifications in general; they were more suited to impressing the viewer and perhaps the gods than to withstanding a determined military attack.[8]

Given a desire to advertise to the world Hattusa's resplendent new face, given the festival-oriented character of Hittite society, we might well expect that the redevelopment of the capital was marked by great celebrations in which subjects and foreigners and gods alike participated, perhaps along the lines of a Great Durbar like that which the pharaoh Akhenaten celebrated in his new city Akhetaten. In any case, official visits to the city by vassal rulers and foreign dignitaries were probably marked by much pomp and ceremony, beginning with their entry to the city. These were no doubt also occasions for the display of tribute arriving from the vassal states—vessels of gold and silver, garments of fine linen, red- and blue-dyed woollen textiles of the highest quality,[9] as well as the gifts brought to the Great King by the emissaries of his brother-rulers.

The Main Gateways

Almost certainly official visitors to the capital entered it via its south-west entrance, the 'Lion Gate', so called because of the pair of

Fig. 12. Lion Gate

lions which appear on the external gate jambs and face directly outwards from the city. Their protomes carved in the round, they are depicted as if in the process of emerging from the solid rock, ready to challenge the city's enemies and roaring their defiance at any who dare approach with hostile intent. That at least is one way of looking at them. They have become a kind of general symbol of the Hittite world, of Hittite royalty in particular, the physical counterpart of the text-images of a mighty leonine ruler who pounces ruthlessly upon his prey. Of course the lion symbol has been adopted by many royal and aristocratic dynasties throughout the ages. The Hittites certainly had no monopoly on it. In European tradition it goes back at least to the Lion Gate at Mycenae (a close contemporary of Hattusa's Lion Gate), whose relief of confronting lions above the main entrance has been called, perhaps not too fancifully, the royal coat-of-arms of the House of Agamemnon, the first coat-of-arms in the Western world.

Though now rather weather-beaten, the Hattusa lions still show clear signs of the care and precision with which they were carved, as particularly illustrated in the minute attention to the treatment of the patterned hair of the mane. But this very stylization is significant. These creatures are hardly of a kind likely to inspire terror in an approaching enemy. They are not, nor ever were even in their pristine state, particularly ferocious of aspect. In fact Hittite lions seldom are,[10] in contrast to the savage brutes depicted in Assyrian relief sculpture or even in miniature on the famous dagger blade from Mycenae. They are generally rather benign-looking creatures. If the Hattusa lions were supposed to reflect the sort of spirit and ferocity which an enemy mounting an attack on the city might encounter from its defenders, the enemy might feel rather more reassured than unnerved. Their image is one of regal dignity rather than ferocity. They are essentially emblematic in function, serving to remind the visitor that he is about to enter the city which contains the royal seat of the Hittite world.

The south-east gate is commonly known as the King's Gate, so named because of the sculpted figure which appears on the left of the inside of the gateway. Over 2 metres high, this monumental figure represents one of the Hittites' finest artistic achievements—so fine in fact that some critics have suggested, quite unjustifiably, that it must have been the work of a foreign artist.[11] In contrast to the flat, low relief of most surviving Hittite sculpture, the figure is modelled in high relief, with much attention to anatomical detail, including

Fig. 13. 'King's' Gate

chest hair and nail cuticles, and with a plasticity which realistically depicts the body's planes and muscular development. The figure is male. His dress and equipment are those of a warrior. He wears a helmet, with long plume and cheek flaps, and a kilt, and carries a battle axe in his right hand and a curved sword at his side. His hair is long in the Hittite manner. Three-quarters of his face is visible, as though he is in the process of turning his gaze upon those who are leaving the city. The expression on his face is one of benevolence. His left arm is raised and his fist clenched, as a salute, or gesture of farewell. Though the sculpture has inspired the name 'King's Gate', it almost certainly represents a god. It may well be Tudhaliya's tutelary deity Sharruma, his presence at the city's exit serving to reassure the king that his guidance and protection will always be with him in the days of military campaigning that lie ahead.

The Sphinx Gate lies between the 'King's' and Lion Gates, at the city's highest point (now called Yerkapı). Providing only indirect access to the outer world, as Bittel notes, well protected against assault by the defences of Yerkapı, it was not in regular use by traffic passing into and from the city. Two pairs of sphinxes were carved on the gateway's jambs, one pair facing outwards from the city, the other inwards. Unlike their Egyptian prototypes, Hittite sphinxes are invariably female. They appear relatively frequently in the iconography, here and at Alaca Höyük (where the sphinxes, over 2 metres in height, are carved on the city's external gateposts) on a monumental scale, with a number of variations in detail. At Hattusa's Sphinx Gate, the inward-facing figures are the more elaborately carved of the two pairs. Again we have the sense of figures in the very process of emerging from the rock, their foreparts almost fully disengaged, the remainder of their bodies, down to their erect tails, presented in high profile. In a pattern of whirls and curves, their headdresses are carved in the form of spiralling branches, their wings unfurled in magnificent fanlike formations. (In this respect they contrast with the Alaca sphinxes, who wear an Egyptian-type cowl which ends in curls over the breast.[12]) From their lofty station, they gaze tranquilly over the activities in the city below. They represent benevolent forces under whose protection the city's inhabitants lie—at least for the time being.

The Temples

Entry to the city via the Sphinx Gate brought one into the central temple quarter. Here some twenty-five temples were clustered, the larger varying in size from 1,200 to 1,500 square metres, the smaller from 400 to 600 square metres. Most were built within the kingdom's last decades, all with similar design and layout: they were square or rectangular in plan, with an entry portal leading to an inner court, with pillared portico, which gave access through a vestibule to the *adyton* or inner sanctuary where the image of the god was housed. This holy of holies was always off-centre, deliberately so designed to ensure there was no direct view into it from the entry portal. A basement room or cellar was often constructed beneath the sanctuary floor.[13] The temples' cult statues have long since disappeared, along with much else of their sculptural ornamentation. However, reliefs featuring lions and sphinxes may once have embellished their walls and pillar-bases and perhaps their entrance portals as guardian figures, to judge from the remains of such creatures which formed part of the architectonic decoration of Temples 2 and 3.[14] A dark green granite-like gabbro was used in the sculptural decoration, which must have served to highlight the figures against their limestone background. The same material was also used in the Temple of the Storm God in the Lower City (here too was found in the temple's south magazine, a large cube-like shape of green nephrite of unknown function). It may well be that this material had a significance which went beyond the purely ornamental. In addition to the cult images, other free-standing figures may have served to decorate the temples, along with painted, or painted stucco, friezes. But nothing remains of such embellishments or of the items used in the temple's rituals and ceremonies beyond a small collection of figurines, libation vessels, and other votive objects.

Excavations have proved more productive of another group of artefacts. The temple cellars seemed to have served as archive rooms, for all the temples have produced a range of inscribed material—stamp seals, clay bullae, seal impressions, and clay tablets recording donations, ritual procedures, and oracle enquiries—generally found on the cellar floors. The largest collections, which have come from Temples 15 and 16, included amongst their contents tablets from a mythological text-series in Hurrian–Hittite bilingual form,[15] and some Akkadian fragments of the Gilgamesh epic. This may provide evidence of the temples' role as centres for scribal training. The temple personnel were no doubt housed in the residential quarters which lay close by the temples. Here too were workshops. As we have already noted, Hittite temples had a range of functions—administrative, economic, and industrial—beyond the purely cultic.

On either side of the central temple quarter was a large temple precinct, Temples 5 and 30 so called. In keeping, it seems, with the Upper City's symmetrical layout, each was close by and perhaps ceremonially and functionally related to one of the city's main access gates. The Temple 5 precinct was located near the 'King's' Gate, the Temple 30 precinct near the Lion Gate. Professor Neve notes that with an area of almost 3,000 square metres, Temple 5 is by far the biggest sacred building in the Upper City, and is also remarkable for its special layout, with temple complemented by a 'palace-annexe' and three small 'chapels'. In one of these ('House A') a relief some 90 centimetres in height was discovered, depicting a warrior in short skirt armed with lance and wearing a horned cap. Above its left fist the name Tudhaliya appears in hieroglyphs. Neve suggests that since the horned cap represents a deified ruler and therefore a dead one, the Tudhaliya so identified is an ancestral namesake of Tudhaliya IV (perhaps his great-great-grandfather Tudhaliya III), and that the so-called chapel complex was dedicated to the king's lineal ancestors—Tudhaliya III, his grandfather Mursili II, and his father Hattusili III.[16] Though clear evidence for Neve's conclusions is lacking, one might reasonably if tentatively conclude with him that Temple 5 was erected as a private precinct of the king, with special chapels dedicated to the worship of his ancestors.

That might in turn suggest a close relationship between precinct and 'King's' Gate, noting again that the sculptured figure on the gate looks *inward*, towards the precinct. Its position gives the gate predominantly the character of an *exit* gate. It is the last image one sees as one leaves the city. For King Tudhaliya this would most appropriately be his tutelary deity Sharruma. Or in line with Neve's suggestion that part of the precinct was devoted to ancestor worship, it could represent one of the king's ancestors, now deified, who might also have served to inspire him as he departed his city. Here in this precinct the king perhaps spent his final hours, in communion with his god and his ancestors, before setting forth on whatever external enterprise lay ahead of him.

All in all, it seems likely that the 'King's' Gate was used primarily if not exclusively for special occasions—ceremonial processions, royal departures on religious pilgrimages, military campaigns, and the like. It is most improbable that it was used by regular everyday traffic, particularly if the Temple 5 precinct was closely associated with it and reserved for the personal use of the king. The obsession with isolating the king from all sources of contamination would surely have required a greater degree of separation from the noise, the dust, the pollution of human bodies than would have been possible if the 'King's' Gate were in regular use by the city's inhabitants and visitors.

That leaves only the Lion Gate as the city's main public entrance.

In fact it is the only gate in the city which has all the characteristics of a public entrance-way. It alone both provides direct access to the city and is embellished by monumental sculptures which face *outwards*, towards the approaching traveller. Further, the lion figures are the only gate sculptures which convey unequivocally to all comers that they are entering a royal capital. Given that Tudhaliya devoted so much time and so many resources to making Hattusa into a show city, he would certainly have ensured that visitors to the city, at least official ones, entered it by the one gateway which really did provide a fittingly impressive introduction to it.

That raises the question of the Temple 30 precinct, which serves as a kind of counterpart to Temple 5, and consists of a separate sanctuary situated the same distance from the Lion Gate as Temple 5 is from the 'King's' Gate. Though possessing some of the features of Temple 5, it was built on a more modest scale. Unfortunately its abandonment after its destruction following the first phase of the building of the Upper City and the replacement of it by simple residences and workshops leave us with virtually no indication of what its purpose and function were. Perhaps, corresponding to what we have suggested for Temple 5, it served as some kind of private sanctuary for the king on his return to the city.

Official Visitors to the Capital

After entering the capital via the Lion Gate, visitors to His Majesty travelled first through the Upper City, either skirting or passing through the central temple district as they made their way towards the acropolis. To the south-west of the acropolis lay the rocky outcrop we have referred to above called Nişantepe. A building erected on the site during the reign of the last known king, Suppiluliuma II, may have been intended as his *hekur*, his final burial place. Here an eleven-line hieroglyphic inscription was discovered, the longest known Hittite inscription in the hieroglyphic script, unfortunately weathered to the point where it is illegible except for its opening words. Nişantepe has, however, produced another rich find. Excavations conducted on the site in 1990 brought to light a 'seal archive' consisting of almost 3,300 items—3,268 clay bullae and 28 land-grant documents, ranging in date from the reign of Suppiluliuma I to the end of the kingdom. Increasing many times over the number of such impressions previously known to us, they serve as a valuable source of information in a number of respects on the history of the kingdom in its last two centuries.[17]

Two viaducts, 85 metres long, linked Nişantepe and the Upper City with the acropolis. They provided access to the palace for functionaries and officials in the king's service who lived outside the palace precincts, for vassal rulers come to pay their yearly homage to the king, and for envoys on diplomatic missions from foreign Great Kings. After being admitted by the sentries on duty at the citadel's south-west gate, the dignitary and his retinue were escorted by royal attendants through a series of colonnaded courts, each with its own entrance portal, to the upper floor of a large two-storey building. (There was another main gate in the south-east corner. A third gate in the southern part of the western wall was suitable for pedestrian traffic between the citadel and the Lower City but was probably not used on official ceremonial occasions.[18]) The ground floor contained a complex of storage chambers. On the upper floor was a pillared hall some fifty metres in length, forty in width.[19]

Here the Great King held audience. When all were assembled, he was announced by the court herald and made a grand separate entrance from the palace's innermost royal apartments. In the Great Hall, vassal rulers appeared before His Majesty, to renew their vows of loyalty and pay their annual tribute. No doubt they also reported to him on the state of their kingdom and the region in which it lay, the king's scribes assiduously recording the details. Here *kuirwana*-kings, rulers of 'protectorate' states, reported and paid their respects.[20] The Great King's own high-ranking dignitaries did them the honour of rising in their presence as a mark of respect, thus maintaining what was largely a diplomatic fiction—that they really were of higher status than mere vassals. Here too envoys from His Majesty's Brother-Kings presented their credentials. In audience with His Majesty they broadly outlined proposals which their king had commissioned them to bring to Hattusa, or they gave responses from their king to proposals which Hittite envoys had taken to their own land. Detailed negotiations would follow at a later stage between them and His Majesty's own representatives. Here, the Egyptian envoy Hani finally persuaded King Suppiluliuma to send one of his sons to Egypt, to become the husband of Tutankhamun's widow and ascend the pharaonic throne. It may have been here too that Suppiluliuma received news of the death of his son Zannanza while en route to Egypt for this purpose. Here Urhi-Teshub rebuffed the overtures from the envoys of the Assyrian king, thus exacerbating the tensions already mounting between Hatti and Assyria in the Euphrates region. Here no doubt King Hattusili III received envoys from the pharaoh Ramesses, sent for preliminary negotiations on the treaty which would formally mark the cessation of all hostility between the two kingdoms.

This Great Hall, which according to Naumann's reconstruction was lit by windows on three sides with entry in the centre of its east-oriented fourth side, appears to have been unique in Late Bronze Age Anatolian architecture. But while its size and spaciousness may well have inspired the admiration and wonder of the king's subjects, envoys from foreign kings, particularly from Egypt, were likely to be less impressed. Professor Bittel has suggested Egyptian influence in the concept and design of the Great Hall, and has compared the Coronation Hall at Akhetaten, though the latter's proportions were far grander. Tudhaliya had undoubtedly transformed his city into an impressive showplace of the Late Bronze Age world. But it could still not compare with the massive grandeur of the traditional royal cities of pharaonic Egypt. No doubt Hittite envoys to the court of Ramesses had this regularly pointed out to them.

The Temple of the Storm God

Even a Ramesses could hardly have failed to be impressed with what is arguably the greatest of all Hittite architectural achievements—the monumental Temple of the Storm God. This vast, sprawling complex was constructed in the Lower City to the north-west of the acropolis, and probably on the site of an earlier temple, during the reign of Hattusili III. Built on a massive artificial terrace of great stone blocks, it once rose to an imposing height above its surrounds, especially on its north and east sides. Covering an area of over 20,000 square metres (160 m. long and 135 m. wide), it is many times the size of any other temple complex within the city. In itself it was a grand enterprise. But Hattusili may have conceived of it as merely a part of something much grander still—the first step towards the realization of a comprehensive new vision for the capital, a vision which, we have suggested, was enthusiastically embraced and brought close to fruition by his son and successor Tudhaliya.

The Storm God's temple complex epitomizes the full and final development of Hittite religious architecture out of the simple

Fig. 14. Temple of the Storm God

domestic structures which probably typified Anatolian building traditions long before the Hittite period. The Hittites may have borrowed much else from their neighbours, but the evolution of their temples belongs almost entirely within native Anatolian tradition. The temples were essentially houses or household shrines built and elaborated on a monumental scale—just as in the Greek world temples were by and large an outgrowth of the simple house-like structures where the images of the gods were sheltered.

The entire complex, surrounded by a *temenos*, or enclosure wall, consists of three main elements typical of a number of Hittite temple complexes—storerooms and workrooms, quarters for the temple personnel, and the temple proper. In a number of respects it represents almost the total antithesis of Western architectural tradition, as epitomized by the Classical Greek temple. In the latter the emphasis is on simplicity of design and function, on symmetry and harmony of proportions. On entering a Greek temple one passes directly from vestibule to *cella*, the inner sanctuary which houses the god's image. And the temple is often located on a site which shows it to its best advantage, enabling the viewer to see and appreciate it in its totality. Generally it served but one purpose—to provide a shelter for the god. By contrast, the Hittite temple complex served a range of purposes, had many different parts to it, and was largely asymmetrical in concept and design.

The route to the temple proper leads obliquely through the outer precinct, so that each part of the complex is in effect screened from its adjacent areas. The complex can never be comprehended in its entirety by the visitor in its midst. Each turn of the route brings into view something new—as if to intensify, by obscuring till the last moment what lies ahead, the sense of awe and mystery felt by those who were privileged to enter the temple's inner world. The temple itself is of a roughly symmetrical rectangular design. After making the appropriate ritual ablutions, one enters it on the south-west side through a *hilammar*, an elaborate gateway flanked by porters' lodges or guard rooms. The gateway gives access to a large open-air plastered courtyard. Here, we may suppose, in the presence of Their Majesties and other dignitaries and priestly officials eligible to enter the precinct's most sacred areas, cultic ceremonies and ritual dramas took place in honour of the deities to whom the temple was dedicated. The courtyard is flanked on its north and south sides by almost identical sets of rooms, perhaps to accommodate the images of those who formed the *kaluti* or divine circles of the temple's chief deities. In the north-east of the courtyard was a small building, corresponding to a similar structure in the courtyard of the temple buildings at Yazılıkaya, where further ritual ablutions were made. For just behind lay a colonnaded entrance which gave access to the temple's inner sanctum. One was now preparing to come before the divine presence.

Though the name we commonly use for the temple suggests that it was associated only with the Storm God, it was in fact dedicated to two deities. In its holy of holies there were two shrines, one for each of the gods who stood at the head of the Hittite pantheon—the Storm God of Heaven and the Sun Goddess of Arinna,[21] now identified in Hattusili III's reign with Hurrian Teshub and his consort Hepat. Two stone bases indicate where the divine images once stood—life-size gold and silver figures, perhaps in human form, perhaps in abstract form, or perhaps in Teshub's case in the form of a bull. Particularly on a fine day, they must have been a resplendent sight. Elsewhere in the Near East, and in Classical Greece, divine images were forever enshrouded in gloom (except on festival occasions), for their sanctuaries were totally shut off from the outside world.[22] But the Hittite deities in the Great Temple's inner sanctuary (as no doubt those in the sanctuaries of other temples) were illuminated by natural light, from windows in the walls behind and on either side of them, very likely reflecting a time when deities regularly received homage in open-air sanctuaries.[23]

Of course windows not only let in the light of the outside world, but also its noise, dust, and smells. Even within the temple precincts there must have been plenty of each. The temple proper was surrounded by bakehouses, breweries, butcheries, workshops, larders for the gods' food and drink, treasuries of spoils won in battle and dedicated to the god, storerooms for the equipment and garments used in festivals and rituals, rooms where divination was carried out. There were also archive rooms containing records stored on clay tablets; the Storm God's temple was an important repository of vassal and international treaties, its most famous item being the 'eternal treaty' which Hattusili drew up with Ramesses II.

A large staff was necessary to perform all the tasks associated with the manifold aspects of a temple's life and activities. The numbers of cult personnel alone who were employed in the service of the Storm God's temple ran into the hundreds[24]—and included both those who performed duties within the temple proper, and those appointed as a kind of temple security force. The latter had the task of patrolling the temple precinct by day and night, to ensure that it was kept secure against all unauthorized entry. Penalties imposed for those who failed to carry out their responsibilities ranged from humiliating to extremely harsh:

> There shall be watchmen employed by night who shall patrol all night through. Outside, the enclosure guards shall watch; inside the temples, the temple officials patrol all night through, and they shall not sleep. Night by night one of the high priests shall be in charge of the patrols. Furthermore, someone of those who are priests shall be in charge of the gate of the temple and guard the temple. . . . If a guard fails to spend the night with his god, in the event that they do not kill him, they shall humiliate him. Naked—there shall be no garment on his body—he shall bring water three times from Labarna's cistern to the house of his god. Such shall be his humiliation.[25]

Cult personnel had living quarters within the temple precincts. But there were many others employed by the temple who may have lived outside the complex in the blocks of houses, separated by small streets or lanes, to the west and north-west of the temple—the butchers, the bakers, the brewers, the kitchen hands, the garment-makers and repairers, the carpenters, the craftsmen, and the cleaners. All formed a community within a community—a city in microcosm. As the temple personnel went about their allotted tasks, as animal carcasses were quartered, repairs made to festival chariots, dough pounded and bakehouse fires stoked, beer poured into large earthenware pots for fermentation, as carts clattered to and fro with fresh equipment and supplies, as bulky items for storage were manhandled up flights of stairs for depositing in storerooms rising at least one and perhaps two storeys above ground level—all this hubbub of daily life cannot have failed to penetrate the temple's innermost sanctum. Yet the gods were obviously not averse to some level of exposure to the noise of human activities (unlike the rancorous Mesopotamian god who was so put out by the din of humanity that he obliterated the lot of it in a flood), especially when such activities were conducted in their honour. As we have seen, they could at times be positively gregarious, on the occasions when they paraded through the city streets and countryside, and shared with their worshippers in the feasting and entertainment of festival programmes.

The People of Hattusa

A question frequently asked by the lay person is how many people lived in the capital. The answer must be depressingly vague and evasive. One can respond by saying it depends on the period, on what precisely is meant by 'living in' the city, on whether or not the city had a large floating population, and on a range of other factors. Estimates suggested by various scholars vary from 10,000 to 40,000. Both figures may well be valid for particular periods of Hittite history, the lower one for an early stage in the city's development, or for the years in Muwatalli II's reign when the city ceased to be the royal capital, the higher figure, or an even higher one, perhaps for the city's final years. But any suggested figure can be little more than a pure guess. We can always hope that the archaeologist's spade will throw more light on the matter. But as students of ancient demography will hasten to point out, evidence provided by ancient residential remains can be susceptible to a wide range of interpretations—to the point where it is of very limited use for demographic purposes. In Hattusa itself the residential areas so far known were probably largely occupied by temple or palace personnel.

We have referred to the closely settled blocks of houses in the Lower City outside the precinct of the Temple of the Storm God. These were probably occupied by the more menial functionaries in the temple's service. The basic Hittite house was a two-roomed mudbrick-and-timber-framework structure on a rubble foundation, with forecourt and sometimes upper storey with external ladder access. When space and circumstances allowed, more rooms could be added. The residential area also contained larger free-standing buildings erected on terraces, probably the houses of higher-ranking personnel. But a large part of the city's population must have lived beyond the city walls, particularly during the city's last decades when its massive redevelopment undoubtedly required a substantially increased workforce. In these final years increasing numbers of the extramural population may have settled within the walls. This is probably reflected in the reuse of the Temple 30 precinct for simple residences and workshops, and the major changes in the temple quarter in general, leading to the haphazard and apparently hastily improvised layout of houses closely packed together on the sites of former temples and on areas hitherto not built upon. Only a few temples, the larger and more important ones, continued in operation.[26] Hattusa was no longer—if it ever had been—a purely sacred, ceremonial city. Professor Neve sees these late changes as a sign of the increasingly deteriorating political and economic situation of the city—which may not least have been caused by the upheavals in the royal house. Or they may reflect an increasing sense of insecurity in general as the city and the kingdom neared its end, and the peripheral population of the capital could no longer feel confident in the king's ability to protect them.

None of this is of much help in estimating the overall size of Hattusa's population. But we can be sure that it was a very mixed and diverse one, in terms of occupations, social classes, and ethnic origins. Even if the city focused predominantly on sacred and ceremonial activities (and we have suggested that it may have been far from unique in this respect), it still needed all the human infrastructural support which any large city requires for effective functioning—to say nothing of the troops essential for its defence in the increasingly insecure last days of the kingdom, and the enormous labour force that was certainly required for the city's redevelopment. No doubt this labour force was widely recruited from beyond as well as within the homeland.

A veritable babel of languages must have echoed through the thoroughfares and byways of Hattusa—royal bureaucrats speaking the official Nesite language, Luwian-speaking descendants of booty people brought back to the homeland from Hittite campaigns in the west, Akkadian-speaking scribes and emissaries from the Babylonian king, merchants and representatives of vassal rulers from the Syrian states speaking a range of languages, Hurrian-speaking priests and diviners in the service of the city's many temples, Egyptian-speaking envoys and their retinues on business from the pharaoh and awaiting an audience with the Hittite king. Even a few persistent echoes of the old Hattic language might also have been heard.

On the official level communications between speakers of different languages could be conducted, whenever necessary, with the aid of bilingual or multilingual interpreters. No doubt a good deal of the king's business with foreign envoys was transacted in this way. But how did people communicate with each other on everyday matters in the street, given the dynamics of the population's composition, and the constant influx into the capital of foreign visitors and new residents speaking different languages? Those who belonged to a particular ethnic group and spoke the same language may well have formed their own social communities and occupied their own residential areas. But there must have been a considerable mixing of the population on a daily basis, particularly in view of the collaboration and teamwork required in the large-scale building projects of the thirteenth century. From the range of languages spoken in the capital a kind of street-speak or pidgin probably developed, made up partly of words and phrases and expressions from the different languages which various population groups had introduced into the city, but also incorporating many new words and expressions developed exclusively within a street-argot context. There must have been common words for common items of food and drink and wearing apparel—the knee-length tunic for men, the ankle-length cloak for women, and the standard footwear of shoes in assorted colours with upturned toes. An extensive repertoire of universally understood obscenities no doubt decorated the language of the large numbers of labourers and soldiers who swelled the capital's population. One would also have needed a basic common language to bargain with street vendors for trinkets, or to negotiate with the makers or purveyors of the fine jewellery much favoured in the Hittite world—earrings, finger-rings, necklaces, pendants, bracelets, little amulets in the shape of human or animal figures or sun-discs.[27]

Fire!

There must at all events have been a common word for what was potentially one of the greatest dangers to the city. Fire! Temple officials were instructed to observe the strictest vigilance in preventing an outbreak of fire in a temple in their charge. The point is emphasized by the severity of the penalty imposed upon an official whose negligence has led to a temple's destruction by fire:

> Be particularly vigilant in the matter of fire. If there is a festival in the temple, keep close watch over the fire. At nightfall, thoroughly extinguish whatever of it remains on the hearth. In the event that there is any flame in isolated spots and also dry wood, and the person responsible for extinguishing it becomes criminally negligent in the temple, he who is guilty of the crime will perish together with his descendants—even if only the temple is destroyed and Hattusa and the king's property are not harmed. Of those who are in the temple (*and thereby share in the crime of negligence*), not one is to be spared; together with their descendants they shall perish. In your own interests, then, be particularly vigilant in the matter of fire.[28]

The concerns are understandable, given the timber-framed mudbrick construction used in the great majority of the city's buildings. In one of her letters to Ramesses Queen Puduhepa refers to a fire which destroyed a major building in the capital, perhaps a royal treasury. She uses its destruction as an excuse for the delay in collecting a dowry and sending the pharaoh his Hittite bride. A major fire in Tudhaliya's reign caused serious damage to part of the walls and temple quarter.[29] And at the very end of its existence, the entire city was consumed in what must have been a spectacular conflagration.

Protection of the city against outbreaks of fire was one of the chief responsibilities of Hattusa's chief administrative official, the *Hazannu*,[30] a term generally translated as 'Burgomaster' or 'Lord Mayor'. The *Hazannu*'s immediate subordinate officers were two officials or town governors (LÚ.MEŠ MAŠKIM.URU-*LIM*), each of whom was given responsibility for one of the two districts into which the city was divided. The *Hazannu*'s duties, specified in a set of instructions,[31] assigned him prime responsibility for the city's security. Watchmen under his charge were stationed throughout the city and at various positions on the city's walls and towers. From their vantage points they not only kept a lookout for the approach of enemy forces but were also able to keep a close watch on activities within the city, directing those at ground level to extinguish unwanted fires and maintain vigilance over those which were to be kept burning. Here and in other regions, lookouts were also stationed in watchtowers outside the city, to give early warning of an enemy force while it was still some distance away.

The *Hazannu* had the further responsibility of ensuring that all the city's gates were securely locked in the evening. When these bronze-sheathed wooden barriers were swung shut, copper bolts were inserted and sealed with the stamp of the authorized officer. The following morning the seal was first inspected to ensure that it had not been tampered with, and was then broken so that the bolts could be removed and the gates opened.[32]

Last Days

In spite of the attention he must have devoted to his new city, there is little indication that in doing so Tudhaliya neglected the affairs of his kingdom at large. We do hear of one major setback in the east where his army suffered a disastrous defeat at the hands of the Assyrian king Tukulti-Ninurta—probably the result of a serious underestimation of the enemy's strength and determination—and he seems to have been faced with mounting threats in a number of parts of the kingdom. Even so, to judge from his own inscriptions, including the recently discovered hieroglyphic text from Yalburt, he dealt with the threats from at least his western subject states with considerable success. So too his son Suppiluliuma (II), the last attested Hittite king, won a number of military triumphs, along the southern Anatolian coast as well as in the waters off the coast of Alasiya (Cyprus).[33] His successes on land were achieved during an extensive campaign which he recorded in a hieroglyphic inscription in Chamber 2 of the so-called Südburg structure,[34] the recently discovered two-roomed cultic complex and sacred pool constructed in his reign in the area south of the acropolis.

Of course a king is hardly likely to proclaim his military defeats on his monuments; an impartial chronicler of the reigns of the last kings may well have indicated a situation a good deal worse than the royal inscriptions would have us believe. Above all, the enormous concentration of resources which Tudhaliya's building operations in the capital must have entailed cannot have failed to diminish his kingdom's ability to defend and maintain itself in other areas. The incentives for engaging in the enterprise, particularly given Hittite kings' sensitivity to the need to husband scarce human resources, must have been very carefully weighed up against the costs.

We have suggested that the rebuilding of the capital was associated initially with Hattusili III's efforts to establish his own family line as the legitimate royal dynasty. But there are other possibilities. Was it due to a burst of religious fervour on Tudhaliya's part, associated with his extensive programme of religious reform? Was it a desperate effort to win the favour of as many gods as possible, at a time when Tudhaliya saw his kingdom beginning to crumble around him, from internal as well as external pressures? Dramatically appealing as such explanations may be, they do not altogether square with the picture we have of an otherwise level-headed, pragmatic ruler who kept his hands on the reins of empire as firmly as was possible in those declining days.

Evidence seems to be mounting for widespread famine in the kingdom in the last years of its existence. There were urgent appeals for grain to be sent to the land of Hatti—a matter of life or death! If there were such a famine, was it necessarily due to climatic conditions? We have suggested that Hatti was becoming increasingly dependent on imported grain in the last decades of the Bronze Age, much of this grain coming from Egypt. The first indication of serious food shortages in Hatti had appeared in one of Queen Puduhepa's letters to Ramesses, urging him to take over as soon as possible the horses, cattle, and sheep forming part of the Hittite princess's dowry because, she claims, 'I have no grain left in my lands.' But chronic shortfalls in Hatti's own grain production may have been due as much to a major redeployment of manpower from its agricultural workforce as to poor rainfall and other factors of nature. It may well be that the substantial number of labourers required for building Tudhaliya's new city were recruited from the land's food-producing population. So long as grain imports could be guaranteed from abroad, however they were paid for, local shortfalls were not a serious problem. But once these imports were disrupted, or cut off altogether, by pirates or hostile coastal cities, a crisis very quickly occurred. If the Hittites then turned to their own vassal subjects for alternative sources of supply, their demands might well have led to food shortages in the lands which supplied them. The local rulers might then have found themselves in a position where they could neither satisfy their overlord's demands nor retain sufficient supplies for their own people.

Ironically, then, the rebuilding of Hattusa might have actually accelerated the kingdom's final decline. Tudhaliya's enterprise marked a brilliant, brief florescence of Hittite culture at the very end of the city's and the kingdom's existence. It took but a few years for Hattusa to reach its spectacular new heights. Within a few years of its builder's death it was a smouldering ruin. The city which had risen up almost 500 years earlier in defiance of Anitta's curse had now ended, abruptly, violently. The curse had taken effect. Anitta's vengeance was complete.

CHAPTER 14

Links across the Wine-Dark Sea

> Greeks and Trojans confront each other on the plains of Troy. In the space in between, two warriors meet—Diomedes, son of Tydeus, from Argos in Greece, and Glaukos, son of Hippolochos, from Lycia in the remote south-western corner of Anatolia. As they prepare to do battle, Diomedes calls upon Glaukos to identify himself, to state his lineage and place of origin. He learns that Glaukos too has ancestral origins in Argos, that there have been close bonds between their families, bonds extending back several generations. Enmity between the two is set aside. They exchange weapons and armour, and pledge to renew their families' traditional links.[1]

From the Bronze Age onwards, there have been many meetings, many links between the peoples of the ancient Greek and Near Eastern worlds—all contributing in greater or lesser measure to the ongoing process of cultural transmission and cultural exchange between east and west. The process involved two-way traffic, sometimes predominantly in one direction, sometimes predominantly in the other. During the middle centuries of the first millennium BC, the Greek world had a profound influence on a number of its Near Eastern neighbours; the remains of the Hellenized cities of the Anatolian littoral are amongst the tangible witnesses of this. In the early centuries of the millennium and in the preceding millennium, the Greeks in their turn derived much from their contacts with their neighbours across the wine-dark sea. Mainland and island Greece lay towards the western end of a cultural continuum which began with the earliest historical societies of Mesopotamia. Customs, traditions, and institutions which first appeared in these societies passed ever westwards, from one generation to another, from one civilization to another, and from one region to another over a period of several thousand years, sometimes undergoing substantial changes and modifications along the way. The Hittites were participants in the process, as they absorbed within the fabric of their own civilization cultural elements drawn from the wide range of civilizations with which they came into contact, either directly or through cultural intermediaries. In their turn they may well have played an important role in the transmission of elements of Near Eastern culture further westwards to the Greek world.

In recent years scholars have been giving renewed attention to the nature and extent of the role played by the Near East in shaping Greek culture in its early developmental stages. With this has come an increasing conviction that Near Eastern poetic and mythological traditions exercised a direct and pervasive influence on early Greek literature, most notably the poems of Homer and Hesiod. We have already noted the parallels between the Kumarbi epic cycle, preserved in a fragmentary Hittite version in the archives of Hattusa, and the works of Hesiod. We shall now turn to some of the parallels and possible links between Near Eastern traditions, particularly those that surface in the Land of Hatti, and the traditions used by Hesiod's near contemporary Homer in the *Iliad* and the *Odyssey*.

Parallels abound between the cultures of the Near Eastern and Greek worlds and have already been dealt with in a range of publications.[2] But no matter how striking some of these parallels may appear to be, they are not in themselves demonstrative of actual east–west contacts. If we are to argue that they are more than mere coincidences, that there are actual links between them, we need first to demonstrate in historical or archaeological terms at least the likelihood of cultural transmission between the different regions where they made their appearance. Some steps have already been taken in this direction, by Professor Martin West and others. And some of the mechanisms of cultural interaction between the Near Eastern and early Greek worlds are already becoming clear. What is still to be determined is whether this interaction was primarily a feature of early Iron Age contacts, or whether it was already in play at least several centuries before, in the Bronze Age.

There is no doubt that in the Late Bronze Age commercial and cultural links were well established between the Mycenaean world and western Anatolia and the Syro-Palestine region, and indirectly extended further east into Mesopotamia. The Ulu Burun shipwreck (see Chapter 5) provides some indication of how these links were maintained. The ship's cargo of copper and tin ingots and luxury items is indicative of the commercial contacts between Egypt, the eastern Mediterranean lands, and Greece in the fourteenth to thirteenth centuries, and the nature of the trade between these regions. But there may have been other cargo as well, not identifiable in the archaeological record—what has been referred to as 'human talent'.

Westward Population Movements

In recent years a number of scholars have postulated a westward diaspora of Levantine craftsmen and merchants in the Late Bronze Age, including entrepreneurs in search of new resources and markets, and travelling along the established trade routes. From our Hittite sources we know that by the middle of the thirteenth century a substantial number of western Anatolians were living in Mycenaean Greece, called Ahhiyawa in Hittite texts. In a letter to one of the kings of Ahhiyawa Hattusili III complains of the resettlement of some 7,000 of his western Anatolian subjects from the Lukka Lands in Ahhiyawan territory.[3] Complementing this information, the Mycenaean Linear B tablets indicate that western Anatolia was one of the regions from which labour was obtained for the Mycenaean palace's workforces, for textile-making and the like. The same region may also have served as a recruiting ground, through raids and other means, for supplementing the substantial workforces required for building the massive fortifications at sites like Mycenae and Tiryns. This would fit neatly with an admittedly late attested tradition recorded by the first-century Greek writer Strabo, crediting the building of the walls of Tiryns to the Cyclopes, giants from Lycia.[4] The Lycians, as the Greeks and Romans called them, were first-millennium descendants of the Late Bronze Age Lukka people, who lived in parts of southern and western Anatolia. Many of these people were resettled in the Mycenaean world around the middle of the thirteenth century, in the period when the Mycenaean citadels were being extensively refortified.[5]

The new arrivals in Greece, whether from western Anatolia or regions further east, no doubt included many who were skilled in manual crafts, as well as healers, seers, and singers or poets—indeed, just as they are listed by Odysseus' swineherd Eumaeus amongst the categories of *demioergoi*, craftsmen who can always be assured of a welcome wherever they travel: 'No man of his own accord goes out to bring in a stranger from elsewhere, unless that stranger be master of some craft, a prophet or one who cures diseases, a worker in wood, or again an inspired bard, delighting men with his song. The wide world over, men such as these are welcome guests.'[6] Through the resettlement of foreign *demioergoi* and their fellow immigrants from the Near East, customs and traditions of the societies to which they had originally belonged would have become known in the Greek world. Indeed these foreign settlers were very likely the most important agents of east–west cultural transmission.

The thousands of Anatolian settlers in Mycenaean Greece very likely included some who had been trained as scribes, and continued to serve as scribes and interpreters in the Mycenaean courts. Their services would presumably have been called upon for communications between their new overlord and his subjects or agents in western Anatolia. They could also have served as channels of communication between the Ahhiyawan king and their former overlord, the king of Hatti. And they may well have brought to their new land something else in addition to their scribal skills. We have earlier remarked that scribes educated in the Near Eastern scribal school tradition would in the process of their education have learnt the 'classics' of Mesopotamia, notably literary compositions emanating from the Sumerian, Babylonian, and Hurrian peoples which found their way into the Hittite world—compositions like the Gilgamesh epic and the Kumarbi Song Cycle. Further to the west, in another world that was clearly receptive to stories of heroes and great achievements from the past as well as the present, it is very probable that narrative traditions from the Near East also became known in Mycenaean court circles—at least partly through the agency of Anatolian scribes who had become familiar with them in the course of their scribal training.

Yet there must have been others too who conveyed stories originating in a Near Eastern context westwards to the Greek world. Episodes from the Gilgamesh epic were probably in wide circulation, especially among travellers. The epic is by and large a traveller's tale. And as we have already remarked, the tales of the Kumarbi cycle with their themes of sex and violence would almost certainly have had widespread appeal at all levels of society. Immigrant craftsmen and artists, itinerant merchants, sailors from vessels which plied their trade throughout the ports of the Mediterranean, indeed any traveller capable of spinning a good yarn, may all have been agents in the process of east–west cultural transmission, in the course of which episodes from the Mesopotamian and Hurrian epics made their first appearance in the Greek world. If so, they may well have exercised, already in the Late Bronze Age, a significant influence on the development and shaping of the traditions which provided the genesis of Homeric epic as well as basic material for the poems of Hesiod.

Gilgamesh and the Homeric Epics

We can readily identify a number of features which the Gilgamesh epic has in common with the *Iliad* and the *Odyssey*. The introductory passage of the Gilgamesh epic which depicts Gilgamesh as a restless hero—the far-journeying wanderer who endures many hardships and gathers much wisdom—reminds us of Odysseus in the opening lines of the *Odyssey*. The very notion of a long journey in which the hero is beset by many obstacles and temptations is as fundamental to the Gilgamesh epic as it is to the *Odyssey*. The alewife-temptress Siduri in the former calls to mind Calypso and Circe in the latter. The divine intervention motif is constantly in evidence in both the Gilgamesh and the Homeric compositions—there are those deities who support and assist the hero, and those who are implacably hostile to him and seek his downfall—for an insult he has committed against them, for an injury done to them or to other members of their family.

The Mesopotamian and Greek epics all have a greater or lesser preoccupation with death and the Underworld, and there is much in common between Mesopotamian and Greek concepts of the afterlife.[7] Achilles' meeting with Patroklos' ghost in Book 23 of the *Iliad* recalls Gilgamesh's meeting with Enkidu's ghost in the twelfth tablet of the Gilgamesh epic. Gilgamesh's summoning-up of the spirit of Enkidu has its counterpart in Odysseus' summoning-up of the ghost of Teiresias in the *Odyssey*. This is of course a common literary *topos*—in which the living seek advice from the dead, as we see also in Aeneas' consultation with the ghost of his father Anchises, or in a biblical context Saul's consultation with the ghost of the prophet Samuel.[8]

What do such parallels really signify? Direct influence of one tradition upon the other? Mere coincidence? Or was there an original common source from which common elements have been independently retained in two divergent cultures? The most sceptical view would have it that the broad similarity in themes observable in the Gilgamesh and the Homeric compositions indicate similar but quite unrelated responses, encapsulated in literary form, to similar problems, questions, hopes, aspirations, and fears raised by the different environments in which human societies evolved and developed. Things like the preoccupation with the theme of death and what lies beyond, and a yearning for some form of immortality which will transcend death; or the tension or conflict between the ephemeral, hedonistic delights of this world, and a desire for nobler, more lasting achievement, whatever hardships and dangers that may entail. Are the themes of the epics essentially independent reflections of what is inherent in human nature?

This view would become less tenable if we had conclusive proof that Near Eastern literary or mythological traditions, like those reflected in the Akkadian epics, were already known in thirteenth-century Greece. Such proof has yet to be found. We can, however, be sure that many people from the regions where the epics were read, copied, recited, and performed in the Late Bronze Age either resettled in the Greek world, or visited it in the course of trading enterprises. If they carried their traditions and folk tales with them, and if at this time the poetic and historical traditions on which Homer drew were already taking shape, it would be perverse to argue that they did so in complete isolation from Near Eastern traditions with which they shared a number of similar features and which were then known in the Greek world.

There are, furthermore, a number of specific points of comparison between Homeric and Near Eastern tradition which seem to go beyond mere superficial or commonplace parallels. In Book 5 of the *Iliad* Diomedes maltreats the goddess Aphrodite, and the goddess complains of this to her parents Zeus and Dione. But her father is not at all sympathetic, and in fact gently rebukes her for making the complaint. We are reminded of Gilgamesh's maltreatment of the goddess Ishtar (Aphrodite's Near Eastern equivalent). Just as Aphrodite had done, Ishtar complains to her parents Anu and Antu of Gilgamesh's behaviour. For doing so she too is rebuked by her father. Professor Burkert comments that the two episodes parallel each other in structure, narrative form, and ethos to a remarkable degree.[9]

In Book 4 of the *Odyssey*, Penelope learns of her son Telemachos' journey to find news of Odysseus, and the suitors' plot to kill him on his return. In great anxiety, she prays to Athene to keep him safe. In the Gilgamesh epic, the goddess Ninsun learns of her son's dangerous journey to fight the giant Humbaba, and she too prays for his safety. Of course there is nothing surprising about a mother praying for a son, especially when she perceives him to be in great danger. But a comparison of the two episodes takes us beyond this mere commonplace. After lamenting her son's plight, Penelope bathes and puts on clean linen, then filling a basket with sacred barley, she goes to the upper storey of the palace, and makes supplication to Athene to keep her son safe. When Gilgamesh goes off to fight Humbaba, his mother Ninsun enters her chamber, she puts on a garment and other adornments, then taking a special herb, she goes upstairs to the roof of the palace, and makes supplication to the Sun God Shamash for her son's safety.[10] Burkert remarks that what elevates this comparison from the commonplace is the fact that here narrative content, structure, and sequence are virtually identical.

We might also take a little further the comparison between Homer's Circe and Siduri of the Gilgamesh epic. Each attempts to persuade the hero to abandon his mission—in Gilgamesh's case the quest for Utnapishtim, in Odysseus' the completion of his journey home—and neither succeeds. Yet there are dual, apparently contrasting aspects of the roles which the temptresses play. Gilgamesh prevails on Siduri, who lives on the edge of the sea and knows its ways, to give him directions which will lead him across the waters to Utnapishtim. Odysseus too entreats Circe to provide directions for his homeward journey; she advises him that to reach his final destination he must first visit the house of Persephone and Hades, and there seek counsel from the spirit of the seer Teiresias. In both cases the dangers of the journey ahead are highlighted. Gilgamesh is warned thus: 'There has never been a ferry of any kind, Gilgamesh, and nobody from time immemorial has crossed the sea (to the realm of Utnapishtim).'[11] Odysseus has similar apprehensions: 'O Circe, who will be the guide for this journey? Never yet has anyone reached by black ship the realm of Hades.'[12] But Circe reassures him. Like Siduri, she is knowledgeable in the ways of the sea. In both cases, the temptresses are not merely obstacles put in the hero's way. They play essential roles in the forward movement of the journey. For the directions they give are critical to the attainment of the hero's goal. In this case too Mesopotamian and Homeric tradition closely parallel each other in concept, structure, and detail.

Cultural Transmission

Near Eastern influence on Homer was by no means confined to the sphere of literary tradition. On a broader level, elements of Hittite and other Near Eastern ritual practices occasionally surface in the Homeric epics. We have already referred to the close parallel between the procedures followed by Odysseus in summoning up the dead at the beginning of Book 11 of the *Odyssey* and the Hittite chthonic ritual in which the deities of the netherworld were summoned from their infernal abode (Chapter 10). One further example may suffice. In Book 23 of the *Iliad* (233–61), Homer describes the funeral rites of the Greek hero Patroklos. His body is disposed of by cremation. This has occasioned some surprise, since inhumation was the regular Greek practice in the Bronze Age, the period in which the Trojan War is set.[13] What Patroklos' burial rites do recall are the procedures laid down for the disposal of the remains of Hittite kings, as described in Chapter 10. In both cases the deceased's body is consumed upon a funeral pyre; the pyre's smouldering embers are quenched with wine before sifting through them for the bones of the deceased; the bones are immersed in a vessel of oil and then wrapped in fine linen. To be sure, there are also differences between the Hittite and Homeric burial procedures. But the features which they share strongly suggest that they are in some way connected.[14] The nature of this connection, and how it came about, remains a matter for speculation. We can but note how remarkable it is that a peculiarly Hittite royal burial practice which as far as we know did not outlive the Bronze Age and was unlikely to have been otherwise preserved in a Greek context should strike such a familiar chord in Homeric epic centuries after its last attestation in the Hittite texts.

Scholars like Walter Burkert and Martin West present at considerable length the case for strong Near Eastern influence on Greek culture. But they tend to focus on a later period of cultural transmission, during the so-called orientalizing period (mid-eighth to mid-seventh century) when itinerant craftsmen and artists from the Near East may once again have brought to the Greek world a range of manual and intellectual skills, including the Semitic art of writing, and a range of literary and religious traditions. On the other hand West concedes that the orientalizing period seems to fall too late to be connected with any major reshaping of Homeric epic. It may well be that much of what Homeric tradition may have owed to Near

Eastern influence was already known and was being used in the Mycenaean period when the traditions incorporated in Homeric epic were beginning to evolve. So too elements of the Kumarbi epic cycle may already have been known in the Greek world some centuries before their reappearance in Hesiod, though a number of scholars have long seen their transmission to the Greek world as a later phenomenon, perhaps due to Phoenician contact with this world.[15]

This is not to deny that later Near Eastern influences also contributed significantly to the final version of the Homeric poems. There are many features or elements of the poems which are clearly of Iron Age origin. And in many respects they reflect the world of the late eighth or early seventh century, as is clear from archaeological material and from numerous allusions contained within them. Above all the introduction of the alphabet into the Greek world must not merely have brought with it the technology of writing. It also drew the Greeks into the whole world of contemporary Near Eastern written culture. Within this culture the Gilgamesh tradition was still very much alive and being freshly recorded in Assyria, in much the same period as the composition of the *Iliad* and the *Odyssey*. In any case, the Homeric poems are now being seen much less as a product of an essentially monocultural environment and much more as the result of complex interactions of a number of factors, many of non-Greek origin.

To what extent, then, are we able to identify the actual building-blocks of the Homeric poems? What can we say is distinctively Greek about them? What is distinctively non-Greek? And where are Greek and non-Greek elements so tightly interwoven that they simply cannot be disentangled? These questions open up very large areas of investigation which we can do no more than touch upon here. And we should do so with some degree of caution.

With regard to the Homeric pantheon Martin West, one of the most vigorous proponents of extensive Near Eastern influence on Greek culture, writes thus: 'It is hardly going too far to say that the whole picture of the gods in the *Iliad* is oriental.' He argues that 'The Homeric and Hesiodic picture of the gods' organization, and of the past struggles by which they achieved it, has so much in common with the picture presented in Babylonian and Ugaritic poetry that it must have been formed under eastern influence. The gods are conceived as a corporation that regularly assembles on Mt Olympos, feasts and discusses human affairs. They have a chief Zeus to whom they make representations, and he makes decisions and gives permissions, sends messengers, and tries to control events. But the other gods are often wilful; they argue vigorously with one another, and Zeus on occasion has to threaten or exert physical violence in order to subdue them. This lively poetic scenario does not correspond with actual Greek beliefs about the gods, who were worshipped and invoked at appropriate places and times; two gods might be associated in a cult, but there was no sense of their being members of a larger assembly, nor of gods squabbling and jostling among themselves.'[16]

There is no doubt that Homer's gods, if not substantially derived from a Near Eastern context, would at least have been fully at home in a Near Eastern environment. But the assumption that they were actually taken over holus-bolus from the Near East may be going too far. In general, we should be cautious about using a line of reasoning which reduced to its simplest proportions seems to work along these lines: Here we have elements which were apparently alien to later Greek society. These elements were a feature of Near Eastern Bronze Age and early Iron Age societies. Therefore their appearance in Homer must be due to Near Eastern influence. To maintain this, we would first have to demonstrate that they were not also some sort of residual feature of pre-Homeric Greek society which survived in Homeric tradition but otherwise disappeared. Homer's divine society may well be a reflection of a widespread set of concepts about how the gods behaved and interacted, as much a part of early Greek and more generally Indo-European tradition as it was of Mesopotamian tradition.

In general terms closer attention to Near Eastern–Homeric text parallels may well give us a good deal more insight than we presently have into the actual processes involved in the composition of the Homeric poems, and a greater understanding of how the poet's compositional skills operated. We could take the view that an eighth-century epic poet was merely the last in a succession of 'Homers' extending back over a number of generations, each of whom contributed to the culling, shaping, and refining of the material, with the last in the series adding the final touches, or bringing the compositions to what West calls their astonishing acme in the eighth and seventh centuries. And Burkert and others may well be right in their claim that this was a period of much more intensive east–west connections and cultural transmission than was the case in the Bronze Age. But this is in no way incompatible with the notion of an earlier stratum of cultural transmission as well.

In any case, the epics drew on a wide range of sources and reflect a wide range of influences over a period extending back well before they reached their final form. The tradition of a Trojan War very possibly has a basis in historical fact. But if so it almost certainly represents a conflation of events, beginning perhaps a century or more before the alleged dates of the war in Greek literature and continuing beyond the end of the Bronze Age. Throughout this period, there was regular commercial and political contact between the Greek and Near Eastern worlds (allowing perhaps for a hiatus of 100 years or so in the eleventh century BC), and undoubtedly a considerable degree of cultural interaction between these worlds.

It has been suggested above that primarily through the agency of large groups of immigrants and traders in Bronze Age Greece, Near Eastern intellectual and cultural traditions became known in this world. It would be remarkable if Near Eastern contacts with and a significant Near Eastern presence in the early Greek world, as attested by both archaeological and written evidence, failed to make any major or lasting impression on Greek civilization. Given that the development of the Homeric epics was a long evolutionary process which incorporated a wide range of historical, social, and cultural elements, we can hardly accept that it could have developed in isolation of social and cultural forces from the East which were impacting on the Greek world during the developmental period of Homeric tradition. Speaking in relation to the impact of the Near East on the development of Greek mythological tradition, Professor Kirk comments thus: 'That Greek myths were infected by Near Eastern themes is of very great importance. Not only because it casts a faint glimmer of light on the development of Greek culture and ideas in their formative stage, but also because it makes it easier to isolate the specifically Hellenic contribution, the particular intellectual and imaginative ingredients that made Greek civilization such a very different phenomenon from those of western Asia and Egypt.'[17]

As yet we are only imperfectly aware of the specific ways in which social and cultural forces helped shape Homeric tradition. But greater attention to the links across the wine-dark sea may well contribute significantly to Homeric scholarship in the future—as we see increasingly how the poet adapted, moulded, and transformed a vast range of disparate material into a coherent, compelling narrative, giving it a character and status which led to its position as one of the great masterpieces of Greek artistic achievement.

Notes

Introduction

1. Herodotos 2.106.
2. In Hebrew their name is *ḫittî* (singular) *ḫittîm* (plural). For a summary of biblical references see McMahon (1989: 71–5).
3. See Hawkins (1998).
4. However, a direct connection is still uncertain. According to Beckman (1996*b*: 24), it is more likely that the name is employed here in the looser Assyrian sense of 'Westerner'.
5. Bryce (1998*a*: 381–91).
6. Hoffner (1980: 331).

Chapter 1: King, Court, and Royal Officials

1. *CTH* 6, ed. Sommer and Falkenstein (1938). The description above is based in part on the reconstruction of events proposed by Melchert (1991).
2. See Bryce (1998*a*: 193–9).
3. In the document commonly referred to as the Proclamation or Edict of Telipinu (*CTH* 19), most recently ed. Hoffmann (1984).
4. *CTH* 81, most recently ed. Otten (1981). A shorter version appears in *KBo* VI 29 (*CTH* 85.1).
5. See the text editions of von Schuler (1957).
6. *KUB* XIII 1, *KUB* XIII 2 and duplics. (*CTH* 261), ed. von Schuler (1957: 36–65). Extract transl. Goetze, in Pritchard (1969: 210–11). See also Beal (1992: 426–35).
7. For references, see Del Monte and Tischler (1992: 160 s.v.). The city of Sapinuwa, suggested as an alternative identification, is probably to be identified with the site at modern Ortaköy, which lay some two days' journey (in Hittite terms) from Maşat.
8. In philological terms they belong to the Middle Hittite period. In archaeological terms they belong to level three of the five-level site.
9. The letters have been published by Alp (1991), and are discussed in some detail by Klinger (1995).
10. See Beal (1992: 406–7).

11. See Bryce (1998*a*: 158–61).
12. See Beckman (1995*a*: 539).
13. For a detailed treatment of their role in the kingdom, see Singer (1984).
14. *IBoT* I.30, obv. 2–5. See also Houwink ten Cate (1992: 87); Haas (1994: 188–90).
15. The expression, of Mesopotamian origin, first occurs in Anatolia in the eighteenth century, when King Anitta uses it of his father (*CTH* 1 obv. 1–2); see Gonnet (1979: 178).
16. *CTH* 42, Suppiluliuma's treaty with Huqqana, clause 2, transl. Beckman (1995*a*: 535).
17. In clause 28 of his Proclamation, where he set out rules for the royal succession; see Bryce (1998*a*: 114–16).
18. See Beckman (1995*a*: 532).
19. Perhaps adopted by the Hittites indirectly from Egypt, by way of Syria.
20. The enthronement ceremony itself is preserved only in meagre fragments (*KUB* XVIII 36 etc.), and apart from these we have to rely on the information provided by the ritual for a substitute king (see Chapter 11) whose enthronement procedures probably closely paralleled those of a genuine coronation.
21. See Beckman (1988: 42) with references cited therein.
22. Haas (1994: 201).
23. Beckman (1988: 42–3) notes that the Hittite king never has the epithet 'shepherd' as do Mesopotamian kings, and that in the Hittite world only the Sun God is said to be the 'shepherd of humankind' or the like, a usage imported from Babylonia. Cf. Haas (1994: 197–8).
24. For a detailed treatment of her role in the kingdom, see Bin-Nun (1975); more briefly, Bryce (1998*a*: 96–8).
25. Our information on the *MEŠEDI* comes primarily from a Middle Hittite text 'Instructions for the *MEŠEDI*', *IBoT* I.36 (*CTH* 262), most recently discussed by Beal (1992: 212 ff.). Only the first tablet of the Instructions has survived, which deals with the *MEŠEDI*'s ceremonial duties. See also Košak (1990: 83–5).
26. There is a single late reference to it in the New Kingdom, *KUB* XXVI 12 + *VBoT* 82 iii 29–31 (*CTH* 255.1), on which see Beckman (1982: 441).
27. It has been suggested that the *halentuwa*-residence, or the palace of the king, was building F and the palace of the queen building E. See Haas (1994: 622–3).
28. From *KUB* XXVI 1 (*CTH* 255.2).
29. *KBo* III 27 (*CTH* 5).
30. See Bryce (1998*a*: 330–1).
31. Cf. Singer's comments (1997: 419).
32. Beckman (1992: 47).
33. No doubt the Hittite royal harem was on a much more modest scale than the royal harems of Egypt. The harem establishment of the pharaoh

Amenhotep III, for example, was reputed to house well over 1,000 women.

34. Proclamation of Telipinu, sec. 28.
35. See Goetze (1957*a*: 94).
36. The usual translation of this term is 'bastard' although in a society where concubinage was practised, at least at the highest levels, the Hittite term does not have the strong stigma of illegitimacy which the English word implies. None the less it was clearly used as an expression of contempt for a person whose status was inferior to that of a 'son of the first rank'.
37. *KBo* III 23 (*CTH* 24.1) iv 7′–10′. See Archi (1979: 39–44).
38. As Archi (1979: 40; see also 1995: 2368) notes, the precepts in such 'charity texts' are comparable with similar royal precepts in Mesopotamian and Egyptian texts. Although the Hittite texts belong to an early period in the kingdom's history, they very likely reflect ongoing concerns by the kings of Hatti to ensure that justice and protection were afforded to all their subjects.

Chapter 2: The People and the Law

1. After Kramer (1964: 336).
2. Ed. Neufeld (1951); Friedrich (1971); Hoffner (1997*a*). See also Hoffner (1995).
3. But note below the possible qualifications applicable to those of slave status.
4. Adapted from clause 10 of The Laws. Cf. Exodus 21: 18–20.
5. See Hoffner (1997*a*: 1); McMahon (1995: 1989).
6. The relevant texts have been edited by Werner (1967). As Hoffner (1980: 284) notes, they contain many examples of personal histories of important as well as minor civil servants. Gurney (1990: 77) comments on the immense trouble taken to ascertain facts, remarking on 'the highly detailed minutes of courts of inquiry in cases of peculation and neglect of duty, which are unique in the literature of oriental peoples and have quite a modern ring'.
7. Collected in *CTH* 8 and 9. Sample texts are quoted and translated by Beal (1983: 123–4) and Ünal (1989: 134–5).
8. All of them damaged to a greater or lesser degree, and even after all the texts are collated there are still some missing portions.
9. Probably from the reign of King Telipinu (*c.*1525–1500).
10. See Hoffner (1997*b*: 214). It contains forty-one clauses conventionally designated by roman numerals.
11. The translations from The Laws which appear below are by or adapted from Hoffner (1997*a*; 1997*b*).
12. Though several scholars have attempted to demonstrate an overall rationale for the arrangement; see Hoffner (1997*a*: 14).

13. The collection was compiled in two parts or series, with one hundred clauses in each. The Hittite scribes designated each part by their opening words: *If a man. . . .* (Part I) *If a vine. . . .* (Part II). This is purely a matter of convenience and has no significant bearing on the contents of each part. The individual clauses are most conveniently identified by numbering them consecutively from 1 to 200.
14. 'Customary law' in that they reflect old customs, as distinct from 'statute law' which results from formal legislation; see Neufeld (1951: 95–6); Güterbock (1954: 21).
15. *CTH* 19, sec. 49.
16. Letter of Hattusili III to Kadashman-Enlil, king of Babylon, *KBo* I 10 + *KUB* III 72 (*CTH* 172) rev. 14–25. Enslavement to the victim's family is also indicated in clause 43 of The Laws, translated in n. 20. This is clearly not a case of premeditated murder since the offender has caused the death of his victim in a moment of panic, in order to save his own skin.
17. See, e.g., clauses 23 and 24 of Hammurabi's Laws.
18. A DANNA is probably somewhere between a kilometre and a mile in extent.
19. Late version of clause 6 of The Laws, based on Hoffner's transls. (1997*a*; 1997*b*), who gives as a less likely alternative interpretation of the penultimate sentence: '. . . he shall take those same (payments from the inhabitants of the village)'.
20. Thus clause 43 reads: 'If a man is crossing a river with his ox, and another man pushes him off (the ox's tail), grasps the tail of the ox, and crosses the river, but the river carries off the owner of the ox, (the dead man's heirs) shall take that very man (who pushes him off)'; transl. Hoffner, who comments (1997*a*: 188) that the vivid details of this paragraph betray its origin as a precedent case.
21. On the role of the Elders in general, see Klengel (1965).
22. Instructions to the *BĒL MADGALTI*, *KUB* XIII 2 (*CTH* 261) iii 29–35, transl. Gurney (1990: 76).
23. *KUB* XIII 2 iii 10–14; also transl. Goetze, in Pritchard (1969: 211).
24. Gurney (1990: 76) suggests that the word 'house' should possibly be translated 'household' and the phrase may refer to a punishment such as that of Achan in Joshua 7: 16–26.
25. *KBo* XXII 1, ed. Archi (1979: 44–8). Cf. Hoffner (1997*a*: 218).
26. See Bryce (1998*a*: 201–3).
27. Singer (1999*b*: 70).
28. Unless prescribed by customary law in the region where the offence had been committed.
29. *KUB* XXI 17 (*CTH* 86) i 1–2. Puduhepa's involvement in the kingdom's judicial and political affairs may, however, have been unusually high for a Hittite queen; cf. Beckman (1995*a*: 537).

30. RS 17.346 (= *PRU IV*, 175–7), discussed by Singer (1999*a*: 665–6).
31. Note, e.g., the accord arranged by Ini-Teshub between the people of Carchemish and Ugarit which sets compensation of three minas of silver for each merchant of one kingdom killed in the territory of the other (RS 17.230, 17.146, 18.115, 18.19 (= *PRU IV*, 152–60)). Cf. Singer (1999*a*: 651–2).
32. e.g. in clause 8 the original penalty for blinding a slave in a quarrel is doubled if the injury caused is wilfully rather than accidentally inflicted.
33. See on this topic Hoffner (1973*b*).
34. Thus in the Instructions to the *BĒL MADGALTI*, *KUB* XIII 2 (and duplics.) iii 14 (von Schuler (1957: 47)); Goetze, in Pritchard (1969: 211). See also *KUB* XXX 34 (*CTH* 401) iv 15ff., a ritual designed to remove all trace of defilement from a town.
35. See Hoffner (1973*b*: 90).
36. From the treaty between Suppiluliuma and Huqqana of Hayasa, *CTH* 42 (ed. Friedrich (1930: 103–63)), secs. 25–6; transl. after Beckman (1996*a*: 27–8).
37. As Hoffner points out, sex between father and son is prohibited by The Laws not because of its homosexuality but because it is incestuous.
38. We might reasonably include them in the 'slave' category, on the grounds that they had been forcibly taken from their own countries, and assigned to a master to whom they were indefinitely bound. For more detailed discussion of the booty people, see Bryce (1998*a*: 236–8) and Chapter 6 below.
39. The clauses that follow have also been interpreted as referring not to the purchase of slaves, but to fees paid by employers for the transfer of the services of *free* persons who have been trained in someone else's employment under a kind of bond arrangement; see Košak (1987: 140–1).
40. An actual amount, ten shekels of silver, appears in only one copy and should almost certainly be emended to a higher figure (Goetze (1957*a*: 105 n. 8) and Hoffner (1997*a*: 141 n. 488) both suggest thirty), in view of the price stipulated for an unskilled slave. Most craftsmen seem to have been attached in one way or another to the palace or temple establishments, receiving their board and wages from these establishments in exchange for the products of their craft made from the materials supplied to them.
41. From *KUB* XIII 4 and duplics. (*CTH* 264); cf. Goetze, in Pritchard (1969: 207–8); Gurney (1990: 57).
42. Cf. Archi (1979: 38–9).
43. Just as in the clauses dealing with runaways (22–4) the person who was obliged to compensate the finder of a runaway was obviously the slave's owner.

Chapter 3: The Scribe

1. See Otten (1956).
2. On the curriculum and methods used in Mesopotamian scribal schools, see Sjöberg (1974); McCall (1990: 33–4).
3. See Beckman (1983*a*: 97 n. 2), *contra* Sjöberg, who believed that such institutions came to an end with the Old Babylonian period.
4. Cf. Kramer (1964: 291).
5. As indicated by a partly preserved text from the building complex south of the temple; see Singer (1998*a*: 34).
6. From *KUB* XXIV 1–2 (*CTH* 377), after Goetze, in Pritchard (1969: 396).
7. *KBo* XI 1 (*CTH* 382), ed. Houwink ten Cate (1967).
8. This follows the reasoning and conclusions of Houwink ten Cate (1968), summarized by Singer (1996: 135).
9. Referred to in sec. 2 of the so-called 'Tawagalawa letter', *KUB* XIV 3 (*CTH* 181).
10. The site lies *c.*50 kilometres south-east of Çorum.
11. See Beckman (1995*c*: 25).
12. From *EA* 32, after Moran (1992: 103).
13. See also Singer (2000: 28–9).
14. Van den Hout (1999: 342) notes that while the Hittites stored older compositions and constantly copied texts, not all genres were systematically preserved. Administrative documents, such as palace and temple inventories, vows, and oracle enquiries, mostly had single versions which were probably discarded after a certain period of time. On Hittite archives in general, see Ünal (1989: 130–1) and Košak (1995).
15. Professor Košak provides the following information in a personal communication: '1931–2000 yielded some 17,000 fragments, plus some 10,000 fragments from the first excavations without find-spots. On average, we need more than ten fragments to reconstruct a tablet. I estimate that the whole of Hattusa contained at the most 2000–2500 tablets, divided among several libraries.'
16. The tablet has been published by Otten (1988).
17. For the remains of these shelf-lists, see *CTH*, pp. 153–93. See also Laroche (1949: 14–23).
18. See references in Laroche (1949: 11; 1952: 16).
19. Colophon to *KUB* XX 8 (*CTH* 610) vi 8–10; see Laroche (1949: 8).
20. See Bryce (1998*a*: 253).
21. See Roth (1997: 2), who refers to such works as *ana ittisu*, a multi-tablet series of thousands of Sumerian and Akkadian legal terms and formulas.
22. *KUB* XIII 7 (*CTH* 258), cited Laroche (1949: 11).
23. Shear (1998) notes information provided by Professor Bass of the remains of two other wooden tablets in the wreck. She also refers to the

discovery of two groups of bronze hinges from Pylos and Knossos of a size and nature comparable to the Ulu Burun tablet-hinges, and thus suggestive of the existence of Mycenaean writing tablets, and a possible Mycenaean origin for Bellerophon's tablet.
24. Hoffner (1980: 285–6).
25. Examples cited by Beckman (1995*c*: 26).

Chapter 4: The Farmer

1. *KUB* XXIV 2 (*CTH* 377) rev. 12′–16′, transl. Beckman (1989: 99).
2. Lloyd (1989: 16).
3. See Hoffner (1974) for a comprehensive treatment of the foods of the Hittite world and their preparation for the table.
4. *KBo* V 7 (*CTH* 223) rev. 28–33, transl. Gurney (1990: 66). The document in general records the grants made to a favoured hierodule Kuwatalla. See also Klengel (1986: 28–30).
5. A speculative calculation made by Klengel (1986: 26), based on the figure of 120 square *gipessar* for apparently a minimum-size landholding as mentioned in texts dealing with the size of fields. See also n. 15.
6. On the allocation of land in this way, and the procedures involved, see Bryce (1998*a*: 92 n. 85), and the references cited therein.
7. Thus Beckman (1995*a*: 538).
8. Thus Beal (1992: 55). For a detailed discussion of the term, see Beal (1988).
9. For the terms *sahhan* and *luzzi* indicating the obligations and services imposed on those who owned or at least occupied certain types of land, see Gurney (1990: 84); Hoffner (1997*b*: 244–5).
10. See Seeher (1999: 332–4; 2000*a*; 2000*b*). In a personal communication, Dr Seeher has indicated that on the basis of radio-carbon analysis, the silo complex at the postern wall should now be dated to the sixteenth century, not to the fifteenth/fourteenth century as indicated in his articles, and that an earlier date should probably also be assigned to some of the silos on Büyükkaya.
11. Seeher (2000*b*: 287) notes the possibility that the extensive *pithos* magazines attached to the Temple of the Storm God in the Lower City were also used for grain storage, as were the magazines at Knossos.
12. Seeher (2000*b*: 295) comments that allowance must also be made for the grain reserved for brewing beer.
13. From *KUB* XXIV 3 and duplics. (*CTH* 376).
14. As indicated in clause 183 of The Laws.
15. The *gipessar* was a smaller unit of measurement, 100 of which made up 3.3 IKU, equivalent to approximately three acres or one hectare; thus Hoffner (1997*a*: 20 n. 19). For calculations of land sizes and other

measurements in metric terms, see Melchert (1980); van den Hout (1990).

16. The price is indicated in clause 185 of The Laws. Cf. clause 107 (dealt with below), which indicates the same area within a formula used for calculating penalties for damage to a neighbour's vineyard.
17. Extracted from clauses 178 and 179 of The Laws.
18. See, for example, Klengel (1986: 28–31).
19. This and subsequent translations of clauses from The Laws are by or adapted from Hoffner (1997*a*; 1997*b*).
20. To judge from clause 6 of The Laws, which indicates that a village's legal responsibility extended up to three DANNAS (a distance of up to three miles) from the village centre.
21. Cf. clauses 98–100, 106. It is not clear whether the reference in the first three of these clauses is to fires started accidentally or deliberately.
22. See Beckman (1988: 35), who notes that wool was commonly used as a magical material in ritual.
23. They and their animals were still regarded as belonging to the Hittite crown, as indicated by treaties which demanded their return to Hittite territory if in border regions they strayed or deliberately moved into the territory of a neighbouring independent state.
24. See clauses 74, 76, 77.
25. See *CTH* 138 and 140, ed. von Schuler (1965: 117–34).
26. Cattle-dogs, other trained dogs (perhaps hunting-dogs), and domestic or farmyard (?) dogs; see clauses 87–9 of The Laws.

Chapter 5: The Merchant

1. Literally, 100 minas; the ratio of minas to shekels was 1 : 40. By comparison, the Babylonian ratio was 1 : 60 and the Hebrew 1 : 50. Clause 181 of The Laws indicates that one shekel of silver = four minas of copper.
2. Clause 5 of The Laws, transl. Hoffner. See also note 5.
3. See Bryce (1998*a*: 21–33).
4. See Bryce (1998*a*: 86) and the references cited therein.
5. Even here the word 'Hittite' is appended to 'merchant' only in the New Hittite version of the law.
6. Hoffner (1997*a*: 172); Klengel (1979).
7. See further on this clause Friedrich (1971: 91–2); Haase (1978: 213–19).
8. *EA* 8.
9. *EA* 7, 73–82.
10. *EA* 39.
11. RS 17.435 + 17.436 + 17.437; see Singer (1999*a*: 693–4).
12. See RS 17.230, 17.146, 18.115, 18.019 (= *PRU IV*, 152–60).
13. Singer (1999*a*: 651–2).
14. RS 17.229 = *PRU IV*, 106.

15. RS 17.133 = *PRU IV*, 118–19; transl. Beckman (1996*a*: 164).
16. In accordance with Hattusili III's request in his letter to the Babylonian king Kadashman-Enlil for a 'gift' of horses (*CTH* 172, most recently transl. by Beckman (1996*a*: 132–7), sec. 17).
17. Whose main export was copper, both as a raw material and in the form of finished products.
18. See Cline (1994: xviii), with respect to the circular pattern of the sea-trading routes.
19. As discovered in the Ulu Burun shipwreck off the coast of Kaş. See the comments of Morris (1992: 103).
20. According to Professor Bass, the Gelidonya ship was a Syrian merchant vessel which sank *c.*1200 BC; see e.g. Bass (1973: 34), who keeps open the possibility that the vessel was of Cypriot origin (1973: 36). The Ulu Burun wreck is probably to be dated *c.*200 years earlier. Cline (1994: xvii) notes that this vessel carried a diverse cargo from Syro-Palestine, Cyprus, Egypt, Mesopotamia, Italy, and the Aegean.
21. See Cline (1994: 70) for details.
22. *KUB* XXI 38 (*CTH* 176) obv. 17–18; *ÄHK* I no. 105, pp. 216–17.
23. *KUB* III 34 (*CTH* 165) rev. 15ff.; *ÄHK* I no. 78, pp. 184–5, II, pp. 280–1. See also Klengel (1974: 167); Singer (1999*a*: 715).
24. *KRI* IV 5, 3.
25. RS 20.212, 17′–26′. See discussion in Bryce (1998*a*: 364–5).
26. See Bryce (1998*a*: 368).
27. RS 18.031; see Singer (1999*a*: 672).
28. RS 17.130 and duplics. 17.461 and 18.03 (= *PRU IV*, 103–5).
29. Ref. as in n. 28. See also Singer (1999*a*: 660–1 with n. 174).
30. The most notable were their seaborne assault on Cyprus during Tudhaliya IV's reign, and their engagements with enemy ships off the coast of Cyprus in the reign of Tudhaliya's brother Suppiluliuma II (late thirteenth and early twelfth centuries).
31. Cf. Beckman (1999: 166).

Chapter 6: The Warrior

1. Based on Thucydides 1.76.
2. Aristotle, *Politics* 1254a.
3. From Year 3 of the 'Comprehensive Annals' of Mursili II (*CTH* 61), Goetze (1933: 70–3).
4. See Bryce (1998*a*: 213).
5. See Bryce (1998*a*: 236–8).
6. Cf. Imparati (1987: 188), who remarks that peace appears as an absence of civil wars, an absence of conspiracies against the royal court rather than as an absence of exterior wars.
7. See Houwink ten Cate (1984: 72–3).

8. See Beal (1995: 547).
9. See Bryce (1998*a*: 140–9).
10. See Bryce (1998*a*: 321–4).
11. As in the case of Mursili II; see Bryce (1998*a*: 219–23).
12. Thus did Mursili II in his Arzawan campaign which extended over the third and fourth years of his reign.
13. On the representation in general of military conflict as a lawsuit to be determined by divine judgement, see Houwink ten Cate (1984: 72).
14. *KBo* VI 29 (*CTH* 85) ii 1 ff., transl. Liverani (1990: 156).
15. From Year 3 of the Ten-Year Annals of Mursili II; Goetze (1933: 46–7).
16. See Beal (1992: 313–17) for the active role taken by the king in campaign decision-making even when he was not actually in the field himself.
17. For the civil duties associated with the office, see Chapter 1. On the office in general, see Beal (1992: 342–57).
18. See Beal (1995: 546–7).
19. See Beal (1992: 197–8; 1995: 548–9).
20. See Beal (1992: 37–55). The terms used for permanent troops are UKU.UŠ and *sarikuwa*-.
21. Thus Beal (1992: 43–4). These additional duties are attested only for the UKU.UŠ troops.
22. Further details in Macqueen (1986: 57–8).
23. Goetze (1964: 29).
24. See Kammenhuber (1961); Starke (1995).
25. From *KBo* VI 34 (*CTH* 427), transl. Goetze, in Pritchard (1969: 354).
26. Further on Late Bronze Age fortifications, see Macqueen (1986: 64–73).
27. Thus Hattusili I in his two campaigns against Sanahuitta; see Bryce (1998*a*: 74, 81–2).
28. See Houwink ten Cate (1984: 68).
29. For discussions of the text, see Houwink ten Cate (1984: 68); Gurney (1990: 148–9); Beckman (1995*b*); Bryce (1998*a*: 77–8).
30. *KUB* XIX 37 obv. ii 15–19, Goetze (1933: 168–9), transl. Roszkowska-Mutschler (1992: 6). See also *KUB* VII 60 (*CTH* 423) iii 19–31, a ritual curse to be laid on an enemy city, transl. Beckman (1999: 168).

Chapter 7: Marriage

1. *KUB* XXIV 7 (*CTH* 717) i 38–40, adapted by Beckman (2000: 11) from a translation by Güterbock (1983: 156).
2. Following Hoffner's interpretation of clause 171 of The Laws; see Hoffner (1995: 567; 1997*a*: 171).
3. On the *kusata*, see Puhvel (1997: 293–5). The two stages of gift-giving prior to the actual marriage are indicated by clauses 28a and 29 of The Laws. For reservations about translating *kusata* as 'brideprice', see Gurney (1990: 82).

4. The translations from The Laws in this chapter are by or adapted from Hoffner (1997*a*; 1997*b*).
5. See Hoffner's discussion (1997*a*: 181–3).
6. For a discussion of both views, see Hoffner (1997*a*: 185).
7. We find too in Roman imperial society a number of instances of a male slave marrying a free woman, very likely because in Roman law the offspring of a free woman were always freeborn, regardless of the status of the father.
8. Beckman (1986: 17) compares the practice with the Mesopotamian *erebu*-marriage by which the father of the bride pays, rather than receives, the brideprice, and the bridegroom therefore becomes a member of the wife's family in inversion of the usual custom.
9. A similar arrangement seems to be reflected in native mythological tradition in which the son of the Storm God, whose maternal grandfather is a poor man, becomes a member of the family of the serpent Illuyanka (see Hoffner (1990: 13)), although it is not clear what benefit the serpent expects to derive from the marriage.
10. Provision for this is made in the Telipinu Proclamation, and very likely also in the appointment of Arnuwanda I as Tudhaliya I/II's son-in-law, adopted son, heir to the throne, and co-regent. At sub-royal level, the Old Hittite land-grant document from Inandık (Balkan 1973) may provide a further example of the practice. In this case Ziti was adopted as the son of Tuttulla and was also married to his daughter; cf. Beal (1983: 118).
11. In a small number of attested cases Hittite princes were also used to establish marriage alliances with vassal or foreign rulers.
12. See Kitchen (1982: 88–9, 110).
13. The Amarna letter *EA* 1 refers to a complaint by the Babylonian king Kadashman-Enlil that his sister had disappeared after her marriage with the pharaoh Amenhotep III, and it was unknown whether she was dead or alive.
14. In clause 31 the word *si-e-li/e-es* (a *hapax*) is tentatively translated by Hoffner as 'lovers(?)', in reference to a free man and slave woman who set up house together. But this is merely a guess based on what would seem appropriate in this context; Hoffner points out too (1997*a*: 184) that another word for 'lover' (*pupu-*) is already known.
15. Laws of Eshnunna, clause 26.
16. The quotation at the end of the clause appears, as Hoffner says, to be addressed to the 'abductor'. But its interpretation remains obscure.
17. Following the interpretation of Tsevat (1975), according to whom the veiling constitutes a reaffirmation of the couple's marriage by symbolically re-enacting her bridal status; see also Hoffner (1997*a*: 226).
18. Deuteronomy 22: 25–7 contains a similar provision.
19. See note 17.

20. RS 17.226, 17.355 (*PRU IV*, 208–10).
21. For a more detailed treatment of the episode, see Bryce (1998*a*: 344–7).
22. In his commentary on this law, Hoffner (1997*a*: 226) gives possible examples of the law in practice.
23. Cf. Genesis 38 and Ruth 4.
24. Thus Imparati (1995: 574).

Chapter 8: The Gods

1. From Muwatalli's Prayer to the Assembly of Gods (*CTH* 381), transl. Singer (1996: 32).
2. For *evocatio* texts, see *CTH* 483 and translations by Goetze, in Pritchard (1969: 351–3).
3. *KUB* XLIII 62 obv. ii 5′–6′. Cf. Haas (1994: 297).
4. Akurgal (1962: 76).
5. As Singer (1995: 349 n. 25) remarks, the custom was current also in the Classical world, comparing e.g. Livy (5. 21) who relates that at the siege of the Etruscan city of Veii, the city goddess Juno Regina was entreated to come to Rome, where a temple would be erected in her honour.
6. Cf. Singer (1995: 346), who cites a passage from the so-called Puhanu chronicle, a text of Old Hittite origin (*CTH* 16b), with dialogue between the Storm God of Halab and the representative of the Hittite king. Singer notes that it is only when the Storm God of Halab acknowledges his satisfaction with the respect bestowed upon him by the conquerors that the takeover of the city may be considered as fully accomplished.
7. Beckman (1998: 3) notes that approximately twenty-five different local varieties of Ishtar are present in the Boğazköy archives.
8. For general treatments of the pantheon, see Gurney (1977: 4–23); Klock-Fontanille (1998: 32–44).
9. Including Tarhunt, the Luwian Storm-God, and Sanda, apparently equated with Babylonian Marduk.
10. Akurgal (1962: 76).
11. *KUB* XXI 27 (*CTH* 384) i 3–4, transl. Goetze, in Pritchard (1969: 393).
12. See Lebrun (1997: 180–2).
13. Cf. Beckman (1989: 99).
14. The so-called cult inventory texts (*CTH* 501–30) may reflect this census. They are apparently reports of commissioners sent out by Tudhaliya IV to collect information regarding the condition of shrines in various regions (thus Gurney (1977: 25)).
15. Though as Beckman (2000: 22) points out, they were more than simply human beings endowed with greater powers and immortality. 'As representatives of natural forces or of societal functions, deities could not be ordered hierarchically in relationship to one another in the manner of men and women within society.'

16. From *KUB* xiv 8 and duplics. (*CTH* 378 ii). Cf. Exodus 20: 5.
17. From the instructions to temple officials, *KUB* xiii 4 and duplics. (*CTH* 264).
18. Mursili II is the earliest known exponent of this form of prayer. Muwatalli's Prayer to the Storm God of Kummanni (*KBo* xi 1 = *CTH* 382), discussed and edited by Houwink ten Cate (1967), illustrates a number of the features of such a prayer.
19. Introduction to the Prayer to the Sun God, *CTH* 372. Full text in Lebrun (1980).
20. Less frequently, the Sun Goddess of Arinna occupies first position.
21. From *KUB* vi 45 + *KUB* xxx 14 and duplics. (*CTH* 381), after Gurney (1990: 115).
22. Singer (1996: 149).
23. See Haas (1994: 423).
24. See Lebrun (1980: 58–9).
25. Equated with Sumerian Ereshkigal, Hurrian Allani, Akkadian Allatum. In general, see Torri (1999).
26. *KUB* xxi 19 (*CTH* 383) i 1–5, transl. Gurney (1990: 115).
27. From *CTH* 376, ed. Lebrun (1980: 155–79).
28. See de Roos (1995: 2002).
29. Already in pre-Hittite times he was honoured by Pithana, founder of the Nesite dynasty, and his son Anitta, as chief god of their realm.
30. From Muwatalli's Prayer to the Assembly of Gods (*CTH* 381), transl. Singer (1996: 40).
31. Thus Singer concludes (1996: 187). On the transfer of the capital, see Bryce (1998*a*: 251–5), and the references cited therein. For a detailed discussion of the god's significance, particularly in the context of Muwatalli's Prayer to the Assembly of Gods, see Singer (1996: *passim*). See also Haas (1994: 325–6).
32. See Wegner (1981); Beckman (1998: 2).
33. For a comprehensive treatment of Hittite mountain-gods, see Haas (1982).
34. Further on the iconography, see McMahon (1991: 4–5).
35. *CTH* 682. The text is discussed by Archi (1975), and edited by McMahon (1991: 83–141). McMahon (1991: 5) notes that all the tutelary deities known by name are probably Hattic in origin; those known only by title are probably of foreign origin.
36. A convenient table of deities, arranged according to their ethnic origin, is provided by McMahon (1995: 1987–8).
37. *KBo* iv 9 and duplics. (*CTH* 612.1), transl. Goetze, in Pritchard (1969: 358–61).
38. See Hoffner (1990: 33–5).
39. Cf. Haas (1982: 23). McMahon (1995: 1985) notes that Inara (Hittite form of the Hattic name Inar; her name was often written with the

LAMMA sign) like Telipinu was accorded a less prominent position in the cult than she was in the mythology.

40. See Starke (1979).
41. See Pringle (1993: 136).
42. Herodotos 5. 102.
43. See Roller (1999: 48–53), who argues that Kubaba and the Phrygian mother goddess were quite separate deities, though there were a number of points of contact between them. She comments that the name Kybele comes from the Phrygian epithet Kubeliya, defined by Byzantine lexicographers as the Phrygian word for 'mountain'. She argues that it has no connection with the name Kubaba, and that the similarity between Herodotos' Kybebe and Kybele of the Greek poets is purely coincidental.
44. The Hittite archives contain both oracle texts in the original Akkadian versions and also Hittite versions of such texts; see e.g. *CTH* 538–40, 547, 551.
45. Extracts from *KUB* VIII 35 (*CTH* 545 II).
46. Bin-Nun (1979: 121) in her review of Kammenhuber (1976) notes that many dreams contain demands for offerings and gifts as atonement for offences, and comments that they too often give the impression of having been fabricated by the priests.
47. Further details in Frantz-Szabó (1995: 2017).
48. Note the comments of van den Hout (1999: 342).
49. See Bryce (1998*a*: 221).
50. From a Hittite oracle text from Alalah (*AT* (= *The Alalah Tablets*) 454 ii 9–10), after Gurney (1953: 117); see also Singer (1998*a*: 35).
51. From *KUB* XV 34 and duplics. (*CTH* 483), transl. Goetze, in Pritchard (1969: 352).
52. From *KUB* XIII 4 and duplics. (*CTH* 264). For a translation of the full text ('Instructions for Temple Officials'), see Goetze, in Pritchard (1969: 207–10).
53. Ref. as in previous note, after Goetze, in Pritchard (1969: 208).
54. In Greek tradition, the fate of the hapless Semele, mother of Dionysos, who asked her paramour Zeus to reveal himself to her in all his divine splendour, provides ample warning of the dangers of looking upon a god face to face.
55. *KUB* XXXVIII 37 (*CTH* 295), ed. Werner (1967: 56–7), rev. 8–10.
56. See also Singer (1986: 245); Haas (1994: 507–9).
57. *KUB* XXXVIII 1 (*CTH* 501) iv 1–5, transl. Beckman (1989: 102).
58. From *KUB* XXI 27 (*CTH* 384).
59. This latter is a common Near Eastern convention, found also in Egyptian, Babylonian, and Assyrian art.
60. Although as McMahon (1995: 1983) points out, the deities depicted

at Yazılıkaya differ in many respects from those listed in the treaties, since the Yazılıkaya assemblage represents a late adaptation of the Kizzuwadna pantheon and cult that were influenced by Hurrian and Luwian religions.

Chapter 9: The Curers of Diseases

1. Cited from K. Sommerfeld, *Healing Hands*, Brisbane, 2001.
2. Beckman (1993: 28) lists eight physicians known by name; one name is of Egyptian origin, one of Babylonian, and two of Luwian.
3. Two are attested: *KUB* XXX 42 (*CTH* 276) i 8 and *KUB* XXXIX 31 19 (*CTH* 450), cited by Beckman (1993: 28). The list of known physicians might suggest that the ratio of male to female was about 4 : 1. But the total number is really too small to be of much statistical value.
4. *KBo* XVII 62 + 63 iv 7′–12′ (*CTH* 478) transl. Beckman (1993: 29). On Hittite birth-rituals in general, see Beckman (1983*b*); Pringle (1993).
5. In general on this topic, see Edel (1976).
6. The fee so stipulated in clause 10 (late version) of The Laws.
7. As calculated by Hoffner, transl. of clause 158a of The Laws (1997*a*: 127).
8. The Hittite medical texts have been collected and edited by Burde (1974). See also Beckman (1993: 27).
9. Cited by D. Okpako, 'Placebos, Poisons and Healing', *Humanities Research* (Humanities Research Centre, Australian National University) 1, 2000: 22.
10. From *CTH* 406, ed. Hoffner (1987), adaptation of Hoffner's translation by Frantz-Szabó (1995: 2014).
11. *KUB* VII 53 + (*CTH* 409) iv 7–14, transl. Gurney (1990: 135).
12. 'through the unwitting stumbling upon the miasma of which someone else had previously rid themselves' (Beckman (1993: 33), in reference to a situation possibly envisaged in clause 44b of The Laws).
13. de Martino (1995: 2664). For the association of medicine, ritual, and magic, see also Burde (1974: 7–9).
14. However, van den Hout (2000: 645) notes that the Hittite expression *tapusa pai-* (lit. 'to go sideways') in a figurative sense simply means 'cease to function' and that we can only guess at what really happened to the king.
15. *CTH* 486, obv. 1–10. The text has been edited by Goetze and Pedersen (1934), and most recently translated by Kümmel (1987: 289–92).
16. Probably a Mycenaean Greek kingdom, or at least a part of the Mycenaean world; see Bryce (1998*a*: 59–63).
17. *KUB* V 6 (*CTH* 570) ii 57–64.
18. Tushratta writes: 'May Ishtar, Mistress of Heaven, protect My Brother

and myself for a hundred thousand years, and may our mistress grant us both great joy. And let us act as friends' (*EA* 23, transl. Tyldesley (1999: 35)).

19. It may have had to do with the terrible state of his teeth and the extreme pain which this must have caused him; see Redford (1984: 52–4); Tyldesley (1999: 35); though Moran (1992: 62) believes that the dispatch of the statue of Ishtar to Egypt had nothing to do with the pharaoh's indisposition but was more likely connected with the solemnities associated with the marriage of Tushratta's daughter.
20. *KUB* XII 58 (*CTH* 409) iii 2–11; see Beckman (1993: 34).
21. From *KUB* XIII 3 (*CTH* 265), transl. Goetze, in Pritchard (1969: 207).
22. Gurney (1958: 114).
23. From *KUB* III 67 (*CTH* 163).
24. Her name in Hittite was DINGIR.MEŠ-ÌR-i (= Massan(a)uzzi); see Bryce (1998*a*: 268 n. 1) and the references cited therein.
25. Based on a passage from *KBo* XXVIII 30, ed. Edel (1976: 67–75; *ÄHK* I: 178–81; *ÄHK* II: 270–2), also transl. Beckman (1996*a*: 131–2).
26. See Bryce (1998*b*).
27. Masturi, king of the Seha River Land.
28. *EA* 49.
29. *Odyssey* 4. 231–2.
30. *KBo* I 10 + *KUB* III 72 (*CTH* 172), transl. Beckman (1996*a*: 137).
31. From the so-called Plague Prayers of Mursili (*CTH* 378), transl. Goetze, in Pritchard (1969: 394–6).
32. The relevant passage from *CTH* 376 has been quoted in Chapter 4.
33. *KUB* III 51 (*CTH* 170) rev.(?) 1′–16′ (= *ÄHK* I no. 2, pp. 16–19). See commentary in *ÄHK* II, pp. 32–4.
34. Puduhepa's Prayer to the Sun Goddess of Arinna, *KUB* XXI 27 (*CTH* 384) ii 25–30, transl. Goetze, in Pritchard (1969: 393).
35. This and the following extract are from *KUB* XXI 27 iii, transl. Goetze, in Pritchard (1969: 394).
36. *KUB* XV 3 (*CTH* 584) i 17ff., transl. Güterbock, in Oppenheim (1956: 255).

Chapter 10: Death, Burial, and the Afterlife

1. A drink frequently mentioned in rituals.
2. See Otten (1958; 1962); Christmann-Franck (1971); Haas (1994: 219–29; 1995: 2023–7). The primary source is *CTH* 450.
3. Thus Haas (1994: 216).
4. The Hurrian name of the queen of the Underworld = Sumerogram ERESH.KI.GAL, Akkadian Allatum, Hittite Lelwani.
5. Transl. Gurney (1990: 137).
6. The term seems originally to have been used to indicate a mountain

summit or rocky peak, but it is found most frequently in contexts associated with the cult of the dead. The texts refer to stone houses for the kings Tudhaliya I/II, Arnuwanda I, and Suppiluliuma I. A number of scholars believe that Chamber B at Yazılıkaya might have been the *hekur* of Tudhaliya IV.

7. See Bittel et al. (1958).
8. Thus Haas (1994: 233) concludes, on the basis of clause 58a of The Laws, which refers to consignment to the pot/*pithos* for an unfree person sentenced to death.
9. Though we do not have clear evidence for this before the New Kingdom.
10. *KUB* XXVIII 6 (*CTH* 731); see Haas (1994: 464).
11. From 'Version 1' of the myth (*CTH* 324), sec. 27 (A iv 14–19), transl. Hoffner (1990: 17). A similar passage appears in 'Version 2', sec. 20 (D iii 3–14) (Hoffner 1990: 19). So too in a prayer to the Storm God of Nerik (*CTH* 671), there is an appeal to the goddess Ereshkigal to 'open the gates of the Dark Earth' (sec. 7, transl. Hoffner (1990: 23)).
12. *KBo* XXII 178 (+) *KUB* XLVIII 109 ii 4′–8′, iii 1–7, transl. Hoffner (1988: 191–2).
13. In marked contrast, it seems, to the Roman emperor Vespasian, who with commendable wit and sangfroid at his point of death is said to have uttered the words 'Oh dear, I think I'm turning into a god.'
14. From *KBo* IV 8 (*CTH* 71), after Hoffner (1983: 188).
15. *KUB* XXIX 1 and duplics. (*CTH* 414) ii 6–9, transl. Güterbock (1961*a*: 149); see also Haas (1994: 372–3).
16. As indicated by the Royal Offering Lists, *CTH* 661, which extend to Muwatalli II. See Otten (1951; 1968: 122–6); Kitchen (1962: 53–5). More recently, lists A, C, E, and D have been edited by Haas and Wäfler (1977: 107–13).
17. Note the reference in The Laws, clause 52, to a 'slave of a stone house'.
18. Homer, *Odyssey* 11. 538–9.
19. *KUB* XXX 24 (*CTH* 450) ii 1–4, transl. Beckman (1988: 44); for the text see Otten (1958: 60–1).
20. Homer, *Odyssey* 1. 572–5.
21. Respectively in *Odyssey* 11; *Aeneid* 6; and *The Frogs*.
22. See Goetze (1957*a*: 169–70) with references.
23. See Puhvel (1991: 25) with references.

Chapter 11: Festivals and Rituals

1. The former was worn in the AN.TAH.SUM festival, the latter in the KI.LAM festival; see below.
2. For a summary of different aspects of the Hittite festivals and a concise review of the main ones, see Güterbock (1964: 62–73).

3. On the prince's role in festival performances, see Ardzinba (1986).
4. For the reconstruction of the processional route, as suggested by Neve, see Chapter 13.
5. For fuller discussions of the musicians and the musical instruments used in such performances, see Gurney (1977: 34–5); Melchert (1988: 230–4); Haas (1994: 682–4); de Martino (1995).
6. Such performers—singers, instrument-players, and dancers—seem to have been permanent members of the personnel of a temple, where they were trained in their skills.
7. On the contribution of dance to Hittite ritual, see de Martino (1989; 1995: 2664–6); Haas (1994: 684–6).
8. A number of the details which follow are based on the festival procedure described in *KBo* IV 9 (*CTH* 612), transl. Goetze, in Pritchard (1969: 358–61).
9. If that in fact is what the expression 'to drink the god' really means. It may simply refer to the act of drinking in honour of a god.
10. 'They divide the young men into two groups and name them; one group they call "men of Hatti", the other group they call "men of Masa". The men of Hatti have bronze weapons, but the men of Masa have weapons of reed. And they fight, and the men of Hatti win' (*KUB* XVII 35 (*CTH* 525) iii 1 ff., transl. Gurney (1977: 27), from the description of the famous mock battle, in the context of the festival for Iyarri of Gursamassa. Masa was an independent kingdom in western Asia Minor).
11. de Martino (1995: 2668) cites the Old Hittite 'Palace Chronicle Text', which refers to those who miss the target in an archery contest being compelled to fetch water naked. Further on the athletics contests, see Carter (1988).
12. Illustrated in Bittel (1976: 186–200, figs. 209–28).
13. See Ünal (1994).
14. Gurney (1994) continues to support Garstang's original interpretation of the Alaca ladder-men as sculptors or masons.
15. Bittel (1976: 191) believes that painting could have compensated for the lack of plastic modelling.
16. For a general description of the festival, see Güterbock (1960).
17. See Haas (1988; 1994: 696–747).
18. Goetze (1957*b*: 91) comments that for such travelling to be done efficiently, there must have been a developed road system on which the chariot, or for longer distances the carriage of the king and his party, could move quickly.
19. See Bryce (1998*a*: 121).
20. See Haas (1994: 697).
21. For a discussion of the festival itinerary, see Güterbock (1961*b*: 90–2).
22. In general on this festival, see Singer (1983–4).
23. As already noted, this is the Turkish name (meaning 'inscribed rock') for the site. Its ancient name is unknown.

24. Bittel (1970: 107).
25. A similar motif is found on royal seals, from *c.*1300 onwards.
26. *KUB* VII 41 + duplics. *KBo* X 45 and *KUB* XLI 8 (ii 15–20), published by Otten (1961).
27. Bittel (1970: 109).
28. It has been suggested that Chamber A was the *huwasi* of the Storm God.
29. Haas and Wäfler (1974) proposed that Yazılıkaya was used for purification rites, a view opposed by Güterbock (1975: 274).
30. Perhaps what in Hittite was called a *hesti*-house, on which see Singer (1986: 249); Haas (1994: 245).
31. Other translations include 'rock outcropping, crag' (Melchert), 'mortuary shrine, ossuary, charnel, mausoleum' (Puhvel), a loan-word from Sumerian É.KUR 'temple, sanctuary' (Silvestri), a loan-word from the Syrian ḫai = kur, 'the house (is) the mountain' (Haas).
32. *KBo* XII 38 (*CTH* 121), ed. Otten (1963: 13–18), obv. ii 4′–21′. See also Haas (1994: 245–6).
33. McMahon (1991: 1 n. 2).
34. The 'Old Woman' who performs the ritual. The female practitioners commonly associated with rituals are discussed below.
35. From *KUB* XXIX 7 (*CTH* 480), transl. Goetze, in Pritchard (1969: 346).
36. Beckman (1989: 105–6).
37. So named from the Sumerogram MUNUS.ŠU.GI used in reference to them, which means 'old'.
38. See Beckman (1983*b*: 232–5; 1993: 37). Gurney (1977: 44–5) comments that the term may be connected with or even synonymous with *hasnupallas* 'midwife'. Pringle (1993: 134) notes the alternance of ŠU.GI and *hasawa* in a ritual text, citing Otten's conclusion that the latter is the Hittite phonetic rendering of the former.
39. On the basis of genealogical data; see Ünal (1988: 65). Beckman (2000: 20) notes that of the seventy-one individuals attested by name as authors of rituals in *CTH*, thirty-eight, or more than 50 per cent, are women.
40. *KUB* LIV 65 + rev. iii 33–4; see Klengel (1984: 176); Haas (1994: 888).
41. In general, see Haas (1994: 206–15), and for the relevant texts Kümmel (1967).
42. Herodotos 2. 39.
43. In order to transfer the affliction to it.
44. From *KBo* II 3 and duplics. (*CTH* 404), transl. Goetze, in Pritchard (1969: 350–1).
45. See also Beckman (1999: 162) regarding the performance of potentially polluting rituals in uninhabited areas.
46. See clause 44b of The Laws.
47. From *KUB* XXVII 67 (*CTH* 391.1), transl. Goetze, in Pritchard (1969: 348).
48. From *KBo* IV 6 (*CTH* 380), obv. 10′–15′, transl. Gurney (1977: 55), who

notes that here Lelwani is the old Hattic god, not a goddess. See also Kümmel (1967: 120–1).

49. *KUB* xv 1 (*CTH* 584), ed. Kümmel (1967: 111–25) i 14–20.
50. *KUB* ix 31 (*CTH* 757), transl. Goetze, in Pritchard (1969: 347), records a similar ritual performed with a substitute ram, on whose head is placed a crown of different coloured wools woven together before it is driven off along the road leading to enemy territory.
51. *KUB* xv 2 and duplics. (*CTH* 421), transl. Gurney (1977: 57–8). The text has been edited by Kümmel (1967: 50–110).
52. The other is *KUB* xxiv 5 + *KUB* ix 13 (*CTH* 419), ed. Kümmel (1967: 7–37), transl. Goetze, in Pritchard (1969: 355–6). See also Gurney (1977: 56–8); Haas (1994: 207).
53. *KUB* xxiv 5 + ix 13 obv. 4′–11′.
54. From *CTH* 121 (Kümmel (1967: 57–8)), transl. Gurney (1977: 57).
55. From *CTH* 119 (Kümmel (1967: 11)).
56. Text and references cited by Kümmel (1967: 181).
57. On magic in general in the Hittite world, see Goetze (1957*a*: 151–61); Ünal (1988); Frantz-Szabó (1995).
58. Frantz-Szabó (1995: 2007).
59. From *KBo* iv 2 (*CTH* 398), a ritual for expelling evil spirits from the royal palace, transl. Gurney (1990: 136); see also Haas (1994: 289).
60. Further on apotropaic magic and its associated rituals, see Haas (1994: 903–5).
61. Clause 111.
62. Hoffner (1997*a*: 217) agrees with Friedrich in seeing analogic magic at work here: 'He who kills the snake probably said something like "As this snake dies, so may so-and-so (i.e. his enemy) also die."'
63. Clause 140.
64. *KUB* xxiv 9 (*CTH* 402) i 39–42, transl. Beckman (1993: 34).
65. From the 'Apology' of Hattusili III (*CTH* 81), sec. 9.
66. From the Proclamation of Telipinu (*CTH* 19), sec. 50.

Chapter 12: Myth

1. *CTH* 324, most recently translated by Hoffner (1990: 14–22). For recent discussions of the tradition, see Kellerman (1986); Haas (1994: 707–19).
2. A grandmother goddess who appears in a number of Anatolian myths, playing a critical role in restoring balance and harmony within the universe. See Beckman (1983*b*: 238–48).
3. This and the following passages are adapted from Hoffner (1990: 15–17).
4. This tree or pole served as an important religious symbol. It was planted or erected outside the houses of those who held important religious offices in the holy cities to indicate their exemption from taxes and other

public services. See clause 50 of The Laws, and Hoffner (1997*a*: 192), with references cited therein.

5. *CTH* 321, most recently translated by Hoffner (1990: 11–14).
6. On the basis of archaic linguistic features preserved in the text.
7. This and the following passage are adapted from Hoffner's translation.
8. Hoffner (1974: 215).
9. Hoffner (1990: 10).
10. The colophon indicates that the story was continued on another tablet.
11. Of the widespread occurrence of the motif in Near Eastern tradition, see Ünal (1986; 1989: 139–40).
12. *CTH* 3. The text has been edited by Otten (1973).
13. Thus Otten (1973: 64); cf. Gurney (1977: 8).
14. If we are to believe what Hesiod himself alleges in his poem 'Works and Days'.
15. Lebrun (1995: 1972).
16. *CTH* 345–6. As Güterbock (1961*a*: 172) notes, it remains an open question whether the existing Hittite version, which dates to the thirteenth century, is a translation of a Hurrian original or is the creation of an author or authors who only drew their subject matter from Hurrian tradition but freely wrote the epic in Hittite. See Güterbock (1951/2) for a detailed treatment of the text of Ullikummi, including transliteration, translation, and commentary.
17. Other episodes include the Song of (the god) LAMMA, the Song of Hedammu, and the Song of Silver. For translations, see Hoffner (1990: 40–61).
18. Transl. Hoffner (1990: 40–1).
19. Güterbock (1961*a*: 160) notes that Philo of Byblos, in the outline of Phoenician mythology which he ascribes to Sanchuniaton, does have a corresponding first generation: Phoenician Elioun, Greek Hypsistos 'The Highest', corresponding to Alalu.
20. See Hoffner (1975).
21. Hoffner (1990: 39).
22. See Hoffner (1990: 39).
23. This and the following passages are translated by Hoffner (1990: 53–6).
24. See Apollodorus, *Bibliotheca* 1. 39–44.
25. Lebrun (1995: 1973).

Chapter 13: The Capital

1. See Bryce (1998*a*: 165–7).
2. Though the restoration of Hattusa as the Hittite capital actually took place under Urhi-Teshub, it is likely that Hattusili played no small part in the decision; see Bryce (1998*a*: 277). In any case he would have had little hesitation in claiming credit for it in later years.

3. Neve (1993: 85).
4. See Neve (1993: 22). For a description of the layout of Nişantepe, see Neve (1993: 58–63).
5. Neve (1989–90: 7; 1993: 18). Cf. Singer (1998*a*: 40).
6. They may of course have had other functions as well. Arinna, for example, was also a centre for gold-, silver-, iron-, and copper-smiths.
7. Mellink (1974: 204–5).
8. Singer (1998*a*: 42).
9. Like the tribute sent by Niqmaddu II of Ugarit (*CTH* 47); the relevant passage is translated by Beckman (1996*a*: 152).
10. For a brief description of representations of the lion in Hittite art, see Akurgal (1962: 113–14).
11. Contrary to this, Kohlmeyer (1995: 2648) points out that the layout of the figure displays all the principles of Hittite depiction of the human form.
12. See the comments of Canby (1989: 121), who notes that this is a version of the Egyptian Hathor headdress.
13. Following the general description and ground-plans in Neve (1993: 23–6).
14. See Neve (1993: 39–40); also Singer (1998*a*: 38).
15. Referred to by Neve (1993: 30), who notes that amongst other things they are concerned with a festival of the Storm God of Ebla.
16. Neve (1993: 36) suggests this on the basis of a stele from the central temple quarter on which a Tudhaliya appears as third member in the genealogy of Tudhaliya (IV), after the latter's father Hattusili and grandfather Mursili. Suppiluliuma I, son of Tudhaliya III and father of Mursili II, should also be included in Tudhaliya IV's successive lineal ancestors. Neve suggests that 'House B' and 'House C' were respectively dedicated to Mursili and Hattusili, noting that there are blocks in these two buildings corresponding to the relief block in A, but without reliefs, probably because they remained unfinished.
17. See the reports of the excavations by Neve (1991: 322–38; 1992: 307–16).
18. See Bittel (1970: 78).
19. This is the building designated by Bittel as Building D. The conclusion that the upper floor contained a large pillared audience chamber was that of R. Naumann, the architect who worked with Bittel on the site.
20. This applied to the kings of the Arzawa lands before their reduction to vassal status, and to the kings of Kizzuwadna and Mitanni (the latter after the Hittite conquest of Mitanni in the fourteenth century and before its takeover by Assyria probably during Urhi-Teshub's reign).
21. As indicated by inscriptions referring to the 'House of Teshub' and the 'House of Hepat' (refs. in Haas (1994: 625 nn. 47–8)).
22. With the notable exception of Akhenaten's temples to the god Aten.
23. Haas (1994: 623) comments that the orientation of the *cella*s seems to

have been arranged to enable the penetration of direct natural light in liturgically important places.

24. Singer (1998*a*: 34) notes that in the building complex to the south of the temple proper, a partly preserved text was found listing 205 members of the cult personnel: 18 priests, 29 priestesses, 19 scribes (DUB.SAR), 33 scribes on wood (DUB.SAR.GIŠ), 35 incantation priests, and 10 Hurrian singers; further items covering the remaining 61 persons are lost.
25. From *KUB* XIII 4 and duplics. (*CTH* 264) after Goetze, in Pritchard (1969: 208).
26. Neve (1993: 32).
27. In the context of the exquisite examples of Hittite miniature art of this period, see the discussion of Alexander (1991) of the Hittite ivory found amongst the cache of ivories at Megiddo in 1937.
28. Extract from *CTH* 264, after Goetze, in Pritchard (1969: 209).
29. Neve (1989–90: 9–10; 1993: 19) suggests that the conflagration, as archaeologically attested, may have been associated with an ultimately unsuccessful attempt by Tudhaliya's cousin Kurunta to seize the Hittite throne.
30. This is an Akkadogram. The equivalent Hittite term is not known. For a more detailed discussion of the official's duties and responsibilities, see Singer (1998*b*).
31. *CTH* 257, probably to be dated to the reign of Arnuwanda I.
32. For a more detailed description of the process along with the relevant passage from the *Hazannu*'s instructions, see Singer (1998*b*: 171–2).
33. For the reigns of Tudhaliya IV and Suppiluliuma II, see Bryce (1998*a*: 326–66).
34. Ed. Hawkins (1995: 21–49).

Chapter 14: Links Across the Wine-Dark Sea

1. Based on Homer, *Iliad* 6. 119–236.
2. See e.g. West (1988; 1997).
3. *KUB* XIV 3 (*CTH* 181), commonly referred to as the Tawagalawa letter; see Bryce (1998*a*: 321–4).
4. Strabo 8. 6. 11.
5. See Bryce (1999: 259–60).
6. Homer, *Odyssey* 17. 382–5, transl. W. Shewring.
7. See e.g. Kirk (1974: 260–1).
8. 1 Samuel 28.
9. Burkert (1992: 97).
10. The relevant passage (from Tablet III) is translated by Dalley (1989: 64–5).
11. From Tablet X of the epic, transl. Dalley (1989: 102).
12. *Odyssey* 10. 501–2.

13. As attested by the tholos tombs.
14. Gurney (1990: 139–40) lists both the similarities and the differences.
15. Thus Güterbock (1948: 133).
16. West (1995: 36).
17. Kirk (1974: 267).

Bibliography

AKURGAL, E. (1962), *The Art of the Hittites*, London.

ALEXANDER, R. L. (1991), 'Šaušga and the Hittite Ivory from Megiddo', *JNES* 50: 161–82.

ALP, S. (1991), *Hethitische Briefe aus Maşat-Höyük*, Ankara.

ARCHI, A. (1975), 'Divinità tutelari e Sondergötter ittiti', *SMEA* 16: 89–117.

——(1979), 'L'Humanité des Hittites', in *Fs Laroche*, 37–48.

——(1995), 'Hittite and Hurrian Literatures: An Overview', in J. M. Sasson, 2367–77.

ARDZINBA, V. G. (1986), 'The Birth of the Hittite King and the New Year', *Oikumene* 5: 91–101.

BALKAN, K. (1973), *Eine Schenkungsurkunde aus der althethitischen Zeit, gefunden in Inandık*, Ankara.

BASS, G. F. (1973), 'Cape Gelidonya and Bronze Age Maritime Trade', in H. A. Hoffner (1973*a*), 29–37.

BEAL, R. H. (1983), 'Studies in Hittite History', *JCS* 35: 115–26.

——(1988), 'The GIŠTUKUL-institution in Second Millennium Hatti', *AOF* 15: 269–305.

——(1992), *The Organization of the Hittite Military*, Heidelberg.

——(1995), 'Hittite Military Organization', in J. M. Sasson, 545–54.

BECKMAN, G. (1982), 'The Hittite Assembly', *JAOS* 102.3: 435–42.

——(1983*a*), 'Mesopotamians and Mesopotamian Learning at Hattusha', *JCS* 35: 97–114.

——(1983*b*), *Hittite Birth Rituals*, *StBoT* 29.

——(1986), 'Inheritance and Royal Succession among the Hittites', *Fs Güterbock II*, 13–31.

——(1988), 'Herding and Herdsmen in Hittite Culture', *Fs Otten*, 33–44.

——(1989), 'The Religion of the Hittites', *BA* 52: 98–108.

——(1992), 'Hittite Administration in Syria in the Light of the Texts from Hattuša, Ugarit and Emar', in *New Horizons in the Study of Ancient Syria*, Bibliotheca Mesopotamica 25, ed. M. W. Chavalas and J. L. Hayes, 41–9.

——(1993), 'From Cradle to Grave: Women's Role in Hittite Medicine and Magic', *JAC* 8: 25–39.

——(1995*a*), 'Royal Ideology and State Administration in Hittite Anatolia', in J. M. Sasson, 529–43.

BECKMAN, G. (1995*b*), 'The Siege of Uršu Text (*CTH* 7) and Old Hittite Historiography', *JCS* 47: 23–34.

——(1995*c*), 'Hittite Provincial Administration in Anatolia and Syria: The View from Maşat and Emar', in *Atti del II Congresso Internazionale di Hittitologia*, Studia Mediterranea 9, Pavia, 19–35.

——(1996*a*), *Hittite Diplomatic Texts*, Atlanta.

——(1996*b*), 'The Hittite Language and its Decipherment', *Bulletin of the Canadian Society for Mesopotamian Studies* 31: 23–30.

——(1998), 'Ištar of Nineveh Reconsidered', *JCS* 50: 1–10.

——(1999), 'The City and the Country in Hatti', in *Landwertschaft im Alten Orient*, Procs. *RAI* XLI, ed. V. Haas, H. Kühne, H. J. Nissen, J. Reuger, Berlin.

——(2000), 'Goddess Worship—Ancient and Modern', in *A Wise and Discerning Mind: Essays in Honor of Burke O. Long*, ed. S. M. Olyan and R. C. Culley, Providence.

BIN-NUN, S. R. (1975), *The Tawananna in the Hittite Kingdom*, Heidelberg.

——(1979), 'Some Remarks on Hittite Oracles, Dreams, and Omina', *Or* 48: 118–27.

BITTEL, K. (1970), *Hattusha, the Capital of the Hittites*, Oxford, New York.

——(1976), *Les Hittites* (transl. from German by F. Poncet), Paris.

BITTEL, K., HERRE, W., OTTEN, H., RÖHRS, M., and SCHAEUBLE, J. (1958), 'Die hethitischen Grabfunde von Osmankayası', *WVDOG* 71.

BRYCE, T. R. (1998*a*), *The Kingdom of the Hittites*, Oxford.

——(1998*b*), 'How Old was Matanazi?' *JEA* 84: 212–15.

——(1999), 'Anatolian Scribes in Mycenaean Greece', *Historia* 48: 257–64.

BURDE, C. (1974), *Hethitische Medizinische Texte*, *StBoT* 19.

BURKERT, W. (1992), *The Orientalizing Revolution*, Cambridge, Mass., London.

CANBY, J. V. (1989), 'Hittite Art', *BA* 52: 109–29.

CARTER, C. (1988), 'Athletic Contests in Hittite Religious Festivals', *JNES* 47: 85–7.

CHRISTMANN-FRANCK, L. (1971), 'Le rituel des funérailles royales hittites', *RHA* 29: 61–111.

CLINE, E. (1994), *Sailing the Wine-Dark Sea: International Trade and the Late Bronze Age Aegean*, Oxford, BAR International Series 591.

DALLEY, S. (1989), *Myths from Mesopotamia*, Oxford, New York.

DEL MONTE, G. F., and TISCHLER, T. (1992), Suppl. to *Répertoire Géographique des Textes Cunéiformes Bd. 6 Die Orts- und Gewässernamen der hethitischen Texte* (1978), Wiesbaden.

EDEL, E. (1976), *Ägyptische Ärtze und Ägyptische Medizin am hethitischen Königshof*, Göttingen.

——(1994), *Die Ägyptische-hethitische Korrespondenz aus Boghazköi* (*Bd I Umschriften und Übersetzungen; Bd II Kommentar*), Opladen (cited as *ÄHK*).

Frantz-Szabó, G. (1995), 'Hittite Witchcraft, Magic, and Divination', in J. M. Sasson, 2007–19.

Friedrich, J. (1930), *Staatsverträge des Hatti-Reiches in hethitischer Sprache, 2. Teil* (*MVAG* 34/1), Leipzig.

——(1971), *Die Hethitischen Gesetze*, Documenta et Monumenta Orientis Antiqui VII, Leiden.

Goetze, A. (1933), *Die Annalen des Mursilis*, Leipzig (repr. Darmstadt, 1967).

——(1957*a*), *Kulturgeschichte Kleinasiens*, Munich.

——(1957*b*), 'The Roads of Northern Cappadocia in Hittite Times', *RHA* 15: 91–102.

——(1964), 'State and Society of the Hittites', in G. Walser (1964), 23–33.

Goetze, A., and Pedersen, H. (1934), *Mursilis Sprachlähmung*, Copenhagen.

Gonnet, H. (1979), 'La titulature royale hittite au IIe millénnaire avant J.-C.', *Hethitica* 3: 3–108.

Gurney, O. R. (1953), 'A Hittite Divination Text', in D. J. Wiseman, *The Alalah Tablets*, London, 116–18.

——(1958), 'Hittite Kingship', in *Myth, Ritual and Kingship*, ed. S. H. Hooke, Oxford, 105–21.

——(1977), *Some Aspects of Hittite Religion*, Oxford.

——(1990), *The Hittites*, London.

——(1994), 'The Ladder-Men at Alaca Höyük', *AS* 44: 219–20.

Güterbock, H. G. (1948), 'Hittite Version of the Hurrian Kumarbi Myths: Oriental Forerunners of Hesiod', *AJA* 52: 123–34.

——(1951/2), 'The Song of Ullikummi: Revised Text of the Hittite Version of a Hurrian Myth', *JCS* 5: 135–61 and 6: 8–42.

——(1954), 'Authority and Law in the Hittite Kingdom', *JAOS* Suppl. 17: 16–24.

——(1960), 'An Outline of the Hittite AN.TAH.ŠUM Festival', *JNES* 19: 80–9.

——(1961*a*), 'Hittite Mythology', in *Mythologies of the Ancient World*, ed. S. N. Kramer, New York, 141–79.

——(1961*b*), 'The North-Central Area of Hittite Anatolia', *JNES* 20: 85–97.

——(1964), 'Religion und Kultus der Hethiter', in G. Walser, 54–73.

——(1975), 'Yazılıkaya: Apropos a New Interpretation', *JNES* 34: 273–7.

——(1983), 'A Hurro-Hittite Hymn to Ishtar', *JAOS* 103: 155–64.

Haas, V. (1982), *Hethitische Berggötter und Hurritische Steindämonen*, Mainz am Rhein.

——(1988), 'Betrachtungen zur Rekonstruktion des hethitischen Frühjahrsfestes (EZEN *purulliyaš*)', *ZA* 78: 284–98.

——(1994), *Geschichte der hethitischen Religion*, Leiden.

——(1995), 'Death and the Afterlife in Hittite Thought', in J. M. Sasson, 2021–30.

Haas, V., and Wäfler, M. (1974), 'Yazılıkaya und der Grosse Tempel', *OA* 13: 211–26.

——(1977), 'Bemerkungen zu [É]ḫestī/ā (2. Teil)', *UF* 9: 87–122.

Haase, R. (1978), 'Zur Totung eines Kaufmanns nach den hethitischen Gesetzen (§§5 und III)', *WO* 9, 213–19.

Hawkins, J. D. (1995), *The Hieroglyphic Inscription of the Sacred Pool Complex at Hattusa (SÜDBURG)*, *StBoT* Beiheft 3, Wiesbaden.

——(1998), 'Tarkasnawa King of Mira: "Tarkondemos", Boğazköy Sealings and Karabel', *AS* 48: 1–31.

Hoffman, I. (1984), *Der Erlass Telipinus*, Heidelberg.

Hoffner, H. A. (ed.) (1973*a*), *Orient and Occident: Essays presented to Cyrus H. Gordon on the Occasion of his Sixty-fifth Birthday*, Neukirchen-Vluyn.

——(1973*b*), 'Incest, Sodomy and Bestiality in the Ancient Near East', in H. A. Hoffner (1973*a*), 81–90.

——(1974), *Alimenta Hethaeorum: Food Production in Hittite Asia Minor*, New Haven.

——(1975), 'Hittite Mythological Texts: A Survey', in *Unity and Diversity: Essays in the History, Literature, and the Religion of the Ancient Near East*, ed. H. Goedicke and J. J. M. Roberts, Baltimore, 136–45.

——(1980), 'Histories and Historians of the Ancient Near East: The Hittites', *Or* 49: 283–332.

——(1983), 'A Prayer of Mursili II about his Stepmother', *JAOS* 103: 187–92.

——(1987), 'Paskuwatti's Ritual against Sexual Impotence (*CTH* 406)', *Aula Orientalis* 5: 271–87.

——(1988), 'A Scene in the Realm of the Dead', in *Fs Sachs*, 191–9.

——(1990), *Hittite Myths*, Atlanta.

——(1995), 'Legal and Social Institutions of Hittite Anatolia', in J. M. Sasson, 555–69.

——(1997*a*), *The Laws of the Hittites: A Critical Edition*, Leiden, New York, Köln, Brill.

——(1997*b*), 'Hittite Laws', in M. T. Roth, 213–47.

Hout, T. van den (1990), 'Masse und Gewichte. Bei den Hethitern', *RlA* 7.

——(1999), review of M. Popko, *Religions of Asia Minor*, Warsaw (1995), *JAOS* 119.2: 341–3.

——(2000), review of T. R. Bryce (1998*a*), *BiOr* 57: 643–6.

Houwink Ten Cate, Ph. H. J. (1967), 'Muwatalli's Prayer to the Storm-God of Kummanni (*KBo* XI 1)', *RHA* 25: 101–40.

——(1968), 'Muwatalli's "Prayer to be Spoken in an Emergency", an Essay in Textual Criticism', *JNES* 27: 204–8.

——(1984), 'The History of Warfare according to Hittite Sources: The Annals of Hattusilis I (Part II)', *Anatolica* 11: 47–83.

——(1992), 'The Hittite Storm God: His Role and his Rule according to

Hittite Cuneiform Sources', in *Natural Phenomena Their Meaning and Depiction in the Ancient Near East*, ed. D. Meijer, Amsterdam, Oxford, New York, Tokyo, 83–148.

IMPARATI, F. (1987), 'La politique extérieure des Hittites: tendences et problèmes', *Hethitica* 8: 187–207.

—— (1995), 'Private Life among the Hittites', in J. M. Sasson, 571–86.

KAMMENHUBER, A. (1961), *Hippologia Hethitica*, Wiesbaden.

—— (1976), *Orakelpraxis, Träume und Vorzeichenschau bei den Hethitern*, Heidelberg.

KELLERMAN, G. (1986), 'The Telepinu Myth Reconsidered', in *Fs Güterbock II*, 115–23.

KIRK, G. S. (1974), *The Nature of Greek Myths*, Harmondsworth.

KITCHEN, K. A. (1962), *Suppiluliuma and the Amarna Pharaohs*, Liverpool.

—— (1969–), *Ramesside Inscriptions, Historical and Biographical I–VII*, Oxford (cited as *KRI*).

—— (1982), *Pharaoh Triumphant: The Life and Times of Ramesses II*, Warminster.

KLENGEL, H. (1965), 'Die Rolle der "Ältesten" (LÚ^{MEŠ} ŠU.GI) im Kleinasien der Hethiterzeit', *ZA* 57: 223–36.

—— (1974), '"Hungerjahre" in Hatti', *AOF* 1: 165–74.

—— (1979), 'Handel und Kaufleute im hethitischen Reich', *AOF* 6: 69–80.

—— (1984), 'Zu einem Ablenkungszauber bei Krankheit im hethitischen Heer (*KUB* LIV 65)', *AOF* 11: 174–6.

—— (1986), 'The Economy of the Hittite Household (É)', *Oikumene* 5: 23–31.

KLINGER, J. (1995), 'Das Corpus der Maşat-Briefe und seine Beziehungen zu den Texten aus Hattusa', *ZA* 85: 74–108.

KLOCK-FONTANILLE, I. (1998), *Les hittites*, Paris.

KOHLMEYER, K. (1995), 'Anatolian Architectural Decorations, Statuary, and Stelae', in J. M. Sasson, 2639–60.

KOŠAK, S. (1987), 'Eine mittelhethitische Handwerkerliste', *ZA* 77: 136–41.

—— (1990), 'Night and Day, in War and in Peace', *JAC* 5: 77–86.

—— (1995), 'The Palace Library "Building A" on Büyükkale', *Fs Houwink ten Cate*, 173–9.

KRAMER, S. N. (1964), *The Sumerians*, Chicago.

KÜMMEL, H. M. (1967), *Ersatzrituale für den hethitische König*, *StBoT* 3.

—— (1987), 'Rituale in hethitischer Sprache', in *Rituale und Beschwörungen I*, *TUAT* II 2: 282–92.

LAROCHE, E. (1949), 'La Bibliothèque de Hattuša', *AO* 17: 7–23.

—— (1952), *Recueil d'onomastique hittite*, Paris.

—— (1971), *Catalogue des textes hittites*, Paris (cited as *CTH*).

LEBRUN, R. (1980), *Hymnes et Prières hittites*, Louvain-La-Neuve.

—— (1995), 'From Hittite Mythology: The Kumarbi Cycle', in J. M. Sasson, 1971–80.

—— (1997), 'Observations concernant des syncrétismes d'Anatolie centrale et méridionale aux second et premier millénaires avant notre ère', in *Les Syncrétismes Religieux dans le Monde Méditerranéen Antique*, Procs. International Colloquium in honour of Franz Cumont, Rome, Academia Belgica, 25–27 Sept. 1997, 179–89.

LIVERANI, M. (1990), *Prestige and Interest: International Relations in the Near East ca. 1600–1100 B.C.*, Pavia.

LLOYD, S. (1989), *Ancient Turkey: A Traveller's History of Anatolia*, London.

MACQUEEN, J. G. (1986), *The Hittites and their Contemporaries in Asia Minor*, London.

MARTINO, S. DE (1989), 'La danza nella cultura ittita', *Eothen* 2.

——(1995), 'Music, Dance, and Processions in Hittite Anatolia', in J. M. Sasson, 2661–9.

MCCALL, H. (1990), *Mesopotamian Myths*, London.

MCMAHON, G. (1989), 'The History of the Hittites', *BA* 52: 62–77.

——(1991), *The Hittite State Cult of the Tutelary Deities*, Chicago, Assyriological Studies 25.

——(1995), 'Theology, Priests, and Worship in Hittite Anatolia', in J. M. Sasson, 1981–95.

MELCHERT, H. C. (1980), 'The use of IKU in Hittite Texts', *JCS* 32: 50–6.

——(1988), 'Luvian Lexical Notes', *Historische Sprachforschung* 101: 211–43.

——(1991), 'Death and the Hittite King', *Fs Polomé*, 182–7.

MELLINK, M. J. (1974), 'Hittite Friezes and Gate Sculptures', in *Fs Güterbock I*, 201–14.

MORAN, W. L. (1992), *The Amarna Letters*, Baltimore, London.

MORRIS, S. P. (1992), *Daidalos and the Origins of Greek Art*, Princeton.

NEUFELD, E. (1951), *The Hittite Laws*, London.

NEVE, P. (1989–90), 'Boğazköy-Hattuša. New Results of the Excavations in the Upper City', *Anatolica* 16: 7–19.

——(1991), 'Die Ausgrabungen in Boğazköy-Hattusa 1990', *AA* Heft 3: 299–348.

——(1992), 'Die Ausgrabungen in Boğazköy-Hattuša 1991', *AA* Heft 3: 307–38.

——(1993), *Hattuša Stadt der Götter und Tempel*, Mainz.

OPPENHEIM, A. (1956), *The Interpretation of Dreams in the Ancient Near East*, Philadelphia.

OTTEN, H. (1951), 'Die hethitischen Königslisten und die altorientalische Chronologie', *MDOG* 83: 47–70.

——(1956), 'Hethitische Schreiber in ihren Briefen', *MIO* 4: 179–89.

——(1958), *Hethitische Totenrituale*, Berlin.

——(1961), 'Eine Beschwörung der Unterirdischen aus Boğazköy', *ZA* 54: 114–57.

——(1962), 'Zu den hethitischen Totenritualen', *OLZ* 7: 230–4.

——(1963), 'Neue Quellen zum Ausklang des hethitischen Reiches', *MDOG* 94: 1–23.

——(1968), *Die hethitischen historischen Quellen und die altorientalische Chronologie*, Mainz, Wiesbaden.

——(1973), *Eine althethitische Erzählung um die Stadt Zalpa*, *StBoT* 17.

——(1981), *Die Apologie Hattusilis III.*, *StBoT* 24.

——(1988), *Die Bronzetafel aus Boğazköy: ein Staatsvertrag Tuthalijas IV.*, Wiesbaden.

PRINGLE, J. (1993), 'Hittite Birth Rituals', in *Images of Women in Antiquity*, ed. A. Cameron and A. Kuhrt, London, 128–41.

PRITCHARD, J. B. (1969), *Ancient Near Eastern Texts relating to the Old Testament*, 3rd edn., Princeton.

PUHVEL, J. (1991), *Homer and Hittite*, Innsbrucker Beiträge zur Sprachwissenschaft, Vorträge und Kleinere Schriften 47, Innsbruck.

——(1997), *Hittite Etymological Dictionary*, vol. iv: *Words beginning with K*, Berlin, New York.

REDFORD, D. B. (1984), *Akhenaten, the Heretic King*, Princeton.

ROLLER, L. E. (1999), *In Search of God the Mother*, University of California.

ROOS, J. DE (1995), 'Hittite Prayers', in J. M. Sasson, 1997–2005.

ROSZKOWSKA-MUTSCHLER, H. (1992), 'Some Remarks on the Execration of Defeated Enemy Cities by the Hittite Kings', *JAC* 7: 1–12.

ROTH, M. T. (1997), *Law Collections from Mesopotamia and Asia Minor*, Atlanta, 2nd edn.

SASSON, J. M. (ed.) (1995), *Civilizations of the Ancient Near East* (4 vols.), New York.

SCHULER, E. VON (1957), *Hethitische Dienstanweisungen für höhere Hof- und Staatsbeamte* (*AfO* Beiheft 10), Graz.

——(1965), *Die Kaškaer*, Berlin.

SEEHER, J. (1999), 'Die Ausgrabungen in Boğazköy-Hattusa 1998 und ein neuer Topographischer Plan des Stadtgeländes', *AA* Heft 3, 317–44.

——(2000*a*), 'Die Ausgrabungen in Boğazköy-Hattusa 1999', *AA* Heft 3, 355–74.

——(2000*b*), 'Getreidelagerung in unterirdischen Großspeichern: zur Methode und ihrer Anwendung im 2. Jahrtausend v. Chr. am Beispiel der Befunde in Hattuša', *SMEA* 42: 261–301.

SHEAR, I. M. (1998), 'Bellerophon Tablets from the Mycenaean World? A Tale of Seven Bronze Hinges', *JHS* 118: 187–9.

SINGER, I. (1983–4), *The Hittite* KI.LAM *Festival*, *StBoT* 27 and 28 (Parts I and II).

——(1984), 'The AGRIG in Hittite Texts', *AS* 34: 97–127.

——(1986), 'The huwaši of the Storm-God in Hattuša', Procs. IX. Türk Tarıh Kongresi, Ankara, 1981, Ankara, 245–53.

——(1995), '"Our God" and "Their God" in the Anitta Text', in *Atti del*

II Congresso Internazionale di Hittitologia, Studia Mediterranea 9, Pavia, 343–9.

——(1996), *Muwatalli's Prayer to the Assembly of Gods Through the Storm-God of Lightning (CTH 381)*, Atlanta.

——(1997), review of T. van den Hout, *Der Ulmitešub-Vertrag*, Wiesbaden, 1995, *BiOr* 54: 416–23.

——(1998*a*), 'A City of Many Temples: Hattuša, Capital of the Hittites', in *Sacred Space: Shrine, City, Land*, Procs. International Conference in Memory of Joshua Prawer, ed. B. Z. Kedar and R. J. Zwi Werblowsky, Israel Academy of Sciences and Humanities, 32–44.

——(1998*b*), 'The Mayor of Hattuša and his Duties', in *Capital Cities: Urban Planning and Spiritual Dimensions*, Procs. Symposium held on 27–29 May 1996, Jerusalem, ed. J. G. Westenholz, Jerusalem, 169–76.

——(1999*a*), 'A Political History of Ugarit', *Handbook of Ugaritic Studies*, ed. W. G. E. Watson and N. Wyatt, *Handbuch der Orientalistik*, Abt. 1, *Der Nahe und Mittlere Osten*: Bd 39, Leiden, Boston, Cologne, 603–733.

——(1999*b*), 'A New Hittite Letter from Emar', in *Landscapes, Territories, Frontiers and Horizons in the Ancient Near East*, Procs. *RAI 1997*, ed. L. Milano, S. de Martino, F. M. Fales, G. B. Lanfranchi, vol. ii: *Geography and Cultural Landscapes, History of the Ancient Near East/Monographs* III, Padua, 65–72.

——(2000), 'Cuneiform, Linear, Alphabetic: The Contest between Writing Systems in the Eastern Mediterranean', The Howard Gilman International Conferences II: *Mediterranean Cultural Interaction*, ed. A. Ovadiah, Tel Aviv, 23–32.

SJÖBERG, A. (1974), 'The Old Babylonian Eduba', *Fs Jacobsen*, 159–79.

SOMMER, F., and FALKENSTEIN, A. (1938), *Die hethitisch-akkadische Bilingue des Hattusili I. (Labarna II.)*, Munich (repr. Hildesheim, 1974).

STARKE, F. (1979), 'Halmašuit im Anitta-Texte und die hethitische Ideologie vom Königtum', *ZA* 69: 45–120.

——(1995), *Ausbildung und Training von Streitwagenpferden. Eine hippologisch orientierte Interpretation des Kikkuli-Textes*, *StBoT* 41.

TORRI, G. (1999), *Lelwani: il culto di una dea ittita*, Università di Roma 'La Sapienza', Dipartimento di Scienze storiche, archeologiche e antropologiche dell'antichità, Sezione Vicino Oriente, Quaderno 2, Roma.

TSEVAT, M. (1975), 'The Husband Veils a Wife', *JCS* 27: 235–40.

TYLDESLEY, J. (1999), *Nefertiti*, Harmondsworth.

ÜNAL, A. (1986), 'Das Motiv der Kinderaussetzung in den altanatolischen Literaturen', in *Keilschriftliche Literaturen*, ed. K. Hecker and W. Sommerfeld, Berlin, 129–36.

——(1988), 'The Role of Magic in the Ancient Anatolian Religions according to the Cuneiform Texts from Boğazköy-Khattusha', in *Essays on Anatolian Studies in the Second Millennium B.C.*, ed. Prince Takahito Mikasa, Wiesbaden, 52–75.

——(1989), 'The Power of Narrative in Hittite Literature', *BA* 52: 130–43.

——(1994), 'The Textual Illustration of the "Jester Scene" on the Sculptures of Alaca Höyük', *AS* 44: 207–18.

WALSER, G. (ed.) (1964), *Neuere Hethiterforschung*, Historia Einzelschriften, Heft 7, Wiesbaden.

WEGNER, I. (1981), *Gestalt und Kult der Ištar-Šawuška in Kleinasien*, *AOAT* 36.

WERNER, R. (1967), *Hethitische Gerichtsprotokolle*, *StBoT* 4.

WEST, M. L. (1988), 'The Rise of the Greek Epic', *JHS* 108: 151–72.

——(1995), 'Ancient Near Eastern Myths in Classical Greek Religious Thought', in J. M. Sasson, 33–42.

——(1997), *The East Face of Helicon: West Asiatic Elements in Early Greek Poetry and Myth*, Oxford.

Index

Bold figures indicate main references